The Alternative
Third World War
1985–2035

Other titles available from Brassey's

LAWRENCE JAMES
Imperial Rearguard

R. J. KRICKUS
The Superpowers in Crisis!: Implications of Domestic Discord

JOHN LAFFIN
Brassey's Battles

JOHN LAFFIN
War Annual 2

KENNETH MACKSEY
Godwin's Saga: A Commando Epic

CHARLES MESSENGER
Hitler's Gladiator: The Life of Oberstgruppenfuehrer and Panzergeneral Oberst der Waffen-SS Sepp Dietrich

J. G. WHELAN & M. J. DIXON
The Soviet Union in the Third World. Threat to World Peace?

STAN WINDASS
The Rite of War

The Alternative Third World War 1985–2035

by

William Jackson

BRASSEY'S DEFENCE PUBLISHERS

(a member of the Pergamon Group)

LONDON • OXFORD • WASHINGTON • NEW YORK • BEIJING
FRANKFURT • SÃO PAULO • SYDNEY • TOKYO • TORONTO

U.K. (Editorial)	Brassey's Defence Publishers, 24 Gray's Inn Road, London WC1X 8HR
(Orders)	Brassey's Defence Publishers, Headington Hill Hall, Oxford OX3 0BW, England
U.S.A. (Editorial)	Pergamon-Brassey's International Defense Publishers, 8000 Westpark Drive, Fourth Floor, McLean, Virginia 22102, U.S.A.
(Orders)	Pergamon Press, Maxwell House, Fairview Park, Elmsford, New York 10523, U.S.A.
PEOPLE'S REPUBLIC OF CHINA	Pergamon Press, Room 4037, Qianmen Hotel, Beijing, People's Republic of China
FEDERAL REPUBLIC OF GERMANY	Pergamon Press, Hammerweg 6, D-6242 Kronberg, Federal Republic of Germany
BRAZIL	Pergamon Editora, Rua Eça de Queiros, 346, CEP 04011, Paraiso, São Paulo, Brazil
AUSTRALIA	Pergamon-Brassey's Defence Publishers, P.O. Box 544, Potts Point, N.S.W. 2011, Australia
JAPAN	Pergamon Press, 8th Floor, Matsuoka Central Building, 1–7–1 Nishishinjuku, Shinjuku-ku, Tokyo 160, Japan
CANADA	Pergamon Press Canada, Suite No. 271, 253 College Street, Toronto, Ontario, Canada M5T 1R5

First English Language edition 1987

Library of Congress Cataloging-in-Publication Data

Jackson, W. G. F. (William Godfrey Fothergill), Sir, 1917–
The Alternative Third World War, 1985–2035.
Includes index.
1. World War III. 2. Great Britain – Military policy – Forecasts. I. Title.
U313.J33 1987   355.4'8   87–15942

British Library Cataloguing in Publication Data

Jackson, W. G. F.
The Alternative Third World War, 1985–2035.
1. World War III
I. Title 303.4'9   U313
ISBN 0–08–034740–1

Printed in Great Britain by Richard Clay Ltd., Bungay, Suffolk

*To Kitty, my granddaughter
whose career I have assumed
without her permission!*

Preface

After completing my *Withdrawal from Empire; a Military View* in 1985, in which I concluded that Britain should avoid over-emphasis on Continental strategy and maintain balanced forces for use anywhere in the world, I was challenged by several eminent military historians to paint a plausible scenario in which Britain, in her post-imperial era, had either the political will or military capability to do more than assist in the collective defence of Western Europe. This is my answer, seen through the eyes of my grand-daughter soon after her retirement from the Army as a lieutenant general in the year 2040. It is a work of imagination. No one has the power to divine the future. History does have a pattern, but it is only visible in retrospect. In prospect, it is the unexpected that usually happens, and our estimates of the time scale of the future are invariably wrong. It has been fun to write: I hope it will be equally interesting to read.

W.G.F.J.
West Stowell

Contents

List of Maps

PROLOGUE

The Revelation

*. . . I looked, and before my eyes was
a door opened in heaven; and a voice
that I had just heard speaking to
me like a trumpet said, "Come up
here, and I will show you what must
happen hereafter."'*

Revelation of St John, Chapter 4
(New English Bible)

1

The Four Horsemen (1985–1998)

> . . . and I heard one of the four living creations
> say in a voice like thunder, "Come!" And
> before my eyes was a white horse and its
> rider held a bow. He was given a crown,
> and he rode forth conquering and to conquer.
>
> . . . I heard the second creature say, "Come!" And
> out came another horse, all red. To its rider
> was given power to take grace from the earth
> and make men slaughter one another; and he
> was given a great sword.
>
> . . . I heard the third creature say, "Come!". And
> there, as I looked, was a black horse; and its
> rider held in his hand a pair of scales.
>
> . . . I heard the fourth creature say "Come!" And there,
> as I looked, was another horse, sickly pale;
> and its rider's name was Death . . .'

The Revelation of St John, Chapter 6
(New English Bible)

In 1986 my grandfather, General Sir William Jackson, published his classic *Withdrawal From Empire; A Military View*. I remember seeing a copy of it on his desk at West Stowell. It looked terribly dull to me at my age. He had written it soon after his retirement from the Army after forty-six years service to the Crown, during which he had been directly or indirectly involved in most of the major events in Britain's surprisingly successful disengagement from her imperial commitments.

He would have been very surprised, but delighted, if he had known that the sequel to his work would be written by his granddaughter on her retirement from the Army in the year 2040. Like my grandfather, I served the Crown for over forty years, but what would have surprised him even more was that I too became a general officer, an achievement unthinkable for a woman in his day. My successful military career not only reflects the enhanced status of women in Western society in the mid-21st century, but also the changing nature of warfare in this age of supra-technology, which dwarfs the high-technology of the last decades of the 20th century.

One thing would not have surprised him, and that is my decision to write this history of the Third World War. We come from a family of soldier-academics in which soldiering has become paradoxically mixed up with scholastic inclinations. We both have Fothergill in our names. The first Fothergill to set foot in England was Sir William de Fothergill, one of William the Conqueror's knights, who commanded the Norman army sent to subdue Northern England during the Conquest. He took York by guile rather than brute force, demonstrating the intellectual military bent that has stayed with the family ever since. Those Fothergills, who did not farm the unrewarding fells of the Lake District, tended to join the Army or the academic world, providing the Masters of several Oxford colleges. They must have been a tough lot in the 18th and 19th centuries because they would mount their horses in Ravenstonedale, in Cumbria, and ride down to Oxford and back at the beginning and end of each term. The names of several who joined the Army are still to be found on tomb stones in neglected British military cemeteries in India.

My account of the Third World War cannot be a definitive history of the conflict since I am writing in 2040, only five years after the signing of the Treaties of London which brought about the latest international settlement. Few official archives have been opened as yet and we are still too close to the events to see them in historical perspective. I have, therefore, given the story a personal ring because I was so closely involved in many of the episodes that I describe, and because I have made very full use of my own diaries.

Lying beside my grandfather's *Withdrawal from Empire* I remember seeing an equally dull looking book by General Sir John Hackett entitled *The Third World War, 1985*. My grandfather used to tap it, saying 'Nonsense; it couldn't happen like that! There can be no political objective that would warrant the risk of mega-deaths and the destruction of civilisation as we know it – not even in the mind of the most senile member of the Soviet Politbureau.' Shan Hackett, as I found out later when I read his book, postulated a short, sharp fifty day war waged in 1985, which ended in a nuclear exchange of Birmingham for Minsk, but not in the nuclear holocaust which most people expected in the 1970's and 1980's.

Hackett's war, of course, did not happen either in 1985 or any other date. As we all now know, the Third World War did occur, but it was a long drawn out affair lasting fifty years rather than fifty days and was ended by supra-technology weapons during the Battle of the Armur River in 2034 rather than by nuclear devastation. On several occasions nuclear brink-manship brought the world close to annihilation, but the sense of self-preservation, so deeply ingrained in all humanity, saved the day.

Hackett's war, if it had been fought, would have been between the 20th century's two superpowers, the United States and Soviet Union, backed by their allies and satellites. The actual Third World War was fought by Afro-Asia and the 'deprived' of Latin America in their long and, in the end, successful struggle for a greater say in world affairs. In my view, it was fought at the end of the 'European' period of world history and at the beginning of what may be seen as its 'multi-racial' successor. However, the Treaties of London, that loom so large in our minds today, may well turn out to be nothing more than a false crest on the way up to some more distant and unseen historical watershed, though I doubt it: the Third World's victory has been so decisive and the London settlement so com-plete. There is even less doubt that Tokyo and Peking have emerged from the struggle as the joint capitals of the third superpower, the Sino-Japanese alliance.

It is not easy to decide exactly when the Third World War actually began. Nasser's triumph over the Anglo-French Suez intervention in 1956 is a possibility; the Sharpville massacre in South Africa in 1960 is another; the collapse of the Portuguese Empire in 1974, of course, changed the face of sub-Sahara Africa; the Soweto uprising in 1976 could be said to be historically more significant than Sharpville; or perhaps it was the over-throw of the Western-backed Shah of Iran in 1979 by the Ayatollah Khomeini. I believe, however, the starting year was 1985, when the South African Government instituted its State of Emergency and the rest of the world declared war upon *Apartheid*. The intervals between the cycles of violence in South Africa, which began at Sharpville, had progressively narrowed until by the crisis period of 1985 violence had become endemic. At that moment the First Horseman of the 21st Century Apocalypse mounted his steed.

Looking back over the half century of the Third World War I find St John's *Revelations* an apt and telling analogy. There were, indeed, four horsemen trying to create a 'New Heaven and New Earth' in the struggle between the powers of Light and of Darkness: Black Nationalism, Islamic Fundamentalism, Latin American Christo-Communism and what I have called the New Shintoism of Sino-Japanese culture. Whether Western Democracy and Eastern Communism were Light and Darkness or vice-versa depends upon your point of view, but the four riders are more clearly identifiable in the war, which had three distinct phases. In the first, the four horsemen rode their separate ways from 1985 to 2017. Then they found common cause and came together in the short second phase from 2018 to 2020. And finally the apocalyptic phase was fought out from 2020 to 2035.

By the time I had taken my degree at Cambridge, where I read

Engineering, and I had become the first woman to be commissioned directly into the Corps of Royal Engineers instead of into the Women's Royal Army Corps in 1997, the identity of the first Horseman as Black Nationalism was already apparent and this was brought home to me when I was posted to the Headquarters of 38th Field Engineer Regiment at Ripon as a trainee subaltern, very much on probation and on sufferance too! My first job was to help in the contingency planning for the support of an RAF *Falcon* squadron, which might be despatched to Kenya at short notice. The *Falcon* was the successor to the highly successful *Harrier* of the Falklands War. It was super-sonic and could carry the latest stand-off weapons, developed from what used to be called Emergent Technology or ET in the 1980's. There is always a price to pay for increased performance, and in the case of the *Falcon* we engineers had to provide stronger launching platforms. Our primary role in 38th Field Engineer Regiment was to support RAF *Falcon* squadrons flown to Germany in times of tension in Europe, but our secondary role was to support them elsewhere in the world if the unexpected happened and British forces were deployed outside the NATO area.

Although I had personally only become involved in Third World War military activity in 1997, there had already been a long 'phoney war' period reminiscent of the earliest phase of the Second World War. The anti-Apartheid struggle, which started the Third World War, had intensified throughout the second half of the 1980's and the first half of the 1990's, but all out civil war had been prevented by United States and British determination that there should be no blood bath. Neither international political and economic pressure, nor guerrilla and terrorist campaigns launched by the African Front Line states, were decisive in themselves in bringing about the dismantlement of *Apartheid*. Coercion drove the White South Africans into the laager of a defiant seige economy in which the challenge of sanction-busting acted as a spur to Afrikaner intransigence; and attempted insurgency was successfully contained by the ruthless efficiency of their experienced Security Forces. Stalemate might have ensued had it not been for one factor: the limited availability of white manpower.

The initial economic and military successes of the South African Government could not be sustained in the longer term. Both depended upon white manpower, which became a declining asset as emigration took hold. A point was reached when the essential manpower requirements of both the Security Forces as well as the needs of the economy could not be met. Although the Security Forces managed to maintain their grip on the Black population, they could only do so at the expense of the economy, which progressively lost its resilience as more and more men were called up for longer and longer periods of service in the Police and the Army. Agriculture, mining and business in general stagnated, and the remorseless economic decline exacerbated the latent enmity which had always existed between the two White tribes: the English and Afrikaner speaking peoples. A movement for radical constitutional advance on multi-racial lines, which had, indeed, begun in Natal in 1986, gathered momentum and spilled over into Cape Province, much to the alarm of Pretoria. In a snap election in 1993, unwisely called by the Government to re-affirm its mandate, the Nationalists were decisively defeated by a coalition of the English-speaking White South Africans and the more liberal minded of the Afrikaners, who were prepared to seek a negotiated settlement with the all embracing African National Congress. Through the initiative of the Indian Prime Minister, Pandit Shastri, a Commonwealth offer of mediation was accepted by both the new South African Government and the African National Congress, and this led to a second Lancaster House Conference in 1994, reminiscent of the first chaired by Lord Carrington in 1979, which brought peace to Rhodesia under its new African name of Zimbabwe.

Under the Lancaster House Agreement of 1995 the Union of South Africa became the Union of Azania with a constitution based upon a universal franchise, majority rule and entrenched safeguards for all minorities, guaranteed by the United Nations and the two superpowers. One of the most important safeguards, which softened White opposition, was the inclusion in that guarantee of fixed numbers of 'white' and 'coloured' seats in the Azanian legislature for a minimum period of 35 years. In effect there had been a redistribution rather than a transfer of power: Blacks assumed political authority, leaving the Whites very much in control of the commanding heights of the economy.

Re-reading an essay that I must have been writing for my Cambridge tutor at the time, I found this prescient paragraph with a large tutorial question mark in the margin:

'The Lancaster House agreement, which was announced today, brings the Third Boer War to an end. The First was fought and won by the British, despite international opprobrium. The second was won by the Boers when Field Marshal Smuts was defeated by Doctor Malan's Nationalists in the South African general election of 1948, enabling them to start imposing **Apartheid**. *The Third has just been won by the Africans, but the Boers are far from defeated. A Fourth Boer War seems almost inevitable.'*

In 1996 the first African President took office with a White Deputy in the Azanian capital which, for obvious reasons, was moved back to Cape Town from Pretoria. Many of the remaining White South Africans had sold up and emigrated, but far greater numbers stayed on and showed a willingness to make a success of the New Azania much as they had done in Zimbabwe.

One important by-product of the Lancaster House agreement was the healing of the rift in the fabric of the British Commonwealth, caused by Britain's efforts to enforce peaceful rather than revolutionary change in

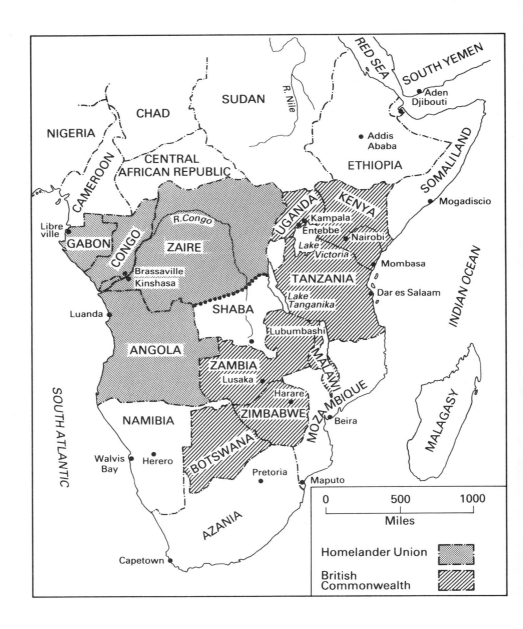

MAP 1: Black Nationalist Africa at the turn of the century

South Africa. At the 1995 Commonwealth Conference held in Accra there were no absentees and a general determination to let bygones be bygones with the final demise of *Apartheid*.

While there was much satisfaction in Britain and the United States that the fundamental error of not entrenching Black majority rights in the original Union of South Act of 1910 had been corrected without a bloody civil war, there was much less enthusiasm for the settlement amongst Black militants and extremists throughout the world, particularly in America and Britain, as well as in Africa itself. The militant view was that Black African interests had been sold down the river. Azania was only a Black country in name. The White minority still held the reins of economic power and were protected in a way that the Black majority had never been in the days of the Union of South Africa.

Out of this world-wide Black dissatisfaction with the Lancaster House Settlement sprang the Black Homelander movement in the United States and Britain, which was a direct descendent of the Civil Rights and Black Power organisations of the 1960's and 1970's that had so reduced racial discrimination in the United States. The Homelanders were led by Noah Johnston, a lawyer from the Bronx, whose oratory matched that of Martin Luther King and his moderation that of Senator Andrew Jackson. It was not a movement of the ghettos but of the Black American middle and upper classes, who wished to export their success back to Africa. It was, indeed, a missionary movement aimed at creating a nucleus Black African state, free from tribalism and in the mirror image of the United States, from which the rest of Africa south of the Sahara could be modernised in time. Noah likened his dreamland to the State of Israel. He hoped it would provide a similar focus for loyalty for Black people all over the world. He also saw his followers as a modern version of the Pilgrim Fathers and the state he hoped to found as the New England of Africa.

In the United States Presidential elections of 1996 both major American political parties courted the Black vote. The opinion polls showed that it would be a close run thing in which the votes of ethnic minorities might be decisive in the outcome. Abraham Rosenberg, the Democratic candidate, had Jewish blood in his veins and was able to show a genuine sympathy for the Homelander Movement. The Republican Karl Nimitz, could point to the acknowledged Republican success in converting White South Africa into Black Azania to secure Black votes. He did not decry Noah's ideas, but he did not enthuse over them either. Azania, in his view, already provided a modern Black Homeland.

The 1996 election proved as close as the polls predicted. Rosenberg just scraped home and was prepared to admit that the balance had probably been tipped in his favour by the Black Homelander vote. In his inaugural address he showed his gratitude by proclaiming his support for Noah Johnston's concept:

'My forebears worked and fought to establish the Jewish homeland – the State of Israel – in Palestine. How can we not support my friend, Noah Johnston's vision of a Black homeland to which all Black people can give their loyalty and their support.'

In the early months of his administration Rosenberg used his slender majority in both Houses of Congress to pass the Rosenberg Doctrine which, when stripped of its constitutional verbiage, pledged U.S. support for the creation of an African State after its own image.

Noah chose Angola for his experiment in creating an African state free from tribalism, not because he saw Angola as particularly suitable for his purpose but because the Angolan president, Victor M'Bundu, invited him to do so.[1] The long drawn out struggle between the Marxist Government with its Cuban supporters in Luanda, the capital, and the South African supported UNITA guerrillas in the bush, had faded away as South African support to UNITA dwindled in the latter years of the anti-*Apartheid* struggle. Once M'Bundu's Government had established control over the whole of Angola, the Cubans were asked to leave as the external threat – the primary reason for their presence – had evaporated. Much to M'Bundu's surprise they did leave, and to his even greater astonishment, his Soviet aid programme was not cut, though the complexion of his regime was clearly becoming more Nationalist than Marxist.

By inviting Noah to establish his Homelander base in Angola, M'Bundu managed to win the best of both worlds. The private capital of wealthy Black American businessmen as well as official American Government funds flowed into Angola. At the same time Moscow continued both its civil and military aid programmes out of fear of losing its hard won foothold on the West coast of Central Africa, which was linked across the Continent to its satellites in the Horn of Africa, and thence across the Red Sea to South Yemen, where Aden had become a fully developed Russian naval base. Moreover, the Soviet government took a cynically realistic view of Noah's chances of overcoming African tribalism. Sooner or later Noah's expatriates from the United States would fall out with M'Bundu's people and the pendulum would swing back in favour of the Marxist camp. Money spent in the right places would not be wasted, though patience would be needed to ensure future dividends.

The U.S. State Department and the CIA had had qualms about Noah's acceptance of M'Bundu's offer, but the chances of re-establishing Western influence on a sounder footing in Central Africa seemed to warrant taking the obvious risks involved. Any attempt to persuade Noah to reject the offer would have alienated many of Rosenberg's Black supporters and, in any case, it would have been contrary to the spirit, if not the letter, of the recently promulgated Rosenberg Doctrine for Africa. M'Bundu was astute enough to sugar the pill as far as the United States Government was concerned by offering Noah the presidency of the Homelander State of Angola, while retaining the posts of Prime Minister and Minister for Defence for himself.

M'Bundu's manoeuvres and ambitions were not lost upon the governments of the British Commonwealth States in East and Central Africa. Expansionist Homelander policies could threaten the existing governments of Kenya, Uganda, Tanzania, Zambia, Botswana and Malawi, if Noah and M'Bundu united the whole of the Congo basin in their Homeland. At the Commonwealth Conference at Harare in 1997 hosted by the grand old patriach, Robert Mugabe, who was in his 73rd year, there was a ground swell of distrust which Mugabe articulated neatly in his closing speech:

'Homelanders, probably, yes: African Hitlers, definitely, no!'

There was no reference to the Homelanders in the final Harare communiqué, but the Commonwealth Secretariat took steps to consult the Old Commonwealth Countries and India about steps which might be taken to help Commonwealth members in Africa if a predator State appeared in their midst. My work in 1998 on *Falcon* support for Kenya was but a small part of the British contribution to the Commonwealth contingency plans made as a result of the Harare conference.

At my lowly level I was quite unaware that the First Horseman, Black Nationalism, was re-mounting his steed. I was equally unaware that the Second Horseman, Moslem Fundamentalism, was already in the saddle. Iran eventually won the war with Iraq that had started in 1979, but not the subsequent peace. The Middle East cauldron continued to bubble in its turbulent, unpredictable and savage way. Iraq became an unruly Iranian satellite, in which the *Sunni* ruling classes were ousted from power by a revolutionary government drawn from and supported by the *Shi'a* working classes. The Ayatollah Khomeini's successor, called the Ayatollah of Tehran, because his real name was so unpronouncable for western radio and TV commentators, was the dominant but not decisive influence in Iraqi post-war affairs. Warring factions took over and Iraq became another Lebanon and Baghdad a reflection of Beirut.

During my days at Cambridge University, I had dabbled in philosophy as a relaxation from the tight discipline of engineering so I was aware that the Moslem world was divided between those who believed in the *Sunni's* interpretation of the *Koran* and those who were brought up in the *Shi'a* traditions in much the same way as Christendom is divided between Roman Catholicism and Protestantism. I was also aware that Islam is a way of life and a system of government as well as a world religion. Only the *Koran*, Allah's revelations to Mohammed, are divine and common to *Sunnis* and *Shi'as*: all the subsequent Islamic texts are accepted as manmade interpretations of Allah's will and, therefore, fallible. Most of the successful Moslem leaders in the past have depended for their political charisma upon fresh interpretations of the divine word. As long as success wreathed their green banners, Allah's will was seen to be done, but when misfortune struck it was the fault of the current interpretation and not of Allah. A return to the fundamental tenets of the *Koran* was deemed vital to the recovery of Allah's favour.

The Arab's humiliating defeats at the hands of the Israelis created just such a surge of Fundamentalism amongst the *Sunnis*. The reverse side of the coin was displayed in the Ayatollah Khomeini's *Shi'a* revolution in Iran. The relatively easy over-throw of the Shah showed that *Shi'a* Fundamentalism had found favour with Allah.

Most successful revolutions are expansionist after they have weathered the reign of terror phase, which so often accompanies them. The *Shi'a* Fundamentalist upsurge in Iran was no exception, as the Iran/Iraq war showed. Most revolutionary reigns of terror also burn themselves out as blood lusts are sated and a dominant personality emerges who can bring order out of chaos. This happened in Baghdad, where a young, thrusting and ambitious *Shi'ite* Mullah seized power with the blessing of the Ayatollah of Tehran, who made him responsible for consolidating the *Shi'ite* Fundamentalist way of life in Baghdad and for bringing about a union of Iran and Iraq in the Federation of Islamic Republics (F.I.R.) based upon the *Shi'a* tradition.

The western media soon christened Iraq's new leader, the Ayatollah of Baghdad, and it was not long before the new Ayatollah began to dream of giving the Islamic world the leadership it needed for success in the 21st century. With the Ayatollah of Tehran's covert encouragement and with the overt blaring of *Shi'a* propaganda over the Baghdad and Tehran radios, he began to flex his muscles by calling together a council of Mullahs at Kerbala (the Mecca of the *Shi'a* on the Euphrates, south of Baghdad) to seek a new interpretation of Islamic Law, which would enable Islam to become a real power in the world once more.

Most of the Moslem states sent representatives or observers to Kerbala, but the more important leaders, including the Ayatollah of Tehran, stayed away, not wishing to be compromised by any failure to reach a united doctrine. But, as events were to show, these cautious men misjudged the abilities, determination and political dexterity of the Ayatollah of Baghdad. He was, in fact, about to usurp the saddle of the Islamic Fundementalist Horse of the Apocalypse.

In the late 1990's the other two horses were, as yet, riderless. The Latin American 'deprived' were still leaderless and the prey to left and right wing extremists, and the Japanese were reluctant to play a role in world politics commensurate with their economic power for fear of bringing about another disastrous military confrontation with the Western world.

In the case of Latin America, Abraham Rosenberg was able to bask in the inherited successes of previous U.S. Administrations, which had brought a semblance of American style government to all countries of Central and South America. He could justifiably claim that there were no military or communist dictatorships left in the Americas. Tragically, the appearance belied the substance. The lot of the great mass of the Latin American people did not improve by being forced into the mould of North American democracy. The United States had been created in the spirit of individual freedom: the Portuguese and Spanish empires of Latin America had been based on exploitation of material and human resources. The Latin tradition could not be changed in a few decades. The poor had only two sponsors: the Catholic Church and the Communist Party. The former was prevented from playing its full part by the Papal encyclical forbidding priests to enter politics; and the latter had been proscribed and forced under ground in most states as the price of American aid. The mould was not to be broken until the Roman Catholic Church and the Communist Party came together under the leadership of a militant priest, Father Ignatious Bolivar. But this still lay in the mists of the future and would not occur until after the election of the Spanish Xavier Vasquez as Pope Xavier 1 in 2002.

In Japan in the 1990's there was still great reluctance to risk the country's outstanding economic successes by alienating either of the superpowers. Having lived and prospered in splendid isolation for over a thousand years, the Japanese had an inbred disinclination to discharge international responsibilities, to run-up a large trade deficit, to over-value their currency or to do any of those things which cost the British and Americans so much at the height of their power. Nevertheless, it was hard for people in the West to believe that Japanese economic success would not lead before long to expansionist political policies. However, in 1998, when I was commissioned, there was still no sign of Japan wishing to export anything other than goods and goodwill. Even the protectionist measures introduced by the United States and the European Community in the 1980's had been accepted by the Japanese as unfortunate but legitimate ways of maintaining the balance of world trade. As western markets became more difficult, the Japanese had turned increasingly to exploit the expanding Chinese, Asian and African markets where standards of living were rising and thus offering greater opportunities for Japanese companies.

There was one cloud on the Japanese horizon no bigger than the biblical 'man's hand'. It was a small party on the right of the Japanese political spectrum that did believe it was Japan's sacred duty to export the Japanese spirit of corporate individualism, upon which their great success was based, to the rest of Afro-Asia and the world for the general good of mankind. The party was led by the great great grandson of General Maresuki Nogi, who took Port Arthur during the Russo-Japanese War of 1904. He called his creed New Shintoism or the New Way of the Gods, fervently believing that Japan had discovered the secret of success in this world from which all races should be allowed to benefit. New Shintoism was to be propagated by peaceful economic co-operation. In 1996 Nogi won a handful of seats in the Japanese Parliament, but he had little support because the people of Japan preferred to enjoy the fruits of their own success rather than risk antagonising other nations by evangelism. In the 21st century it turned out to be the world that antagonised Japan rather than vice versa. Nogi would, in fact, be the Fourth Horseman but no-one could have foreseen this before the turn of the century.

Throughout the 21st century apocalypse the two existing superpowers continued their efforts to impose their political vision on the world, but each still had to fight with one hand held behind its back clasping its nuclear arsenal, and with one foot planted in and shackled to its half of Europe. Neither dared move for fear of triggering a fatal strategic nuclear exchange. This was because President Reagan's Star Wars Research Programme had shown that his proposed defensive shield could never be more than ninety per cent efficient. The ten percent was a sufficient margin for mutual nuclear annihilation to be a very strong probability, if a nuclear exchange were to occur. The philosophy of nuclear deterrence thus retained its validity into the 21st century. The lid was still kept firmly in place on conflicts of the scale of the First and Second World Wars. Those who wished to disturb the peace of the world still had to do so on tip-toe to avoid springing the nuclear trap.

Regrettably, the proliferation of states possessing nuclear weapons accelerated during the 1990's as the French pursued chauvinistic policies in their efforts to regain the self-confidence they lost in the Second World War, in Indo-China and in Algeria. French nuclear know-how enabled Israel, Pakistan and India to join the Nuclear Weapons Club. Azania took over existing South African weapons. The stockpiles of these countries were limited and their means of delivery modest. Only Britain, France and China had world class strategic delivery systems, but these too were modest in comparison with the superpowers' arsenals.

France remained a political enigma. By the 1990's she had become the wealthiest country in Western Europe, and yet political stability eluded her. The chasm that has always existed between the Left and Right in French politics was widened rather than narrowed by economic success: arguments over the distribution of wealth were waged more bitterly than ever. The French needed a Louis XIV, Napoleon or de Gaulle to unite them. No such figure emerged and France remained a law unto herself throughout the Third World War: rich but selfish in external as well as internal affairs.

By contrast, Britain remained economically weak in relative terms, though politically far more stable than her French rival across the Channel. She veered between enjoying being an off-shore island of the United States and of the European Community. Her Commonwealth concept, although still valid, had more downs than ups. It had never developed the political punch in world affairs proportional to the size of the populations which it embraced within its membership. And yet its continued existence with its bi-annual Prime Ministerial meetings did, on occasions, have an impact on British policies. Despite Britain's difficulties in absorbing her Black communities in her inner cities, she remained multi-racial in inclination and practice. The Lancaster House settlements of Zimbabwe and Azania confirmed the Commonwealth's usefulness in helping to create a more equitable multi-racial world.

Militarily Britain's defence policy dilemmas were eased, though not solved, by the Anglo-U.S. Gibraltar Accord of 1996, which had as little to do with the Rock as Nassau had with the Kennedy-Macmillan agreement of 1962, which gave Britain access to Polaris technology. The Foreign and Defence Secretaries of both countries met 'in the margins' of a NATO Council meeting, held in Gibraltar to review plans for the defence of the Southern Flank in the Mediterranean. After the other delegations had left at the end of the conference, the British and American teams stayed on for bi-lateral talks, which were held in the Convent, the Governor's residence.[2]

The talks were held at the Americans' behest. Their Joint Chiefs of Staff were becoming increasingly anxious about the future of NATO because the Treaty of Brussels had only a fifty year life and was due to expire in 1998 – in just two years time. They were in no doubt that the continued existence of NATO was vital to the defence of the United States as well as Western Europe. Despite all its warts and imperfections, NATO had helped to keep the peace in Europe for half a century and the chances of devising anything better were not encouraging. Working on the basis of 'the Devil you know . . .', the Joint Chiefs recommended to the Presidents' Security Adviser that every effort should be made to extend NATO's life *sine die*. They feared that, if the United States did not take the initiative, the North Atlantic Alliance would collapse through its own internal tensions and lack of leadership once the bonding of the Brussels Treaty was removed. They suggested that ways should be sought to make the extension of the Treaty attractive to the NATO membership. The quest should be pursued through bi-lateral talks with each ally. The Gibraltar talks were the first of this series of negotiations.

In the preliminary discussions in Washington before the talks began, the President's security advisers were confident that Britain would support the extension of the Treaty whole-heartedly. They were, however, anxious about two trends in British politics. The Labour Party's hostility to United States bases in the United Kingdom had not abated; and there was a body of opinion in all three of the major political parties that questioned the wisdom of pruning back Britain's maritime capability to maintain the strength of Rhine Army and RAF Germany. This school of maritime strategists believed the Continental countries should take over more of the Central front, for which they were better suited and better placed, so that Britain could concentrate on defending the Eastern Atlantic and on supporting the Northern Flank in Scandinavia. In the view of the Joint Chiefs of Staff these trends could be neutralised if the United States were to offer to pay substantially more for its bases in the U.K. The increase should be large enough to enable Britain to maintain both her Maritime and Continental efforts at their current level, but not be so large as to suggest that Britain was on the way to becoming the 51st State of the Union.

The actual talks took place in the great dining hall of the Convent, which had been a Spanish Franciscan friary before the British took the Rock in 1704. I was only a babe in arms when my grandfather was Governor, but I have often looked at the oil painting of that room, which hangs in the house at West Stowell. It is pregnant with history. Around the alcoves of the high bay windows are the names of 752 years worth of Moorish governors and the coats of arms of another 242 years of their Spanish successors. Circling the room itself, just below the open timbers of the roof, are the emblazoned shields and pennants of the fifty eight British military governors, spanning the 286 years of British sovereignty. The walls themselves are hung with contemporary portraits of men who made Gibraltar's history, including the principal officers present during the Great 14th Siege (1779–83), which gave Gibraltar its reputation of impregnability with the cachet 'as safe as the Rock'. At the end of the long dining table, flanked by its twenty six blue leather backed chairs, embossed with the Royal arms in gold, lie the massive keys of Gibraltar, nestling on their velvet cushion in front of the Governor's chair. In 1996 the Governor was a general so the cushion was scarlet. When there is an Admiral or Air Marshal as Governor, the colour is changed to dark or light blue as the case may be.

The agreement, which was thrashed out around the Convent dining table, was elegant in its simplicity. The offset costs of the United States bases in Britain – a euphemism for rent – would be fixed at one half percent of the United Kingdom's Gross Domestic Product (GDP), provided the British defence vote was not allowed to fall below the level of five and a half percent of the GDP, and Rhine Army was kept at a minimum strength of 55,000 men. At one point in the negotiations the American team tried to insist that their half per cent – £2,000 million at 1996 prices and level of British GDP – should be spent only on projects approved by Congress, but, in the end, they accepted the counter-argument that such a requirement would infringe the sovereignty of the British Parliament. The only string attached to the deal was the proviso that the United States money must be used on weapon procurement. In effect, this raised the British Defence effort to a minimum level of six per cent of GDP, only one per cent lower than the American level and two and a half per cent higher than that of France and Germany.[3]

Had it not been for the Gibraltar Accord, Britain would have been faced with some hard strategic choices in the 1990's in trying to balance her Defence budget. Cuts would have had to be made in her Continental or Maritime capabilities or, more likely, a combination of the two. The £2,000 million rental for United States bases was just ten per cent of the Defence vote, but it made all the difference between military solvency and bankruptcy caused by ever escalating equipment costs. Britain was able to enter the 21st century with her forces at much the same level as they had been during the Falklands campaign in 1982. All the ships lost had been replaced – belatedly it is true – and none of her experienced regular forces had been lost to the Western Alliance through financial stringency. Britain was still able to defend herself and to back her foreign policy with modest but efficient military forces.

What that foreign policy was to be as the post-imperial era developed was still ill-defined. Dean Acheson's quip in the 1950's about Britain, having lost an empire and being unable to find a role, was as valid as ever. The 21st century apocalypse was to thrust a role upon her.

In defence policy there was more clarity, but no easy solutions. Admiral of the Fleet, Sir John Fieldhouse, who had been Commander-in-Chief Fleet during the Falkland campaign, used to say in his talks to Staff College students when he was Chief of Defence Staff in the latter half of the 1980's.

'The most serious threat, against which we must prepare, lies in Western Europe and the Eastern Atlantic, but it is, at the same time, the least likely to require us to take action.'

He would then continue:

'We must go on devoting the greater part of our military effort and resources to meeting our NATO obligations, but we must also maintain a capacity to operate nationally or with allies outside the NATO area, should the occasion arise.'

His successors in the 1990's did not demur. The Gibraltar Accord made it possible for them to fulfil Britains' military commitments as they arose during the Third World War. It also led to the successful re-negotiation of the Brussels Treaty and the extension of NATO's life for a further fifty years.

Notes

1. Noah would have preferred to have started his experiment in Mozambique. Marxist – Leninism had disintegrated there and, out of the debris, had come the first authentic African state of the post-colonial era.
2. Spain still pursued her claim to sovereignty over the Rock, but Britain remained steadfastly

loyal to her pledge in the Gibraltar Constitution that there can be no change of sovereignty against the freely and democratically expressed wishes of the people of Gibraltar. As I write in 2040, the Gibraltarians still have no wish to become part of Spain.

3. See the *Statement on Defence Estimates 1986*, page 41, Fig 8, for a comparison of scales of defence expenditure in terms of the GDP.

PART I

Riding separately

'After this I saw four angels stationed
at the four corners of the earth, holding
back the four winds . . . Then I saw
another angel rising out of the east . . .'

Revelation of St John, Chapter 7
(Revised English Bible)

2

The Unexpected Always Happens (1999–2003)

'I have learnt the meaning of fear.'
Diary entry for 23rd January 2002

I shall always remember listening to my grandfather talking to his contemporaries at lunch parties that my grandparents used to give at West Stowell in the early 1980's when I was in my late teens and already showing an interest in military affairs. As each annual Defence White Paper was published, he would criticise it for being far too heavily biased towards Western European Defence, convinced, as he was, that Britain's interests lay, as they had always done throughout her long history, beyond the narrow confines of Europe. He acknowledged that the security of the British Isles depended directly upon the successful defence of NATO's Central and Northern Fronts, but he believed that the real threat to the British and indeed the Western way of life lay outside the NATO area.

'*They're* besotted with Europe,' he used to say, stressing the *They* – the powers that be in Whitehall – rather forgetting that he had belonged to *them* for so many years!

'Europe's never been so secure,' he would continue, 'Only a real break-through in the Star Wars programme would change things and there doesn't seem to be much sign of the creation of an effective anti-missile shield good enough to do more than swing the balance between offensive and defensive systems slightly in favour of defence.'

'But do we really want success,' he would muse, 'Europe would lose the security of the balance of nuclear terror, which it has enjoyed since 1945. We would be at the mercy of the Warsaw Pact's vast conventional superiority. The only answer then would be chemical and biological weapons, which God forbid!'

'No, the real threat that our military should be thinking about lies in the world at large. Our kith and kin, who spilled out of our islands and out of Europe over the last three centuries, and those people of other races who have espoused our way of life, circle the globe. They are the people most likely to suffer from the political instabilities that abound throughout the world, and from predator nations who believe they should swallow up their neighbours.'

Some of his guests used to challenge his post-imperialist theories by questioning whether he thought that Britain in her straightened circumstances would ever wish to intervene again overseas or, in fact, be asked to do so. Such actions were the prerogative of the superpowers and perhaps one or two chauvinist states like France. He would immediately mount his hobby-horse:

'You may think the chances of us doing another Falklands are minimal; and I would agree with you that we are not likely to deploy another Naval Task Force 8,000 miles away in a hurry, but from my own personal experience I can say that the unexpected always happens in military affairs. In the 1960's when I was D.D.S.D.[1] in the old War Office, I lost three Christmases in a row scrambling intervention forces. If we could have foreseen the emergencies in Cyprus at Christmas 1961, in Brunei at Christmas 1962 and in Aden at Christmas 1963, we would certainly have reacted earlier – but we could not and so I spent those Christmases in the Army Operations Room in Whitehall instead of at home!'

I am afraid that I and any of the younger generation present were highly sceptical. Our lives seemed to be developing on such easily predictable lines, and Britain was so immersed in her own internal problems that my grandfather's views appeared no more relevant to the 1990's than a Crimean War general's would have been. Britain no longer had imperial responsibilities to discharge. She had only her own 'enlightened self-interest' to consider as our political theorists at school used to put it. In the Imperial era Britain had a service which she believed it was her moral duty to give to 'the lesser breeds without the law'. The imposition of 'good government', or certainly better government than existed at the time, was her gift to her dependent people. All that had changed, but it was hard for my grandfather's generation to accept that it would not come back in some new guise. The grim fact was that Britain in the 1990's had nothing new to give to the world. People like the Germans and Japanese had much more to offer, but were chary of doing so for fear of alienating their erstwhile conquerors yet again. Our generation in 21st century Britain had enough to do carving out a modest prosperity for ourselves in the fiercely competitive world.

To give my grandfather his due, he had thought through an alternative defence strategy. The crux of his policy was the simple axiom that you cannot tell what tomorrow will bring. So in peace, or in pseudo-peace of the type we were living in at the end of the 20th century, you should always maintain balanced defence forces able to react to the unforeseen. Military crises which could be predicted rarely occurred, because deterrent measures could usually be taken to forestall them, provided, of course, there was the political will to do so. In his view, Britain's Defence Forces in the 1990's were too hog-tied to the defence of Western Europe and were, in consequence, over-specialised and lacking in strategic mobility and tactical flexibility.

His solution was to pull back 1st (British) Corps from its defensive sector of NATO's Central Front east of Hanover into Northern Army Group Central Reserve between the Weser and the Rhine, so that it could be equipped as a highly mobile force able to play its full part both in the defence of Western Europe and in defence of Western interests beyond the NATO boundaries in the world at large. He was one of those who believed that the Central Front should be held with the relatively cheap conscript forces of our Continental Allies so that the very expensive and highly trained British troops could be equipped for more mobile operations. If this were done, some of the tanks and conventional artillery regiments could be replaced by helicopters and the latest missiles and other advanced equipment that conscript forces found difficult to handle effectively.

He realised that politically his solution was difficult to sell. Britain would be seen as 'perfidious Albion', preparing to fight to the last drop of her Continental Allies' blood. Others would accuse her of risking the unravelling of the delicate skein of NATO co-operation. But he used to counter by pointing out that the Continental armies had a far greater stake in the forward defence strategy than the British. They would after all be fighting for 'hearth and home'. Moreover, it was militarily sounder to reduce the number of international corps boundaries in the defence of the vital North German plain. Such boundaries are always a source of weakness in a defensive front. In any case, what was forward defence in Europe? Nothing more than an alarm system able to deter minor incursions and to identify major aggression before springing the strategic nuclear exchange. The regular troops of 1st (British) Corps were not needed for that.

I remember one of our guests asking:

'What about the 300,000 regular American soldiers in Southern Germany? Will the U.S. Government not wish to pull them into reserve for the same reasons?'

The reply was short and sharp:

'They are there as the American guarantee to Europe. 55,000 British troops are hardly in the same league!'

While my grandfather felt the British Army was over equipped with heavy armour and under equipped with advanced equipments and helicopters, he was equally sceptical about the Royal Air Force equipment policies. One of his classic quips was:

'Tell the Air Marshals to remember the horse.'

Between the two World Wars the Army's veneration of the horse had all but stifled the introduction of the tank. Having invented the tank in the First World War, the Army's conservatism handed the lead in armoured warfare over to the Germans. Rommel's victories in the Western Desert stemmed from having better tanks than we did and knowing how to use them.

'The RAF's "horse" is pilot seats' my grandfather maintained. 'No Air Marshal worth his salt is going to admit that cruise and stand-off missiles will do the job better than a piloted aircraft, but that is the truth. Front end guidance has improved enormously. *Tornado* is an expensive nonsense, as is the new European fighter aircraft. The RAF should become a missile force, with pilots only flying Army close support aircraft, the larger helicopters and transport aircraft, which can double the role of missile launch platforms and troop and cargo carriers.'

He was kinder to the Royal Navy. He felt they had got their surface ship/submarine mix about right, and he sympathised with them over the delays in replacing the ships of the Falklands era. The three anti-submarine carriers, *Invincible, Illustrious* and *Ark Royal* were still in service as were the aged assault ships *Fearless* and *Intrepid*, though the keels of two new assault ships had been laid down quite recently. Great strides had been made in planning the quick conversion of specific ships owned by British companies for war purposes. The ship owners were only too happy to accept the subsidies offered in the fierce competitive environment of world shipping. The Army's two logistic ships lost in the Falklands had been replaced. Thanks to Britain's commitment to reinforce NATO's northern flank in Norway the amphibious forces had not wasted away. The Royal Marine Commandos had survived many a penny-pinching Defence Review.

Towards the turn of the Century, my own career and world events had such a predictable ring about them that I felt my grandfather's views on the stability of Europe and the inevitability of the unexpected were misguided. In my own case, any starry-eyed hopes I may have had about commanding fighting troops were dashed at the end of my probationary period in 38th Field Engineer Regiment by my CO telling me that he intended to make me Regimental Intelligence Officer, as he felt it was neither in my interests, nor in those of the Sappers, to have a female field troop commander. In his view it was far too rough a life for a woman, although I had all the necessary qualifications. And so I was sent off to the Intelligence Corps Training Centre at Ashford in Kent on a Regimental Intelligence Officers' course. Though I had hoped not only to be the first woman commissioned direct into the Royal Engineers but also the first to command troops, I think the decision was as right as it was predictable, and, looking back, I have no regrets.

In Europe, the German problem, which had been the curse of the Continent since Bismarck's day and had been at the root of the two world wars, again began to threaten world stability in a predictable way. The winds of change generated by Mikhail Gorbachev in the late 1980's could not be confined to the Soviet Union. They rekindled hopes of re-unification that had been smouldering underground in the peat of the German subconscience since 1945. Re-union became thinkable once more to the younger generations on both sides of the Iron Curtain, and political leaders began to refer to Teutonic unity as their rightful heritage. Not unexpectedly, the Berlin crisis of 1998 brought the flames to the surface. The German authorities in the Eastern and Western sectors of the divided city reflected the mood of the times and found more common ground than usual in their dealings with the occupying powers. The Western Commandants took the growing pressure in their stride, but the Soviet authorities were alarmed and reinforced their troops and air forces in Eastern Europe. Moscow made it quite clear that German re-unification was not an option open to anyone. It would not be tolerated under any guise. Memories of the seven million dead that Russia had suffered in the Great Patriotic War, as they called the Second World War, had not faded. On the contrary, time had magnified rather than softened anti-German feeling, making any favourable re-assessment of the post-war Germanies as unpalatable to the Soviet people as it was appetising to the Germans.

Moscow had other reasons for building up their military strength in Eastern Europe. The Gorbachev reforms also encouraged thoughts of greater freedom in Poland, Czechoslovakia, Hungary and Rumania. Dissidence was on the increase and governments more prone to compromise. Revolt of some kind seemed probable in one or more of the Soviet's East European satellites and the Kremlin was taking no chances.

Again, predictably, the Americans responded to the Soviet reinforcement of Eastern Europe with a deployment of part of their Rapid Deployment Force to Western Europe, and there was renewed anxiety in the West about the inadequacy of NATO's conventional forces. It was certainly not the time to make any of the radical changes in the composition and deployment of the 1st (British) Corps, which my grandfather had advocated. Although the crisis subsided without nuclear brinkmanship, stability in Europe could not be taken for granted as long as the 'wild card' of German reunification could be picked up by either side in the superpower poker game.

The 1998 Berlin crisis had other foreseeable consequences. In the United States the Pentagon's 'knee jerk' reaction to the emptying of its reserves by the deployment of more troops and aircraft to Europe, was to regenerate a campaign in Congress for an expansion of United States conventional forces, coupled with a drive in the NATO Council for a build up of Western European conventional strength as well. The approach in

Europe was met with platitudes and no action, and in America Rosenberg's Administration was embarrassed by the logic of the campaign. His election platform had contained promises of reductions in United States Defence spending, whereas the Republicans had continued to trumpet their policy of negotiating from strength. The Pentagon's demand could only be met by reintroducing conscription, the hated 'Draft', and this Rosenberg was not prepared to do. Instead he instructed the State Department and Pentagon to seek economies elsewhere so that the United States could stay strong in Europe. And again, quite predictably, the eyes of the two departments fell upon the burgeoning surpluses of their Japanese economic rivals, who were only spending a fraction of their gross national product on defence of the Free World compared with the United States.

The idea of killing two birds with one stone is always attractive in any walk of life and especially in government circles. If Japan could be cajoled into increasing her Self-Defence Forces, not only would the competitive edge of her economy be blunted, but the United States would be able to reduce its Defence expenditure in the Far East. America's Pacific allies disliked the idea intensely. The ASEAN States, together with Australia and New Zealand, protested as vigorously as they could but to no avail. After several months of hard bargaining between Washington and Tokyo, an agreed package emerged. None of the major Japanese political parties liked the deal, but, as usual with Japanese decisions, an internal consensus was reached that it was time for Japan to stand more firmly on her own military feet and depend less for her defence upon her friendship with the United States. The only political party which openly welcomed the deal was Nogi's New Shintoists, who increased their seats in Parliament as a result, enabling Nogi to start influencing the Japanese political consensus. Nogi's support for the deal certainly did not go unnoticed by Western Intelligence agencies, who were always on the alert for any sign of the re-emergence of Japanese militarism.

One of the reasons for the Berlin crisis not generating superpower nuclear brinkmanship was the long running crisis in space. Both the superpowers had cricks in their necks from watching the other's space activities and this reduced their interest in the political activities of lesser power on earth. Star Wars research had led to some technological breakthroughs in laser and particlebeam weapons in space, but the problems of computer capacity and power generation still limited the extent and effectiveness of practicable anti-missile defences. Nevertheless, production and deployment of rudimentary systems generated endless international debate, superpower summitry and anti-Star Wars protest in the last year of the 20th century.

Britain staked out her claim to be a Space power by successfully launching the earliest version of her $HOTOL^2$ Space Vehicle in 1999 in co-operation with the Japanese. Efforts had been made in the early 1990's to find European partners for the project, but they were cold-shouldered because Europe was already committed to and had spent billions on the French *Ariane* rocket, satellite launcher. The Anglo-French collaboration had, in any case, been soured by their experience developing *Concorde*; and the Americans were not slow to discourage other Europeans from collaborating with a rival to their space shuttle. The Japanese, however, were looking for a space partner, and were attracted by the HOTOL concept and the chance of collaborating with British Aerospace. It was a decision which was to have far reaching consequences.

Back on earth, life went on. Even in Africa, events were unfolding in a predictable way. There were rumours about difficulties being experienced by Noah and M'Bundu as they tried to develop their Homelander concept. Many of the American Blacks who came in with Noah were over-bearing and tactless towards the local people, but most of the reported friction was wishful thinking by hostile journalists. The unpalatable fact was that Noah's rhetoric and economic backing were combining well with M'Bundu's political flare and organisational abilities. While Noah concentrated on winning hearts and minds through the liberal use of American capital, both private and Government funded, M'Bundu was organising Homelander youth on para-military lines and building up the security forces with the help of his Soviet advisers and Soviet aid. The resulting mix was not far removed from an African version of Hitler's National Socialism. Indeed, many Western intelligence reports drew the parallel between the methods of the Nazis and Communist Parties in Germany during Hitler's early days. His Nazi party was just the more successful of the two and came out on top. The same would probably happen in the Homelander Movement but it was too early to predict who would eventually win. In the late 1990's it was Noah to whom people listened perhaps because M'Bundu preferred organisation to polemics.

While the United States and Britain remained relatively unconcerned with developments in Angola, the French began to show increasing signs of nervousness about their investments in Central Africa and, in particular, in the mineral rich Shabah Province of Zaire, formerly Katanga in the days of the Belgian Congo. There was also growing concern amongst the British Commonwealth Prime Ministers when they met in Delhi at the end of the year. Mugabe reiterated his earlier warnings, but it was Pandit Shastri, the Indian Prime Minister, hosting the conference, who took the initiative and led the debate on Africa. While he congratulated the Commonwealth Secretariat on the contingency planning done since the Harare meeting in 1997, he felt that things had not been taken far enough. The Homelanders were consolidating their foot hold in Africa and their expansionist policies were becoming more and more obvious as the months sped by and yet no counter-measures were being taken by neighbouring states to check their ambitions. As far as the Commonwealth contingency plans were concerned no forces had been assigned, no logistic preparations made and no commander or staff designated. He then made a surprising offer. India would provide base facilities for a Commonwealth Indian Ocean Task Force set up to bring rapid support to any Commonwealth country in Africa which called for help to defend itself against Homelander aggression or any other predator who might appear. The Russians had been good friends to India, but India would support any African member of the Commonwealth keen to preserve its independence, whether the threat came from Angola or from the Soviet supported regime in Ethiopia.

The Indian offer was too generous to be left lying on the table. Here was the Commonwealth, at last, coming together to protect its members' interests rather than letting the United States do so, as had happened in the Caribbean in the 1980's when the U.S. Marines ousted the Marxist regime in Grenada. The idea of a Commonwealth Indian Ocean Task Force was not new. Such plans used to be discussed at the Commonwealth Chiefs of Staff 'Unison' exercises run in the United Kingdom by Admiral Lord Mountbatten in the late 1950's and early 1960's before Britain started the final stages of her withdrawal from empire. The last one was held in 1967. The withdrawal from Aden and Singapore made it clear that Britain was no longer able to take the lead in Commonwealth defence planning and so each country turned to which ever superpower offered it the best deal. Now, thirty years later, the concept of Commonwealth military co-operation was being reborn at the behest of what used to be called the New Commonwealth countries to distinguish them from the Old Dominions of Canada, Australia, New Zealand and, in those days, South Africa.

The communiqué issued at the end of the 1999 Commonwealth Conference did mention this time the agreement on military contingency planning as a warning to Noah and M'Bundu. The ink was barely dry on it when the unexpected did start to happen. In January 2000 the world was startled by the murder of the Prime Minister of Zaire. Those journalists who had equated the Noah/M'Bundu regime with a new form of fascist dictatorship, were quick to draw the analogy of Doctor Dolfuss's murder in Vienna in 1934, which was followed by the German *Anschluss* with Austria. They were soon proved right. Three co-ordinated Homelander coups took place almost simultaneously in Kinshasa, capital of Zaire, Libreville, capital of Gabon, and Brazzeville, capital of the Congo.[3] Noah announced that the three States had voluntarily joined the new Black Homelander Union of the Congo, the capital of which would be Kinshasa. The Congo *Anschluss*, as it became known, was highly successful with a genuine ground swell of popular support to sustain it. The most disturbing element in the whole affair was the appearance of M'Bundu's well trained and tightly disciplined troops, carrying Eastern Bloc weapons and equipment, who would not have shamed Hitler's Wehrmacht when it entered Vienna in 1938.

The Hitlerite analogy was far too apt for comfort as far as the Commonwealth countries of Africa were concerned. It was not, however, the Commonwealth which reacted first. The French Government was not prepared to see its own and Belgian assets in Shaba seized by the Homelanders. Without any reference to their allies or to the United Nations, a French Foreign Legion parachute force was flown into Lubumbashi (Elizabethville in Belgian days) and a secessionist regime was set up, supported by a large French military build up.[4] The Zimbabwe, Malawi, Botswana and Zambian governments breathed a very private sigh of relief. Their northern frontiers were now covered by French dominated Shaba. The Homelanders would have to deal with the French before they could be reached. Kenya, Uganda and Tanzania had no such protection and felt remarkably naked. There was, as yet, no Commonwealth Task Force in the Indian Ocean, but the spur to action was there and permitted no delay.

Offers which came into the Commonwealth Secretariat were remarkably generous. India placed 4th Indian Division of Keren fame at the disposal of the task force commander as the main land force, as well as agreeing to provide some naval units and base facilities at Bombay and Madras. Britain agreed to provide an amphibious intervention force. And Australia offered an air component with strike and transport aircraft and a range of helicopters. Canada backed off on the grounds that she was too closely involved with the Americans in the Caribbean and Latin America to disperse her meagre military resources into Africa as well. New Zealand felt she must confine her external military effort to supporting the ASEAN states with her contingent in Singapore.

The British Chiefs of Staff were faced with a major dilemma in advising the Government on the size and composition of the British contribution to the ComTF, as the Commonwealth Indian Ocean Task Force became known in official jargon. For a balanced intervention force they would have to send at least a carrier, an assault ship with commandos embarked, several frigates, Army logistic ships and probably a number of bulk carriers taken up from the trade, as well the usual Fleet auxiliaries and oilers. Such a force was within the planned level of forces available for use outside the NATO area, but there was the problem of endurance to be taken into account. A crisis in Africa would certainly last for months, if not years. A relief force of a similar size would be needed, and that would cut into the amphibious forces assigned to NATO for operations on the Northern flank in Norway. In view of the recent Berlin crisis, there would certainly be resistance from Britain's NATO Allies if she requested the withdrawal of assigned forces for use in the Indian Ocean.

In Whitehall there was a general reluctance to face up to the crisis as there had been at the time of Munich in 1938. Noah assured the British Ambassador in Kinshasa that he had no further territorial claims to make on his neighbours. He and M'Bundu had quite enough on their hands bringing the Congo basin into the 20th, let alone the 21st century. His main problem, he frankly admitted, was to get the French out of Shaba. In inter-Commonwealth consultations it was generally agreed that deployment of the ComTF was probably premature.

But Whitehall, Delhi, Canberra and even Harare were living in a fool's paradise. In Nairobi and Dodoma, the capitals of Kenya and Tanzania, the situation was seen in a very different light. The attractiveness of the Homelanders' philosophy, the ease with which they had taken over the Congo basin, and a general wish to jump on a successful political band wagon, were all factors influencing many disgruntled East Africans, particularly amongst the Kenyan Kikuyu with their *Mau Mau* traditions. At the request of the Kenyan Government, the 2001 Commonwealth Conference was brought forward from November to June. Such was the pressure for deterrent action from the African Prime Ministers present in Sidney, where the Conference was held, that deployment of the ComTF was agreed. The clinching argument was the need for acclimatisation and work up of the Force, a point accepted as valid by the British Chiefs of Staff. The question of endurance could be tackled later if the situation continued to deteriorate and if the despatch of the force to Bombay did not have the hoped for deterrent effect.

I was personally involved in the mounting of the British component of the ComTF. The Chiefs of Staff decided that nothing less than a Commando Brigade of two commandos with some artillery, armoured cars, helicopters and engineer support was needed to seize and hold a point of entry, through which 4th Indian Division could be landed either by sea or air, if a *coup d'état* had taken place before the force arrived. Anything less was unlikely to have the necessary deterrent effect. Both assault ships and extra Army logistic ships were assigned to the Task Force which was based upon the Carrier *Ark Royal* with *Falcons* embarked. An undisclosed number of nuclear and conventional submarines were to give underwater protection. The NATO council reluctantly accepted Britain's case for withdrawing both assault ships and Commando Brigade from Northern flank contingency plans, provided the ships were replaced with requisitional North Sea ferries and Army units temporarily assumed the Commandos' operational commitments.

My involvement stemmed from 38th Engineer Regiment being ordered to send a small regimental headquarters and a reinforced field squadron to support the Commando Brigade. I was, by now, Regimental Intelligence Officer and so went down from Ripon to London with the CO, Lieutenant Colonel John Cunningham, to be briefed on our tasks. There had been some discussion behind the scenes as to whether I should not hand over to a male officer because the Royal Navy, for quite understandable reasons, still did not embark female officers for long periods in warships. The regimental headquarters, however, would be sailing in one of the Army's logistic ships. I was given the option by the CO of accompanying his HQ or staying behind. I was in no doubt about the choice. I was part of the team and had no wish to lose the chance of active service experience. In any case I had found that the men always respected us and our need for privacy. Having been in the sixth form of a boys' public school, then at Cambridge and finally at Sandhurst, I had no qualms about setting off in the LSL *Sir Gallahad II* for the Indian Ocean – a chance of a lifetime.

I will not go into all the details of our embarkation. Suffice it to say that we sailed from Southampton in early August 2001 in company with the converted bulk carrier *Atlantic Warrior*, carrying the helicopters and most of our engineer equipment, and with other supply ships and oilers. The Task Force itself, with Rear Admiral White flying his flag in *Ark Royal*, had sailed a day earlier and was to go round the Cape to avoid the risk of confrontation with the Russians in the Red Sea. We, on the other hand, were to transit the Suez Canal to *rendezvous* with the Task Force at Bombay where we were to work up with our Indian and Australian colleagues.

The voyage was totally uneventful, apart from our passage down the Red Sea and past Aden. We were shadowed from Suez southwards by a Soviet frigate and intelligence gathering trawler. As we came abreast of Aden, we could see a number of large Russian warships at anchor in the roads. Aden itself looked as uninviting as ever. Thank goodness we no longer garrisoned its barren, inhospitable rocks.

The welcome we received in Bombay was ecstatic. It was as if the years of bitterness before Indian Independence in1947 had never happened and we were back as partners with India as we had been in earlier times. The Indian military organisations, customs and ways of doing business were still based upon the British tradition and there was virtually no language problem: most of the Indian officers spoke faultless English though with the Indian lilt which we have grown accustomed to hearing in British cities and-towns. The main problem we had to face was the handling of Russian equipment with which most of the Indian units were equipped.

By Xmas 2001 we were paying our first visit to Mombasa. The force had been divided into two groups. *Ark Royal* with *Fearless*, three frigates and *Sir Gallahad* were in Group 01 off the African Coast, while *Intrepid*, *Atlantic Warrier, Sir Tristan* and three frigates were in Group 02 held back as relief group at Bombay. It was intended that the two groups should relieve each other at three monthly intervals. India provided three frigates for each group and her aircraft carrier *Vikrant* (the ex-Soviet carrier *Kiev*) for Group 02.

Apart from the surprise that the Commonwealth had acted in such a concerted way and had achieved a degree of military co-operation, events were still unfolding fairly predictably. The arrival of the ComTF at Mombasa seemed to have a stabilizing effect. Homelander propaganda increased its tone of sweet reasonableness, and the United Kingdom press began to question the need for the Task Force's deployment. The *Guardian* was naturally scathing about British 21st century gunboat diplomacy. Even the *Times* ran a series of leaders questioning the validity of the Commonwealth action, taking the line that African problems were for Africans and not for Britons, Australians and Indians to solve. There was also some restlessness in NATO over the deployment of so many British warships which should have been in the Eastern Atlantic, east of Suez. The general opinion within the Task Force was that it would not be long before costs and political pressure would be turning us homewards.

Christmas at Mombasa was enlivened for us by the unexpected arival of a French naval squadron under command of Admiral de Merville, flying his flag in the nuclear powered aircraft-carrier *Richelieu*. She was accompanied by four Type C70 frigates and the assault ship *Foudre*. I was on the bridge of *Ark Royal*, talking to our admiral's Intelligence Officer, Lieutenant Commander Sandy Gibson, when the French ships sailed into the anchorage. Our conversation was punctuated by the crash of the gun salutes as the two fleets paid the usual courtesies to each other's admirals' flags.

'What are *they* doing here?' I asked, laying the emphasis on the *they*.

'Oh! The god-damn frogs are always sticking their long noses into other peoples' affairs,' Sandy replied in a tone of disdain. 'Ever since they achieved naval parity with us in 1998 when the *Richelieu*, over there, was first commissioned, they have been showing the flag with her when and wheresoever they catch the scent of trouble – especially if it is American or British trouble! There's no love lost between us!'

'But, where have they suddenly sprung from?' I asked, revealing how little attention I had been paying to French items in our Intelligence summaries.

'They've been cruising in Pacific waters where the American run-down and the Japanese build-up have tempted them to scavenge for political influence and markets for the French armament industry. Their last port of call was Nagasaki. They fancy themselves as the one Western European power which is free from all American influence and can act independently without bowing to Washington or Moscow!' I sighed with envy as he warmed to his subject.

'The French are bent on re-establishing the glory of *La France*, whatever the cost. They see themselves at the centre of the cross-roads of the world's two geo-political axes: East/West and North/South. They have built up their navy to match their vision of France in the 21st century, and it is now considerably larger than ours – bless them!'

Knowing how much Britain depended on the Gibraltar Accord to maintain her Maritime forces, I could barely stifle a pang of jealousy. There had been a time in the Thatcher era when it had been fashionable for economic pundits in places like the London School of Economics to predict that Britain would slip out of the Top Ten by the turn of the century, and would be overtaken by Italy, Spain and even Austria. This did not happen because their estimates had given too little weight to the Thatcherite revolution in Britain's economic psychology, which, though slow to bite, had, in the end, reversed our decline. By 2001 our *per capita* Gross National Product was rising, but we had a long way to go before we could overhaul our French rivals. It was cold comfort to be reminded by Sandy that *per capita* gross national products were not everything: such factors as political will, national morale and military efficiency all had a part to play in the relative dynamics of competing states.

A few days before Christmas, Admiral White gave a reception in *Ark Royal* for local government dignitaries and the officers of the French Squadron. It was a colourful affair in formal mess kit and evening dress on *Ark Royal*'s flight deck, which had been especially decorated with bunting and flood-lit for the occasion. It was a lovely cool clear tropical evening, ideal for a 'get to know you better' party. All the officers of the British Task Force had been detailed to host specific guests in the early stages until the flow of alcohol thawed inhibitions and the party became self-generating. My guest was the Navigating Officer of the *Foudre*, who turned out to be a disaster as far as I was concerned. I knew his name was Jacques Gensoul, but my knowledge of French, and indeed British, naval history was too sparse for alarm bells to ring in my subconscience: and no-one warned me to be on my guard!

Jacques Gensoul turned out to be pretty unprepossessing and, though not actually rude, was certainly off-hand. He spoke little English and found my schoolgirl French incomprehensible. In desperation, I caught Sandy Gibson's eye and he came over to help. Gensoul recognised a fluent French speaker and let flow all the pent-up emotion bottled up within him, which he had found he could not express to me.

This was the first time that Lieutenant Gensoul had set foot on a British warship. He had vowed never to do so in order to honour the memory of his great uncle whose squadron had been sunk by Admiral Somerville's Force H at Mers-el-Kebir in 1940 with the loss of 1,300 French lives. I asked what had made him change his mind? He smiled for the first time since he had come aboard, and out came another cascade of tumbling words, which Sandy translated briefly as: 'We are now strong enough to return the compliment, should it ever prove necessary!'

Before I had time to think of a temporising reply, the Flag Lieutenant came up and asked me if I would come and meet the British High Commissioner to Tanzania, who had come up from Dodoma specially for the party. Again my ignorance betrayed me. I expected to meet a man. Instead I was introduced to her Excellency Dame Elizabeth Harding, whom I learnt later had been one of the leading feminists at Oxford in the 1960's. She had made a highly successful career for herself in the Diplomatic Service, and was delighted to meet and encourage another young aspirant like herself in the Services. Though I was no feminist, even in my Cambridge days, I must confess to being inspired by her. If she could make it, so could I!

The reception ended with the traditional ceremony of lowering the colours after the Royal Marine Band had beaten Retreat. Playing the Marseillaise, followed by our own national Anthem, seemed incongruous to me after my brief encounter with Jacques Gensoul. British membership of the EEC and the opening of the Channel tunnel had done little to dispel mutual suspicion in Anglo-French relations. The French were still frogs to us in the Services, and regrettably very powerful frogs at that!

I had another 'brief encounter'. We were all given three days shore leave on a rota basis after Christmas. Sandy Gibson's leave period coincided with mine and he asked me to spend it with him at the Diani Reef Hotel along the coast. Our holiday lasted just one glorious night, which we danced away, ending up with a bathe in the fluorescent sea just before dawn.

Then quite suddenly the unexpected began to happen.

The telephone was ringing as I got back to my room, having said a fond goodnight to Sandy. It was the duty officer in *Sir Gallahad* ringing to tell me to return to the ship at once. There was trouble in the Persian Gulf, but he did not know what it was. All he knew was that the Task Force was sailing at mid day.

Any plans that Sandy Gibson may have had of getting to know me more intimately evaporated with that telephone call. We returned to our ships as quickly as we could, in no fit state to start pouring over Intelligence reports and getting briefing material together on the Persian Gulf for our respective masters.

I think we had all been so involved in the assessments of events in Africa and in the analysis of whether a Black Hitler existed in the Congo basin, that we had been ignoring events in the Middle East since the end of the Iran/Iraq war. When I reached the ship, Colonel Cunningham told me that there had been a *Shi'ite* revolution in Riyadh, the capital of Saudi Arabia. The King and his closest relatives had been murdered and their naked bodies dragged through the streets as King Feisal's and Nuri-es-Said's had been in Baghdad in 1958. The leaders of the coup were claiming that they were acting on the inspiration of the Ayatollah of Tehran for the imposition of his brand of conservative Islamic Fundamentalism throughout the Arab world. Most Europeans were said to be safe, but many Americans had been taken into 'Revolutionary Custody' as hostages to prevent American military intervention. The Task Force was to head for the Persian Gulf to be in a position to rescue British and European nationals, if their lives were endangered.

As Regimental Intelligence Officer, I put away all the Intelligence

MAP 2: The Middle East at the turn of the century

Summaries on Africa and went over to *Ark Royal* to pick up as much as Sandy Gibson had on the Middle East, which was not much. However, he told me that the latest reports were coming in by satellite facsimile and I would get copies as soon as they arrived.

Looking through the basic material, which I had picked up in *Ark Royal*,

I saw that the coup was not as unexpected as I thought. There had been doubts for some years as to whether the Royal houses of Saudi Arabia and Jordan could survive in the turbulent environment of Islamic politics, with so many ambitious men wishing to lead the Moslem world back to its former glories. The general view, however, expressed in the summaries was that both monarchs had such a firm grip on their people and, more importantly, on their armed forces that it would be difficult to topple them. The United States had lost much of its popularity in Saudi Arabia, due to its continued support of Israel and its refusal to supply weapons which could be used against her. The British had, on the contrary, become *persona grata* in Saudi Arabia since Margaret Thatcher's '*Tornados* for oil' deal in the 1980's; and their long standing links with Kuwait and the other Gulf States were still strong.

When the latest Intelligence Summaries came in, we were able to build up a fuller picture of what was happening and of the complex struggle for power which had led to the Saudi revolution. At the heart of the matter lay doctrinal differences within the *Shi'a* Council at Kerbale but, in practice, the theological arguments were but symbolic of the intense rivalry which had developed between the young, thrusting Ayatollah of Baghdad and the senior and ultra-conservative Ayatollah of Tehran. The doctrinal point at issue was the future status of women in *Shi'ite* society. The Ayatollah of Baghdad argued that Islam could only develop its full potential in the modern world if women played a larger part in Moslem public life. He quoted the successes of Golda Meyer, Indira Gandhi and Margaret Thatcher, but he was on firmer ground when he claimed that there was nothing in the *Koran* to support the man-made rules about the treatment of women. The Ayatollah of Tehran, being the successor of Ayatollah Khomeini, would have none of it: women, he claimed, had no right or desire to be equal with men. Who would win the argument was unlikely to depend upon the scholarship of the mullahs supporting either view. It was the political battle for the leadership of the Arab world that would decide the doctrinal issue. In the 1950's Nasser's Cairo had beaten Nuri-es-Saids' Baghdad in the leadership struggle. Now Baghdad and Tehran were vying for the leadership. Tehran had won the first round by engineering the Saudi coup.

As we sailed north the CO and I were flown over to *Ark Royal* by helicopter for briefing on the latest position. Intense negotiations were going on between the British Ambassadors in Riyadh and Tehran and the revolutionaries. There were some three hundred United States citizens being held hostage, and, although the British and other European residents were free to leave, all Saudi international airports were closed. Convoys were being organised to take them overland to Kuwait and Bahrein, where they could be flown out by civilian airlines. An American aircraft carrier group was deployed east of Aden watching the Russians, but could not intervene for fear of endangering the lives of the United States hostages in Riyadh. Our orders were to make for Bahrein and Kuwait to assist in the evacuation of Europeans and to help the Americans in any way that we could.

Admiral White had some difficult decisions to take. He could not risk *Ark Royal* in the narrow and easily mined waters of the Gulf, and yet he could not send *Fearless* and *Intrepid*, which had joined us from Bombay, into the Gulf without air cover. The problem was solved for him by the Kuwait Government, which was becoming increasingly worried about Tehran's intentions. The Ruler asked for British military support ostensibly to ensure the safe evacuation of European refugees, but in reality to prop up his own regime. The British Government, after some hesitation and a great deal of diplomatic cabling between the British embassies in Riyadh, Kuwait and Bahrein agreed that *Ark Royal* should fly off eight of her *Falcons*, which were to provide air cover first from Bahrein and then from Kuwait for the passage of the amphibious force to Kuwait. If the British Ambassadors in the two capitals could negotiate the release of the U.S. hostages, they would be flown out to Kuwait in *Atlantic Warrior*'s four heavy lift helicopters.

The whole scenario seemed fraught with political and military difficulties and had many similarities to the British intervention in Kuwait in 1962. Then we still had bases in Kenya, Aden and Bahrein and were able to fly in five battalions and land two squadrons of tanks from the amphibious squadron in the Gulf to deter the threatened Iraqi invasion of Kuwait. The deployment of the British force on the Mutlah Ridge north of Kuwait City had the desired deterrent effect and the Iraquis did not attack. This time we had only two commandos, an armoured car squadron, a light gun battery and a squadron of engineeers. There could be no question of holding the Mutlah Ridge again. The most we could do was to secure the airfield through which the evacuation of refugees could be carried out. Fortunately, being January, we did not suffer from intense heat as our predecessors had done. In 1962 a number of men died of heat stroke.

While there were undoubted similarities between 1962 and 2002, there was one critically important difference. In 1962 the British troops and airmen who took part were battle experienced, whereas the Iraqis were not. There was every confidence that an Iraqi attack could be decisively defeated. In 2002 our servicemen had not seen military action since the Falklands campaign twenty years earlier, whereas the Iraqis had been fighting Iran for the whole of that time and were battle-wise. I do not think any of us were conscious of our shortcomings as we reached Kuwait in the early morning, and the Commando Brigade disembarked to secure the airfield. The *Falcons* were already there and the heavy-lift helicopters were flown ashore as well. As each ship unloaded, it pulled back into the Gulf to await events.

At first all seemed to be going well. Several British Airways and British Caledonian aircraft arrived, loaded their refugees and departed. From the bridge of *Sir Gallahad* it was just possible to see what was happening through field glasses. In the foreground was the Dallas-like concrete and glass jungle of 21st century Kuwait with the airfield just visible in the grey misty drabness of the desert beyond the city. We saw the heavy-lift helicopters leave the airfield and head southwards towards Riyadh, and assumed, correctly as it turned out, that our Ambassador had successfully struck a deal with the Revolutionary Council over the release of the American hostages. We saw them complete the first turn round and heard on the BBC midday news that the United States hostages were being flown out via Kuwait, which struck me at the time as a premature and thoroughly ill-advised announcement, as only about half the hostages could have been carried in the first lift.

I was up on the bridge again in the evening and thought I could hear the second hostage lift returning. Then all hell broke loose over the airfield area. The ship's anti-aircraft missiles were being fired as action stations were being sounded in the ship. In minutes there was nothing but a thick pall of dust engulfing the desert where the airfield had been. Up through it spiralled a number of columns of jet black oily smoke from burning aircraft. Then, out to sea, where the frigate *Broad Sword* had been cruising there was a blinding flash and another mushroom cloud of smoke. We were all relieved to see *Broad Sword* sail out of the smoke but we could see her bridge was little more than a heap of jagged, tangled wreckage. She did not catch fire as *Sheffield* had done in the Falklands, nor did she sink. We learnt later that she had been hit by a fanatical female *Kamikazi* pilot of one of the extremist Shi'ite sects. Her Captain and twelve officers and men had been killed, but her Commander managed to get her back to Bahrein under her own power. It was a fine effort.

For a time we, in *Sir Gallahad* could not tell in the fading light what was happening ashore. We could hear reports coming through on the Commando Brigade radio net and from it we realised there had been a surprise Iraqi attack on the airfield. Much later, we heard that the BBC broadcast about the evacuation of American hostages through Kuwait had alerted the rabidly anti-Western governor of Basra, who was a fervent supporter of the Ayatollah of Baghdad and who deemed it to be his sacred duty to intervene and stop the evacuation. He had a helicopter borne infantry regiment in the Basra garrison and a number of helicopter gunships to support it. Flying low across the desert, they had been screened by the Mutlah Ridge and took the Marines on the airfield by surprise. Four of the *Falcon*'s were airborne at the time, escorting the heavy lift helicopters with the last of the U.S. hostages on board. The others were refuelling.

In the first few minutes of the Iraqi attack there was indescribable chaos. A British Airways plane was hit by missiles from an Iraqi helicopter gunship and burst into flames. One *Falcon* was also destroyed and two were damaged on the ground. Then the Iraqi infantry started to pile out of their helicopters and were decimated by the fire from the dug in Marines. Several of the troop carrying helicopters went up in flames, adding to the inferno. Those Iraqi helicopters that could do so re-embarked what men they could and the whole force withdrew, having achieved its aim of stopping the evacuation at a price.

Admiral White, who had transferred his flag to *Fearless*, when *Ark Royal* was left in the Indian Ocean, was again faced with the difficult decision as to whether to advise immediate withdrawal under cover of darkness or stay until it was clear that no further humanitarian work could be done rescuing refugees and evacuating wounded. His decision was made more difficult by reports from the British Embassy that part of the Kuwaiti Army had mutinied and run up the Saudi Revolutionary Council's flag over the government buildings. The Ruler and his family had escaped to the Embassy and had requested evacuation in HM ships.

Admiral White, rightly in our view, decided to risk bringing the two assault ships and two logistic ships into the port for a rapid evacuation and, if need be, a fighting withdrawal by the Commandos, so that he could have his ships out to sea again well before dawn. London agreed and we started to nose our way into one of the Kuwait Oil Company quays with just enough depth of water to allow the four ships to lower their loading ramps onto the jetties.

That night, I think, I grew up. Though most of the worst casualties brought in from the airfield were loaded onto the assault ships, we had enough badly burnt refugees and wounded Marines in *Sir Gallahad* to make me realise the true horror of war. At about two in the morning, the assault ships were ordered to withdraw. *Sir Tristan* was to be the next to go and *Sir Gallahad* would be last, embarking the Marine rearguard not later than 4 a.m. before pulling back into the Gulf.

The departure of the big ships seemed to be a signal for panic ashore. A milling crowd of local inhabitants tried to rush our ramp and were only stopped by a warning burst of fire from the Marine guard. Then we saw the figures of three or four Marines struggling through the crowd, trying to reach the ramp. They had lost their helmets and were without weapons. As the Master at Arms had them pulled out of the crowd one of them shouted that their mates had all been killed; they were the only survivors; and the Kuwaiti mutineers were close behind them. Looking at them, as a burly Petty Officer tried to knock some sense into them, I saw for the first time the real face of fear. They were youngsters and had lost all self-control. There were no mutineers behind them.

Fortunately the Brigade Command net was was 'loud and clear', and we knew that thinning out had begun and the rearguard was under no immediate threat. As four o'clock approached, the files of Marines of the last

Company ashore came up the ramp. They were begrimed with dust and oil, but elated with their day's work. One of the Naval officers standing close to me said:

'The only difference between this lot and the Liverpool supporters is discipline. They get stuck in and enjoy a fight!'

They certainly looked it. The soccer hooligan has his uses if properly trained. They are from the same stock as the men who manned Nelson's broadsides at Trafalgar and fought in the squares at Waterloo.

The ramp started to rise as the rearguard commander reported that all his men were aboard. *Sir Gallahad* went astern and the bow doors closed. Britain's second Kuwait intervention was over. In 1962 the Iraqis had been deterred. This time they had struck us a sharp blow. The cost when calculated later had been grim. About one hundred and fifty refugees had died in the British Airways plane; one helicopter load of some thirty American hostages had been lost; the Marines had had over fifty casualties; and we had lost three *Falcons*, a medium lift helicopter and, of course, *Broad Sword* would be out of commission for some time.

As we withdrew from the Gulf, political rows started in London and Washington as to why British forces had been involved in a strictly Arab affair, and why so many British and American citizens had been killed. Few of us heard the announcement from Rome that Pope John Paul III had died.

Notes

1. Deputy Director of Staff Duties, who used to be responsible for the executive deployment of the Army world-wide.
2. Horizontal Take Off and Landing space vehicle developed by British Aerospace.
3. See Map 1 page 8.
4. The French plan to phase out their military commitments in Africa, made in the 1980s, died with their intervention in Shaba.

3

The Rise of the Militants: (2004–2006)

*'The world is suffering its worst economic crisis since
1929 and yet beggar my neighbour has become the favourite international sport..'*
Diary entry for 12.2005

The Saudi Revolution of 2002 did not, of course, end with our withdrawal from Kuwait. The initial unity of the Shi'ite Revolutionary Council in Riyadh soon splintered into factions loyal to Tehran and Baghdad, and their internal squabbles were added to by the recovery of Saudi Army and Air Force units loyal to the Hashemite dynasty who began to fight back with the help of Jordan's armed forces. Saudi oil production came to a shuddering halt as civil war engulfed the oil producing areas. The world suddenly found itself short of oil for the first time since the oil glut of the middle 1980's. The price of oil rocketed even faster than it had done after the Arab/Israeli war of 1973 because alternative sources of supply like the North Sea oilfields were already in decline and the Chernobyl accident in Soviet Russia in 1986 had stunted the growth of the nuclear power industry. The world economy, which had benefited from cheap oil for so long and had reached a peak of activity, nose dived into one of the steepest declines since the Wall Street crash of 1929.

Periods of economic depression are apt to spawn political militancy rather than increased collaboration and the crisis of 2003 was no exception. The great depression of the early 1930's brought forth Hitler, Mussolini and Togo: the depression of 2003 to 2007 gave the four horsemen of the 21st Century Apocalypse their chance and imprinted their charcters upon the pages of the history of Third World War. They were to be the men who would eventually throw down the gauntlet, challenging the super powers to create a fairer and more prosperous 'New Heaven and New Earth'.

When the British amphibious element of the Commonwealth Indian Ocean Task Force arrived back at Bombay, having left most of the

41

refugees, hostages and wounded at Bahrein and Muscat to be flown home, Admiral White found that our services were no longer needed. The Indian C-in-C of the Commonwealth Force had appreciated that our diversion to the Persian Gulf meant that he no longer had an intervention force equipped and ready to secure points of entry in East Africa if a sudden Homelander coup occurred. The very absence of the British ships off Mombasa and Dar-es-Salaam might well encourage the Homelanders to bring forward any coup they were planning to launch at a later date. With the Governments of Kenya's and Tanzania's blessing and the Indian Government's agreement, a brigade of 4th Indian Division was sent by air to both ports to help secure them and their airfields in case help was needed. The Australians provided most of the air transport for the move before withdrawing their RAAF contingent back to Australia.

It was with some relief that the British Government found themselves able to sail the naval task force back to Britain. In their place it was agreed that contingency plans should be prepared for the despatch of 5th Infantry Brigade from the United Kingdom to Kenya if the Indian C-in-C had to call for reinforcements at any time. Otherwise the main British military presence would be the small British Services Training Teams which had been in East and Central Africa since our withdrawal from empire.

The year 2003 was a hectic one for me as I had to sit the Staff College exam. I was successful and was lucky enough to be selected for the 2005 course; the year that will go down in history not as 'the year of revolution', like 1848, but as 'the year of the Militants'. Being at Camberley at the time meant that you heard all the best speakers lecturing on the events as they unfolded, and you could listen to the discussions about their implications amongst the wide cross-section of students drawn from all over the Commonwealth and from the armies of our European allies.

It was during my time as Intelligence Officer with the Task Force in 2002 that I had decided to keep a diary, a thing which is usually frowned upon in the Service for security reasons. Thank goodness I did. The habit became a permanent one and I have been able to use it in writing this history, not so much for factual data, for which I rely on the Public Record Office and Ministry of Defence Historical Sections, but for the feel of the times. Contemporary diary entries are free from hindsight, which makes them immensely valuable in recreating the environment of the day.

Apart from the Saudi Civil War, which triggered the oil crisis of 2002, one of the most significant contemporary events was the death of Pope John Paul III, which occurred while we were on our way home from the Gulf. I must confess that it only merited one short sentence of regret in my diary at the passing of a world figure and no more. He had been a man of great humanity but like his far-travelled predecessor, John Paul II, he had no wish to see the Roman Catholic priesthood involving itself in the world's political affairs. In consequence, the Catholic Church stayed very much on the side of the establishment, particularly in Latin countries, and it was in Latin America that his death was to have the greatest impact.

It is perhaps wrong to say that it was his death that mattered. That would be unkind. What did matter was the appointment of his successor. When the College of Cardinals met in Rome to elect the new Pope, the internal debate was more acrimonious than usual because there was a deep division of opinion amongst all Christians, not just among the Roman Catholics, on the question of the Churches' involvement in politics. The Church of England's bishops had tried unsuccessfully to influence the debate on Nuclear policy in the 1980's and had been politely but firmly put in their place by the Thatcher Government. Pope John Paul II had had a difficult row to hoe in Poland and had not been able to do more than prevent an open schism between the Church and the Communist Government. These failures added impetus to the feeling amongst committed Christians that more forthright leadership was needed if the Church was to fulfil its duty to mankind as it used to do in earlier centuries.

In the College of Cardinals in 2002 opinion seemed remarkably evenly balanced. Indeed, several ballots were forecast before a final selection would be made. The choice lay between the so-called 'Political' and 'non-Political' candidates. The leading contender of the 'Political' Group was a former Spanish Jesuit, Cardinal Xavier Vasquez, who had served his apprenticeship in the Latin American priesthood. He believed fervently that the Church could not minister to people's souls without caring for their material well-being. There had to be both leadership and discipline in any successful society, but there also had to be a sense of compassion and equality of opportunity as well. While he believed in rendering unto Caesar the things that are Caesar's, he held also that the Church had the right to ensure that Caesar ruled according to Christian principles.

In the debate it appeared that Xavier Vasquez was on the losing side. After two conservative Popes in succession it was not easy for many of the Cardinals to take an openly liberal line in debate for fear of showing disloyalty to the accepted orthodoxy. But when the first ballot was taken white smoke appeared from the chimney of the Cistine Chapel, signifying a decisive majority had been achievedd by one man – but who? Much to the surprise of the world media, which had been predicting another conservative, it was Xavier Vasquez who had been elected and who chose to break with tradition by using his own Christian name in his title, Xavier I. His election, with an overall majority in the first ballot, showed that there was a ground swell of opinion that accepted the indivisability of the spiritual and material needs of mankind.

The message of the election was not lost on the priesthood in the new Pope's former parishes in the mountains of Colombia. Not only did the church there bask in the reflected glory of his election, but it felt a sense of relief that their problems of ministering to their backward and

MAP 3: The northern half of Latin America at the turn of the century

impoverished flocks would be better understood in the Vatican. No-one
was more jubilant than Archbishop Ignatius Bolivar, the Roman Catholic
Primate of Colombia, one of the poorest countries of Latin America. It
was he at whom Pope John Paul had wagged his finger during the Papal

visit of the 1980's in disapproval of his political activities. He had only been in his early thirties at the time and so had had the mental agility to mend his ways as the Holy Father directed. He put left wing politics behind him and concentrated upon his very considerable successes as a preacher, pastor and organiser of Church affairs in his native province. His spiritual charisma, his genuineness of purpose, and his administrative abilities brought their rewards with his steady advancement to Bishop of Cali and then Archbishop in Bogota.

But with Ignatius's promotion came an equally progressive realisation that Christians could not stand back and watch the corruption of society by ambitious politicians, to whom power and wealth were synonomous, and to be fought for, irrespective of the needs of the people they were supposed to represent. To Ignatius, the root cause of the evils that beset Colombia was the all pervading influence of the United States. The Americans were backing a party of so-called 'Democrats', who were, in reality, nothing more than ambitious place-seekers of the *ancien régime* with that happy knack of ensuring that a 'reasonable' percentage of all American aid was syphoned off into their own pockets in 'Commissions'.

Decisive changes in the careers of many great men quite often come about through a random coincidence of events. In Archbishop Bolivar's case it was a chance meeting with an aged and very senior priest of the Greek Orthodox Church in Bogota during an ecumenical seminar. The Greek was, in fact, a Cypriot, who, as a young man, had been one of Archbishop Makarios's secretaries during the anti-British struggle for *Enosis* – union of Cyprus with Greece in the 1950's. The two men drew parallels between Cyprus in the 1950's and Colombia at the beginning of the 21st century. Both were dominated by a paternalistic alien power, which did not reflect the true wishes of the local people. In Cyprus the Church allied itself with Colonel Grivas's Greek nationalist guerrilla organisation, *EOKA*, to force Britain to quit. The Colombian Church, the Cypriot suggested, should combine with the only effective opposition in the country, the outlawed Communist guerrillas. He suggested Ignatius should read the biographies of Archbishop Makarios and of Colonel Grivas. Ignatius was fascinated with the analogy and did read everything he could lay his hands on about the Cyprus struggle, but could see little hope in being able to become the Makarios of Colombia, the man who would drive out American influence and re-establish a true Latin society once more in the mirror image of Spain as he imagined it to have become since the death of Franco.

The election of Xavier Vasquez as Pope opened the way. Ignatius had been brought up and went to school with the local Communist guerrilla leader, Domingo Garcia, and until Pope John Paul II had wagged his finger, the two men had been close collaborators in local politics. Both had done their utmost to expose political corruption and to improve the lot of the local peasantry. They had parted with regret in the 1980's when the Colombian Army mounted an anti-Communist drive through their district. Now, twenty years later, Ignatius Bolivar, the Archbishop, sought a secret meeting with his erstwhile friend Domingo, the *Caudillo* of one of the strongest guerrilla forces in Latin America with established links through Cuba to the Soviet Union. Garcia, besides being a successful guerrilla leader, also had Colombian Indian blood in his veins, which Ignatius did not; and so he could act as an effective link between the Latin establishment and the impoverished Indians who knew and trusted him.

No copy of the Concordat of 2004 between Archbishop Bolivar and Domingo Garcia has ever been published. That one existed and was probably known to both the Vatican and Moscow can hardly be doubted: the circumstantial evidence of subsequent events provide sufficient proof. The two men agreed to respect each other's ideology and to work together in the common cause of ridding their country of American influence and in improving the lot of the ordinary people. Domingo could only expect covert support from the church; but priests, who collaborated with the Government at the expense of the people, would receive no mercy from the guerrillas. The Archbishop would keep a trusted representative at Domingo's headquarters and Domingo nominated one of the Archbishop's young and ambitious secretaries to act for him in ecclesiastical councils. These two 'liaison' officers were to be the controllers of their respective networks of informers and couriers.

The first evidence that some concordat existed between the Church and the Communists came in the local elections of 2006. In many provincial centres that had previously elected establishment figures, the voting patterns were reversed and the left wing candidate emerged victorious. It was not long before the Government was receiving reports that priests had been advising their flocks to vote for those 'who looked after their interests'. Though there was suspicion that the Archbishop was the instigator of the anti-government swing, there was no hard evidence to prove that this was so. When challenged by one of the Ministers, he replied with studied care that he hoped all good Christians had read the debate which had led to the election of Pope Xavier I. In a true democracy, like Colombia, it was the wishes of the people that mattered. Unfortunately, it had turned out that they were not over-impressed with the Government's performance. He and the Church could not be blamed for that.

Like the *EOKA* campaign against the British in Cyprus, it was the guerrilla leader's pseudonym, 'El Caudillo' that appeared on all subversive leaflets and hoardings, and in whose name terrorist attacks were made. But the brains behind the campaign of violence which was about to begin was that of Ignatius Bolivar. He and not Domingo was the Latin American Horseman of the Apocalypse. No-one as yet had coined the phrase 'Christo-Communist'. In retrospect it can be seen that the concordat of

2004 marked the beginning of the Christo-Communist campaign in Latin America.

The African nationalist Horse still had two riders in 2004 and was feeling the strain of two pairs of hands tugging, often in different directions and certainly with varying shades of emphasis, upon the reins. There was a general feeling in Kinshasa that the Noah/M'Bundu partnership could not last much longer.

Noah began to appreciate from his influential contacts in Washington that the Congo *Anschluss* had been launched too soon and with too little preparation of public opinion in the United States. His aggressive Hitleresque performance had not sat well with his earlier declarations of making his African State a mirror image of the United States. 2004 was again Presidential election year and Rosenberg was particularly sensitive to the charge that he had acted as midwife at the birth of the unruly Homelander child in Africa. He had helped to bring forth a most disagreeable fascist monster. Noah had, therefore, begun to appease American and Western opinion generally with conciliatory statements, assuring the rest of Africa that his movement had no further territorial ambitions except for the recovery of the secessionist Shaba Province. He looked to the United States and Britain to lead the Security Council in condemning French and Belgian aggression in Shaba, but otherwise he would concentrate on developing the wealth of the Homelander Union of the Congo on American political and industrial lines.

While M'Bundu accepted the need to placate U.S. opinion in the electoral year, both he and his Soviet backers saw Noah not only as a necessary embarrassment but also as a growing threat to their planned transition of the Homelander concept from its capitalist origins to its Marxist future. The decision as to when to strike would depend upon the outcome of the United States Presidential election. If the Democrats won, it would be worth playing along with the Americans for another four years, benefiting from governmental and private capital injection. But, if Karl Nimitz, the Republican candidate, won, there would be no point in carrying on the charade much longer. M'Bundu's known links with the Soviet Bloc would put an end to American aid under a Republican Administration.

Karl Nimitz's victory for the Republicans in the 2004 United States Presidential Elections was Noah Johnston's death warrant. A new American Ambassador arrived in Kinshasa early in 2005. In his first interview with Noah, the Ambassador made it very clear that in the current economic climate in the United States, aid, to use American slang, was 'as scarce as hens' teeth' and had to be earned. The next *tranche* of United States aid would only be released in return for 'copper bottomed' assurances that Homelander expansion had reached its limits and a positive approach would be made to establishing cordial relations with neighbouring states. If

Noah would clear a draft memorandum of understanding with his colleagues in the Homelander Government, President Nimitz would invite Noah to Washington to sign a new aid agreement in April.

Noah gave the United States draft to M'Bundu to set before his Cabinet. When he was assured by M'Bundu that it had the unanimous support of Government ministers, he accepted the President's invitation, assuring the Ambassador that he saw no insurmountable problems in establishing friendly relations with the new United States Government.

Noah's visit to Washington followed the well established routine of a fanfare welcome on the White House lawn, speeches stressing coincidence of political views and bilateral confidence, and the public signing of the mutual aid document. Only the size of the financial package was announced in the public communiqué. The political protocol curbing Homelander ambitions was undisclosed, to avoid souring the occasion.

Noah set off home with a glow of satisfaction. During his visit he had been feted by the leaders of Black communities in major American cities and had received further generous pledges of financial support from large corporations. Some, of course, were not entirely altruistic, because the donors hoped for preferential treatment in establishing offshoots in the Congo Homeland, but, for the most part, the support was genuine. Despite the economic climate, Noah felt he could not have been more generously treated. The price he had paid for United States Government aid had been well worth it. Even M'Bundu had acknowledged that, for the next few years, priority must be given to internal economic development. The protocol restricting further external expansion was, in reality, irrelevant.

While Noah and his wife enjoyed the comfort and luxury of their First Class tickets on their return flight from Washington to Kinshasa, a copy of the political protocol was leaked to the press. Splashed across the front page of the leading Kinshasa newspaper, *The Homelander*, was the single word TRAITOR in bold block type. Noah was depicted as an underhand schemer who had sold the Homelander birthright to expansion for a handful of American dollars. A large and angry crowd assembled at the airport, not to give him the noisy welcome that he expected, but to howl for his instant dismissal. Dismissal was not to be his fate. As he left the aircraft, he was seen to crumple and fall forward on to his wife. No-one heard the shots that hit him above the clamour of the crowd because they were fired from a silenced rifle from the top of the air terminal building. Like President Kennedy in 1963, he died in hospital without recovering consciousness. And again, like Lee Harvey Oswald, Kennedy's probable assassin, the police caught a man with the murder weapon but he, too, was killed before he could give evidence. Noah's assassin, however, was not shot on his way to stand trial as Oswald had been by Jack Ruby. He died in a police cell!

M'Bundu's elevation to the Presidency was almost as quick as Lyndon

Johnson's. A vast crowd appeared on the streets of Kinshasa, together with massed contingents of M'Bundu's Homelander Youth Movement, all shouting for their leader's promotion to president. The Homelander Assembly carried through his unanimous election by a show of hands and general acclamation. M'Bundu was, however, astute enough to recommend the election of another Black American lawyer, Ernest Conway, as his deputy. The post of Prime Minister went to one of M'Bundu's supporters, a well known local Marxist. The Communist revolution had been completed with the loss of only two lives, Noah's and his assassin's. M'Bundu had every right to be proud of his achievement.

There was initial consternation in the American Embassy in Kinshasa at this unexpected turn of events. The Ambassador's advisers recommended caution. They knew M'Bundu could not afford to jettison the U.S. aid package, and they noted that, in his acceptance speech in the House of Assembly, he had not publically repudiated the political conditions attached to it. He had, in fact, praised the negotiating skill of his predecessor and admitted that his Government had accepted the deal before Noah left for the States. The United States Ambassador was not entirely reassured, but decided to await events.

'By their fruits ye shall know them,' he said to his advisers as he set out to pay his first call on the new Homelander President. 'I hope he is a nationalist, using Marxism for his own ends. We will see!'

M'Bundu had unseated Noah Johnston and would henceforth be riding the Black Nationalist horse of the Apocalypse alone.

In the Middle East, the Saudi civil war smouldered on, with occasional bursts of fighting, for almost three years. Initially, it was a contest between the *Shi'ite* revolutionaries loyal to the Ayatollah of Tehran and the remnants of the Saudi regular forces still loyal to the Hashemite dynasty. Jordanian intervention had not been successful in turning the tide. Nor had the United States intervened. At the time of the rescue of the American hostages by our British Task Force, which had ended so tragically, there were strident demands for action from Congress, from the American media and from the American public. But, on the advice of the State Department and Pentagon, Rosenberg declined to act for two very good reasons.

The first reason was the eye-ball to eye-ball confrontation which was going on between the United States and Soviet fleets in the western Indian Ocean, off the Yemeni coast, and the forthright announcement by the Kremlin that Russian sympathies lay with the legitimate aspirations of the Saudi people: an indication of Soviet support to the Ayatollah of Tehran, and a sentiment that the United States could hardly condemn.

And the second reason was the difficulty in forecasting on whose side the United States should intervene. The old order in Saudi Arabia had been under threat for many years, and it would be unwise for the American Democratic Administration of Abraham Rosenberg to be seen to be propping up an unpopular and outdated regime. On the other hand, the Revolutionary Council was split betwen those loyal to Tehran and to Baghdad. The Ayatollah of Tehran's supporters were in the majority on the Council, but Iraqi troops loyal to Baghdad and, of course, nearest to Riyadh, had done most of the fighting and were in occupation of the oil fields. The Arabists in the State Department advised that, until the struggle for power in the *Shi'ite* world between Tehran and Baghdad was resolved, the United States should make no attempt to unfreeze Aramco's and other American assets by negotiation with either faction.

One strand of American policy in the Middle East, however, was prospering. Israel seemed to be the main beneficiary of the Saudi revolution. Fear of further *Shi'ite* aggression gave Tel Aviv common cause with Cairo, Amman and Damascus. At the time of the 2002 coup in Riyadh it had been too soon to suggest a *Sunni*/Israeli Pact, but by the time Karl Minitz entered the White House at the end of 2004, such a pact seemed to offer the United States a new base from which to open negotiations with whichever faction came out on top in the Iran-Iraq-Saudi *Shi'ite* 'conglomerate'.

The *Shi'ite* power struggle was not resolved in Riyadh, Tehran or Baghdad but in Kerbala. The eminent Mullahs and Imams, who were debating the new interpretation of Islamic law, were far from immune to the political charisma of the rival Ayatollahs or to the military successes of their followers. The venerable sages sensed that the success of the Iraqi troops in Saudi Arabia pointed to Allah favouring Baghdad. The younger and more ambitious amongst them trimmed their sails accordingly and a majority emerged for the Ayatollah of Baghdad's reforms, including the emancipation of women. The traditionalists, however, fought back and it was agreed that the new interpretation of the Law should be put to specially summoned conclaves of the *Ulema*[1] in the three capitals for sanction or rejection.

The Ayatollah of Tehran called his conclave together early in 2005, ahead of the others, in an attempt to set a pattern of rejection of the proposed reforms. He journeyed especially from Qum to Tehran to preside over the meeting and to ensure that support for the new ideas was minimal amongst the Iranian Mullahs, who owed their positions to his patronage. But he did not consider and, if he did, he underestimated female reaction to a rejection of their emancipation. There were a number of influential women in Tehran, who, in their youth, had taken part in the rallies organised in 1979 against Ayatollah Khomeini's rescinding of female rights after the overthrow of the Shah. They had been angered and disillusioned by the way in which their leaders had caved in to the pressures exerted by the revolutionary fanatics of those days, and they were determined that there should be no similar surrender this time.

The female rights activists had one advantage that their predecessors had lacked. The Iran/Iraq war had so drained the country's manpower resources that the Ayatollah had granted special dispensation for the recruitment of women into the Revolutionary Guard. Most of its units had at least one company of fully armed women as well as the usual quota of female cooks, medical orderlies and so forth. The women, who came forward to carry arms, tended to be revolutionary zealots. They were thought to be totally loyal to their senior male officers. As the secret police had found no evidence of female activist penetration of their ranks, the Islamic theocrats, responsible for staging the debate on the *Shari'ah* of Kerbala in the *Majalis* building in Tehran, took no special anti-female security precautions. The male companies of the Revolutionary Guard battalion on duty at the *Majalis* were deployed, as usual, on external guard duties, while the female company took post inside the building mainly for ceremonial rather than operational purposes.

On the day the conclave was due to open, the streets of Tehran were filled with women wearing their *chadors* (those voluminous black dresses), making their way to the *Majalis*. The crowd seemed good humoured enough as it began chanting its slogans in favour of female rights and calling for the Ayatollah to appear to accept their petition.

Instead of the Ayatollah appearing, the women saw extra Revolutionary Guards taking up positions around the building. The mood of the crowd grew ugly and the chanting more in unison, creating the ominous baying sound of mass emotion. The windows of the main balcony opened and the crowd thought the Ayatollah was coming out to hear their message. With an ear rending shout they threw back their *chadors* from their heads as a gesture of defiance. One of the guards panicked and fired his rifle. Others, thinking they had not heard the order to fire, opened up as well. Disregarding the dead and wounded, who fell amongst them, the crowd turned and surged away from the fire, trampling many more unfortunate women under foot.

Inside the *Majalis* it was men who had to dive for cover. A group of the female Revolutionary Guards, in a spontaneous reaction, opened fire on the podium, killing the Ayatollah and four or five of his immediate aids instantly. In the ensuing chaos, the assassins slipped out of the building and were swept away into anonymity by the crowd outside.

Order was eventually restored by the Iranian regular army. Subsequent police investigations claimed that the Ayatollah had been murdered by a deranged woman, who had later committed suicide. Few people believed the police account. Western Intelligence concluded that there had been a feminist cell in the *Majalis* security battalion that had only intended to act if the debate was seen to be going in favour of the Conservatives. Hearing that their male colleagues had opened fire on the women outside the building, they acted on furious impulse rather than a carefully premeditated plan. The consequences were to be as far reaching as the murder of Noah Johnston.

In most orthodox Moslem minds, such terrible happenings could only occur if they were the will of Allah. They must be his way of signifying approval of the Ayatollah of Baghdad's reforms. Some people saw him as the 12th or Hidden Imam of the *Shi'ite* faith.[2] He himself claimed to be no more than a lowly instrument of Allah's will. Nevertheless, he assumed the leadership of the *Shi'a* people with the assent of the Ulema of Tehran, Baghdad and Riyadh. In his moment of triumph he was, indeed, a man of great humility. He was now the undisputed rider of the Islamic Horse of the Apocalypse. How long his humility would last was debatable.

Nowhere were the effects of the world economic depression more keenly felt than in Japan. The Japanese economy had been too successful and had grown too fast to be able to ride the sudden drop in the world's purchasing power and the upsurge in protectionism that flowed in the wake of recession. Japanese under-employment rose at such a pace that even the corporate spirit of Japanese industry could not carry the burden any longer and had to shed labour. People who had thought they were in the employment for life suddenly found themselves paid off with generous farewell bonuses it is true, but ejected, nevertheless, through no fault of their own, from the major corporations to which they had intended to devote the whole of their working lives.

In these dire circumstances, it is not surprising that Nogi's New Shinto-ism gathered momentum and supporters. In his view, the post–1945 Japanese Governments had made the fundamental error of concentrating too much on the American and European markets which had now absorbed her know-how and were counter-attacking. Japan was an Asian and not a Western country and should have put her emphasis on leading Asia rather than trying to become pseudo-European. Japan should be seeking willing Afro-Asian co-operation in building a Third World co-prosperity sphere, which could compete with the two superpowers and their satellites on equal terms. Japan had made the greatest mistake of all in 1941 by trying to do this by military means. Such methods were anathema to Nogi. Japan had the scientific, technological and industrial skills to make Togo's dreams come true by commercial means. Nogi's New Shinto-ist philosophy of the export of Japanese excellence would achieve what Samurai valour had failed to do with so much loss of life.

In the Japanese elections of 2005, Nogi won enough seats in the Japanese Parliament to become the leader of the Opposition parties. The main division between Government and Opposition lay in the Japanese vision of their position in the world of the 21st century. The Government parties continued to stress the need to co-operate with the other major industrialised countries to pull the world out of the recession. They argued that this was the surest way to reduce Japanese unemployment and to bring back the prosperity of the 1980's and 1990's. Nogi and the Opposition parties sought the more limited objective of helping Asia onto its feet as

Japan's real partner and market. While Government ministers dutifully attended economic summits in Washington, London, Paris and Bonn, Nogi and his friends sought allies in China, India and the ASEAN countries.

Both sides of the Japanese political spectrum were on common ground in their opposition to Soviet Communism. To Nogi it was an alien philosophy practiced by a hostile race. He was, however, prepared to tolerate Chinese Communism largely because it was Asian, and because China would replace the United States as Japan's major political and trading partner if he ever came to power. He was not, he claimed, anti-American, but only pro-Asian. He appreciated the importance of the large Japanese stake in the United States and European economies and had no wish to endanger the Japanese capital which had been sunk in them. A drive for Asian co-operation need not, in his view, be exclusive. Japan's credo under his leadership would be peaceful co-prosperity with all those who did not pose a threat to Japan.

Though Nogi in his public speeches showed himself to be a liberal internationalist, many of his followers were not so tolerant. There was a crusading spirit in his New Shintoism which attracted those with a militarist streak in their make-up and a wish to hark back to Samurai elitism. By 2005, however, it was clear to me that he had a message which could attract support. He was not yet in the saddle of the Asian horse of the Apocalypse, but he had his foot in the stirrup.

Looking back from this year of 2040, it is easy enough to see that M'Bundu, Archbishop Bolivar, the Ayatollah of Baghdad and probably Maresake Nogi had emerged in 2005 as the Four Horsemen of the 21st century Apocalypse. Rereading my diary for 2005, written while I was at the Staff College, I can find no evidence that I thought so at the time. All four are mentioned, but only M'Bundi and Bolivar seem to have attracted my attention mainly, I think, because many of our outside lectures were given by men whose job it was to stress the Communist threat as the main danger to world peace and to the NATO alliance. All four were nationalists, but M'Bundu and the Archbishop were depending upon Communist support: the Ayatollah and Nogi were not.

Any sympathies we might have had for M'Bundu as a nationalist were swept away in the middle of the year when he published his equivalent of Hitler's *Mein Kampf*, entitled *My Africa*. I and most of my fellow students struggled to read it, but it was as rambling and indigestible as Hitler's gospel had been. If you read it closely enough, the experts told us, you could discern his three phase plan for the creation of the United States of Africa. With Noah's help he had achieved the first phase of his plan in the creation of the Congo Homeland. In his second phase, he believed the people of East and Central Africa would seek admission to his promised land.

His strength would by then be so overwhelming that he would be able to take over Azania without much difficulty in his third and final phase and reduce the White minority to servitude. M'Bundu had the same racial ideas as Hitler with a Black instead of an Aryan master race. He was also a great admirer of men like Pandit Nehru, Nasser and Sukarno, who had been adept at blackmailing the superpowers by manipulating the fiction of non-alignment. He believed Noah had lent too heavily towards the capitalist camp: he intended to tread the Marxist road; but his final goal was an African Africa.

Archbishop Bolivar's Christian Marxism excited less interest at Camberley because, since Simon Bolivar's day, when Britain helped in the liberation of South America from Spanish and Portuguese rule, Latin America had lain within the U.S. sphere of influence, protected by the Monroe Doctrine. The general attitude at Camberley was 'The Archbishop is a United States problem: Britain should not become involved'.

More attention might have been paid to the Ayatollah of Baghdad and to Nogi if they had posed a Communist threat to British interests, but they did not. The Middle East was anathema to us because Britain had burnt her fingers so often meddling in its affairs, and we no longer had the power to influence events there. Japan, however, held a fascination for us as the other off-shore island at the far side of the Eurasian Continent.

At the end of each Staff College course at Camberley there was a final term called 'New Look'. All the overseas students departed before it began so that the staff and high level lecturers from Whitehall could let their hair down on future British defence policy. The most important lecture to be given to my year of 2005 was the final address by the Chief of Defence Staff. The economic crisis had brought on one of those painful Defence Reviews which is, in theory, meant to consider strategy but, in fact, is little more than a study of how to reduce the impact of financial cuts upon the Defence Services. The 2005 Review had just been completed before the Chief of Defence Staff came to speak to us so we were the first to hear what could only be unwelcome news. We knew cuts would have to fall somewhere, but hoped our own careers would be less affected than other peoples'.

I could listen to the CDS's talk with a measure of detachment because I had just got engaged, not to Sandy Gibson, with whom I had only been able to keep in touch fleetingly since we left the Persian Gulf, as he was at sea so much, but to a Green Jacket on the course. We had decided that if we could not stay together, I would leave the Service. Fortunately, we had both been posted to the Ministry of Defence after the course, so I did not need to resign my commission as yet. I had been lucky enough to be given a high B grading for my work at Camberley (A's are very rarely given as few commandants have the confidence to declare that they have discerned such excellence in any student!), and I was going to the Intelligence Staff in the

Ministry as a major. My future husband had not done quite so well with a C+, but he too was being promoted to major in the Directorate of Army Training, so face was saved!

In my pre-postings interview with the Commandant I had asked for an Intelligence appointment because I had enjoyed my time as IORE in the Commonwealth Indian Ocean Task Force and felt I knew a bit about the Middle East. I had hoped for a job in a branch dealing with the Persian Gulf which was so indelibly etched on my memory. Postings, however, depend upon which appointments are becoming vacant at the time. I was given Intelligence, but in the branch dealing with Latin America, about which I knew nothing. I accepted the job with some misgivings and fore-boding, though I did not know why.

Like any politician, civil or military, when faced with an unpleasant task, the Chief of Defence Staff started his talk with an ingenuous effort to sugar the pill. He claimed that the Chiefs of Staff had managed to persuade the Government that the world recession was increasing instability around the globe and that it was not the time to reduce Defence Expenditure.

There was an audible sigh of relief in the hall. But then he said: 'This means that the Defence vote will be cut by the same amount as the Social Services rather than considerably more as the Treasury had originally proposed. We will be losing three per cent per year for the next three years!'

Not having served in Whitehall as yet, few of us students appreciated what that apparently small cut would mean. The Directing Staff, sitting behind us, were all too well aware of its implications from past experience. Some major commitment would have to be axed and the strength of the Services reduced unless important re-equipment programmes were jetti-soned, which none of us wanted to see happen because we were already slipping behind other middle powers like France and Germany.

As the Chief of Defence Staff developed his theme it became clear that what was left of our ability to operate outside the NATO area would have to be sacrificed.

'First things must come first,' he pontificated, 'the security of the United Kingdom depends upon the successful defence of Western Europe and the Eastern Atlantic. Anything not needed for these two tasks will have to go. Operations like the Falklands and the recent Kuwait show will just not be on in the future. The Government has accepted this regrettable consequ-ence of our financial retrenchment plans.'

In specific terms, he said, the building of the assault ship replacements would stop; our frigates, which had stood at just under fifty since the Falklands war, would be cut to under forty; one carrier would be put into reserve; the Army would be reduced to 120,000 men from around 136,000; the remaining regiments of the Brigade of Gurkhas would be disbanded; and the Royal Air Force would lose most of its transport fleet.

One of the Directing Staff asked whether the Gibraltar Accord remained valid in the light of the cut back in Defence expenditure? 'Yes, that was why the Prime Minister made his hasty trip to Washington last month,' he replied. 'President Nimitz was sympathetic and agreed to maintain the Rock offset at half a per cent of GDP, provided we do not cut back on the Continent. The United States are as badly hit by the recession and Congress is not in an over-generous mood.'

When the CDS had finished we filed out of the hall in silence. Was it worth staying in a Service tied to European Defence? Then I remembered my grandfather's words:

> *'The unexpected always happens; whatever you do, retain balanced forces able to meet the unforeseen!'*

The Chiefs of Staff were breaking the rule of balanced forces. I hoped they would be caught out again. I and my future husband would await events before resigning our commissions. We had no wish to leave the Army which our families had served for five generations.

My decision to get married had not been an easy one. I was already wedded to the Army and, like a nun, determined to pursue my chosen calling, though I knew in my heart of hearts that I might succumb to the temptations of marriage one day. One of my childhood memories was of my grandfather recounting how he had met and married my grandmother; despite being an avowed misogamist. I can still hear him saying:

> *'I believed that he rides fastest who rides alone!'*

Then he would add as an excuse for the existence of us, his grandchildren:

> *'But riding alone is a lonely life. There comes a time when companion-ship begins to have its attractions!'*

He met my grandmother in the Far East at the end of the Second World War. With the excitement of active service fading away, he began to feel the need for that companionship earlier than he expected and in an unexpected way.

He was one of the General Staff officers of Headquarters 14th Army – the 'Forgotten Army' of Field Marshal Bill Slim – and was lucky enough to be present at the Japanese surrender in Singapore in 1945. Headquarters 14th Army then became Headquarters Malaya Command, and as it transformed itself into a static headquarters in Kuala Lumpur he heard that ATS officers were to be posted into the staff. He applied at once for a transfer to a field formation and was ordered to report to 25th Indian Division in Sumatra. He never got there.

Fate had taken a hand in his career. General Headquarters Allied Land Forces South East Asia (ALFSEA) had arrived in Singapore from Ceylon. A vacancy occurred for a GSOI, and my grandfather found himself diverted to fill the post on promotion. He could hardly refuse, but had he known that ATS officers were already in post in the General Staff branch, which he was to take over, he most certainly would have done – or so he claims!

One of the first things he noticed on taking over was the signature on many of the outgoing signals from his branch: *Joan M. Buesden, Joan M. Buesden, Joan M. Buesden* was repeated on signal after signal. Not only was he unaccustomed to Christian names on official signals, but female ones were more than he was prepared to tolerate. With new broom-like efficiency he summoned the owner of the signature, who was the staff officer responsible for the vast order of battle of the British and Indian Armies in the Far East – no mean task for an ATS officer.

Junior Commander J. M. Buesden ATS duly presented herself in his office to be told curtly that Christian names should not be used on official signals and documents. She coloured slightly as she accepted her rebuke. When she was outside the office again, she stamped her feet, saying: 'Either he goes, or I do!'

Neither went: they married six months later. She stayed on in the Army until my uncle was born in 1946. She lost her career, but they both found companionship for the rest of their long married lives together. He always maintained that he was captivated by her glorious smile. In truth he fell to that indefinable thing called love.

I fell for exactly the same reason. I felt fulfilled and had few qualms about the future. We were married in the small Anglo-Saxon church at Huish, near West Stowell, where my parents had settled after my father retired in 2001. The peace and beauty of the vale had changed little since my grandparents' days. At one time there had been fears that Wiltshire would be urbanised by the development of the 'Silicon Valleys' down the M3 and M4. One of the few benefits flowing from the awful AIDS epidemics of the 1990's was a decline in population pressure, which, coupled with the success of inner-city renewal and conservation policies, left the West Stowell area as it had always been, inhabited by more sheep than human beings.

As I left the church on my husbands arm, I looked down on the plaques, marking the burial place of my grandparents' ashes, lying side by side near the path. I, too, had given up riding alone sooner than I had expected.

Notes

1. *Ulema* is the corporate term for Moslem doctors of the Islamic sacred law and theology.
2. According to Shi'a tradition, Mohammed ibn Hasan did not die but was concealed from the sight of men and will return.

4

Reaping the Harvest of Recession: (2007–2012)

*'It is an ill wind that blows nobody any good.
The world economic recession has certainly breathed
new life into the failing Communist system.
World Revolution is back on Moscow's priority list.'*
Diary entry for 20th November 2007

Mikhail Gorbachev will probably go down in history as one of the luckiest Russian leaders. Not only did he retain power well into his eighties but he saw more of his dreams come true than most of his predecessors. At first this seemed unlikely to be so. In his early years as Russia's leader he revitalized Soviet society through his own personal charisma and forthright leadership. The dead-weight of Russian bureaucracy, the insidiousness of political corruption and the wastefulness of alcoholism were all pruned back with a beneficial effect for Eastern Block productivity. But the harder he worked and the more successful he was within the Socialist world, the more standards of living fell behind those in the capitalist West during the boom years of the 1980's and 1990's. Then his luck changed. Communist economies withstood the storms of the oil led world recession far better than their capitalist rivals. The planned economies of the Eastern Bloc had not been so over-expanded during the boom years and did not have to contract their activity so disastrously when they collapsed. Moreover, the Soviet Union's vast resources of natural gas and oil tided them over the energy crisis caused by the steep rise in oil prices. By 2007 Mikhail Gorbachev was able to pose as the father figure of the Communist revival.

During his frustrating early years, the credibility of the Marxist ideology was badly dented, particularly in the Third World. M'Bundu's invitation to Noah in 1997 to set up the Black Homelander base in Angola had been a symbol of Marxist loss of confidence. M'Bundu felt an instinctive urge to re-insure with the West. By 2007 the tide had turned and gradually confidence began to seep back into Communist Parties throughout the world, not so much because the Socialist countries were doing so well, but because the Capitalists were doing so badly. It was a very confident Gorbachev, who addressed the United Nations' General Assembly in November 2007 and reminded the West of Nikita Kruschev's threat to bury capitalism.

'I repeat', he said with his characteristically cynical smile and his mannerism of stroking the birth mark on his head, 'I repeat, *we will bury you.*'

Gorbachev's words were no idle threat. Their substance lay in the minds of the Kremlin's geo-politicians whom he had directed some months earlier to prepare plans for a rejuvenation of the world Marxist/Leninist revolution, which had been flagging since he came to power and had been concentrating upon curing the malaise within Soviet society.

It is unfortunate that Western historians are never likely to be given access to Kremlin planning files so that they can build up a balanced picture of Gorbachev's last offensive. The most we can do is to extrapolate probable Soviet intentions and plans from contemporary intelligence reports and from the actual events as they unfolded between Gorbachev's challenge of 2007 and his retirement in 2011. We have, however, one other invaluable source to guide us. Anatoli Pushkin, the Soviet Ambassador in Kinshasa at the time, eventually defected to the West and published his memoirs. I have made full use of them in this account in default of primary sources.

According to Pushkin, the Kremlin planners examined five areas of strategic importance which, in their view, showed revolutionary promise: Western Europe, Sub-Sahara Africa, Latin America, the Middle East and Eastern Asia. There was no disagreement about Western Europe. Though the economic depression had created opportunities for left wing activists, the Euro-Communist parties had not attracted many new voters. If anything, the right had done better by being judged more competent and more likely to bring about economic recovery. Nevertheless, Western Europe should remain the Soviet Union's primary target in order to tie down Western military resources and to ensure the security of the Russian homelands. Every effort must continue to be made to destabilise the EEC and NATO, though the chances of success were minimal.

There was less unanimity about the order of priority of the other four. However, the Kremlin planners eventually recommended Sub-Sahara Africa and Latin America as the areas which offered easiest opportunities and quickest returns. Pushkin says they rejected the Middle East because, like the Americans, they were uncertain which side of the Islamic Fundamentalist schism would come out on top. As the Americans were supporting the *Sunni* States and Israel, Moscow would continue to sup with the *Shi'ites* but with a long spoon. They rejected Eastern Asia for the time being since they hoped that the Sino-Soviet Alliance of the 1950's could be rebuilt now that Marxist/Leninism had proved itself so resilient during the World Depression. Their Vietnam base would be retained; Vietnamese ambitions would be encouraged so as to keep up Soviet pressure in South East Asia; and, of course, their major bases at Vladivostok, Sovetskaya Gavan and Petropavlovsk would be maintained to tie down American and Japanese forces in the Pacific, in much the same way as NATO forces were being pinned in Western Europe.

Pushkin was intimately concerned with the Sub-Sahara African plan. When he saw the first draft he was disgusted. He says he minuted his staff:

'*Large fingers on small scale maps never produce practical plans. We must put* **them** *wise to the realities of life in Africa.*'

Pushkin's *them* were the Kremlin planners. They had suggested using M'Bundu's Homelanders in the west and the Marxist Ethiopian and Somali regimes[1] in the east as bases from which to develop a great strategic pincer movement that, if successful, would create a swathe of Socialist states across the waist of Africa from the mouth of the Congo on the Atlantic Coast to Mombasa and Dar-es-Salaam on the Indian Ocean.

Pushkin was enough of a politician to know that it is never wise to ridicule a higher headquarter's plan, and certainly not one emanating from the Kremlin. In his reply he praised the concept of using the two bases and then suggested that the Kremlin might wish him to fill in the details of the Congo operation. He was sure his colleague in Addis Ababa would do the same for the Ethiopian/Somali threat.

In Pushkin's view it was premature to contemplate an East/West link up. M'Bundu would never be able to carry his American backers in such a move. He pointed out that, although Noah's assassination had given M'Bundu the leadership of the Black Homelander Movement in Africa, it had not reduced the influence of the large number of Black professional people who had followed Noah to Africa and whose mission in life it was to create an advanced Black African state upon American lines. Noah's death had hardened their attitudes and they were all the more determined to create such a state in his memory. M'Bundu still had to tread very warily. Over-emphasis of his Marxist leanings could well trigger his own murder at the hands of Black American militants, seeking revenge for Noah's death. He must be allowed to wrap himself in the cloak of Black nationalism, irritating though this might be to the Kremlin.

But the main reason, Pushkin explained, for M'Bundu not being able to thrust eastwards for the time being was the American aid agreement. The planners might not be aware, he suggested, that the unpublished protocol, which lead to Noah's death, had forbidden any further territorial aggrandisement by the Black Homelander Union. There was nothing in the

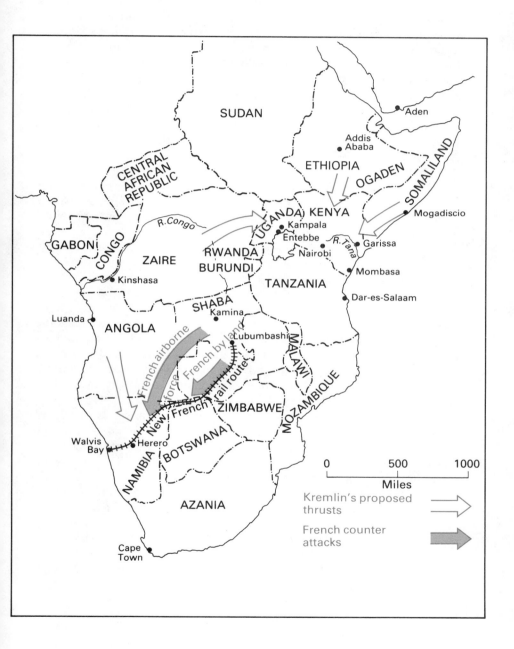

MAP 4: The Kremlin Plan for Africa in 2008

agreement to stop neighbouring states joining the union voluntarily so expansion might still be possible through carefully orchestrated subversion, provided the CIA could be hoodwinked. In Pushkin's view, the assembly of the Commonwealth Indian Ocean Task Force in 2002 showed that it would be risky to attempt another take over in East Africa too soon, but Namibia presented a possible target and, of course, the French supported separatist Government of Shaba was wide open to attack as a neo- colonialist regime. Pushkin recommended that the offensive launched from the Congo should aim first to subvert Namibia and then unseat the French in Shaba. If these operations went well, the Kremlin could then consider the easterly thrust.

Pushkin's views were acknowledged without warmth by the Kremlin director dealing with Africa. He would be sent fresh instructions after the views of Addis Ababa had been received. Victor Kerensky, Soviet Ambassador to Ethiopia and Somaliland, minced few words about the impractibility of the Kremlin's plan. It was geographically and ethnically naive. The most he could promise was a revival of the Somali claim to Northern Kenya. Mussolini had tried it on the British in the 1930's before the Second World War and had been singularly unsuccessful. Since the Second World War there had been half hearted attempts by Somalia to have the northern boundary of Kenya redrawn in its favour, but the Kenyan Government had always rebuffed them. It might be worth another try with better equipped Somali forces. If the Somalis were successful, the Ethiopians might be encouraged to join in a partition of Uganda and Kenya, but the prospects would have to be excellent before they would move. Destablizing Kenya would be better done by the Black Homelanders.

Pushkin and Kerensky, 'P & K' as they became known in the British Ministry of Defence, received their instructions in January 2008. Three preliminary operations were to be mounted: Pushkin was to encourage M'Bundu to engineer a coup in Namibia; the Kremlin itself would orchestrate French discomfiture in Shaba; and Kerensky was to press the Somalis into a military invasion of Kenya for which a team of military advisers and the necessary equipment would be provided from Aden.

M'Bundu accepted Pushkin's suggestions about Namibia without much quibbling. The idea seemed to fit well with his outpourings in his *My Aftica*. He had never liked the idea of taking on the French and he was only too willing to adopt the easier option of subverting Namibia rather than fighting for Shaba. Namibian elections were due in April 2008 and his agents assured him that it would not be difficult, given enough cash, to unseat the existing government and replace it with a more compliant regime. Namibia had been relatively stable since the Azania/South African settlement. The people were delighted to see the end of the civil war. Their economy had been given a boost by the development of an alternative overland route, by the French with Zambian help, from Shaba to Walvis Bay on the Atlantic coast via Herero (Windhoek of colonial days) in case the Indian Ocean ports were ever closed to French and Belgian traffic. It was a feat that rivalled the Chinese construction of the Tan-Zam Railway from Dar-es-Salaam to Lusaka in the 1970s. M'Bundu's henchmen in Namibia found recruiting militant activists difficult until the economic depression reduced commodity prices and brought Namibia's mini-boom to an end. Since then local political unrest had increased and their chances of a successful coup had improved.

The Kremlin's African offensive started on schedule with the clandestinely rigged elections in Namibia. Using a combination of strong arm tactics, an appeal to xenophobic dislike of French and Afrikaner influences, and an existing popular ground swell for change, M'Bundu achieved the election of the pro-Black Homelander government which Pushkin wanted. Within ten days of taking office, the new government of Namibia made a formal request to be allowed to join the Black Homelander Union as its fifth state. Much to the annoyance of Washington, Paris and Cape Town, M'Bundu despatched units of his Marxist trained and equipped troops to give fraternal support to the new Namibian Government while negotiations to consummate the Union were taking place. Herero airport and most of the more important strategic points in the Namibian capital were soon in Black Homelander hands.

Washington hesitated. M'Bundu was in flagrant breach of the United States Aid Agreement of 2005. Republican Members of Congress demanded its termination. The President himself had always had his suspicions about the African legacy bequeathed to him by Abraham Rosenberg and saw M'Bundu's action in Namibia as a heaven sent opportunity to be rid of the incubus with good grace. His advisers from the State Department and CIA agreed that M'Bundu was a Marxist masquerading as an African Nationalist, *but.* . . . There were three big *Buts*: to drop him now would be to jettison all the hard work done over the last few years in weaning Central Africa away from the Communist bloc; it would also alienate the Black American vote in Presidential elections in November; and it could trigger a Black Power terrorist campaign in the United States which the FBI had been worried about for some time. Of the three *Buts*, the probability of loss of Black votes concerned Karl Nimitz most. Elections had been won and lost by mishandling the Jewish vote over the birth of Israel. The same could happen through alienating the Black vote through misjudging the emotional repercussions of ditching M'Bundu and the Black Homelanders. Though he disliked the Communists just as much as Senator Macarthy had done in the 1950's, Karl Nimitz opted for caution. The Secretary of State was directed to find a suitable face-saving formula acceptable to Congress and the Black voters.

The White House and the Kremlin had both overlooked the probable reaction of the French supported government of Shaba to the Namibian coup. Most of the Ministers in the overthrown Namibian government sought refuge in Lubumbashi, where they were well received and treated as *personae gratae*. In Paris, there was no Black Homelander lobby to worry the French right wing government in power in 2008. On the contrary, Paris was the *rendezvous* and chosen place of exile for many anti-M'Bundu African politicians, who had decided the French capital was better for their health and continued existence than Kinshasa. The French Government, without their prompting, had already concluded from its own Intelligence sources that the Kremlin was meddling in Black Homelander affairs. In its view, the Namibian coup was part of a Soviet plot to undermine the French position in Shaba, to counter which it had worked out contingency plans in great detail. Without consulting any of its allies, the French Government ordered its Resident Commissioner in Lubumbashi to re-establish the former Namibian Government in Herero and to prepare fresh elections within six months. He was authorised to use all available French troops and aircraft in Central Africa immediately. They would be replaced and reinforced from France within the week. The *Richelieu* squadron in the Indian Ocean was being sailed to Walvis Bay to support the French counter-coup.

The French operation of June 2008 against the Black Homelanders in Namibia outshone the Israeli raid on Entebbe airport in the 1970's in its speed, decisiveness and sheer audacity. The world could but admire the French political *élan* and military skill. Herero airport was secured by a parachute drop at dusk. During the night the main French army and air striking force was landed. And by dawn the capital was firmly in their hands. In the few encounters that occurred, M'Bundu's men decided discretion was the better part of valour. Next day it became fashionable to be anti-M'Bundu. The Ministers of the M'Bundu regime and all Homelander troops who could be rounded up, were bundled into civilian buses and driven under French escort to the frontier in a long, hot and uncomfortable five hundred mile drive. Five days later the *Richelieu* with her escorts sailed into Walvis Bay and the *Foudre* landed her marines to help consolidate the French action.

Though the audacity of the French operation echoed the Entebbe raid, world opinion reflected the Anglo-French landings at Suez in 1956. Here were the French trying to put back the clock of world history once more. They had tried in Indo-China, in Algeria, at Suez and in Chad. Would they never learn? But France of 2008 was not the France of Sedan in 1870, of the mutinies of 1917, of the capitulation of 1940 or even of the withdrawal from Suez in 1956. France was again the France of Louis XIV, of Napoleon, and of de Gaulle – confident and utterly determined to look after her own interests without help from anyone, least of all the United States.

So well had French plans been laid that the French delegation at the

United Nations forestalled the Soviet Union in demanding an emergency debate on Namibia, accusing Russia of interfering in Namibian internal affairs. In the debate, however, France had few friends. Though her action could be justified in terms of the corruptness of the elections in Namibia, in Afro-Asian eyes it was none of her business. It was up to Africans to manage their own affairs. The days of neo-colonial tutelage were long passed. Africa was for the Africans.

When the vote on the French resolution was taken France stood alone. The United States and Britain abstained. Then France used her vote to veto the alternative Soviet resolution, condemning French aggression and demanding the withdrawal of French troops. In the Afro-Asian press and most particularly in the Japanese media, the French veto was seen to symbolise the inadequacy of the United Nations. A vote representing only sixty-six million Frenchmen could quash fourteen other votes representing perhaps 1,000 million people. Was this true democracy or just an abberation at the end of the European period of world history? The sooner the veto was abolished in the Security Council the fairer the world would become.[2]

Such thoughts were fully justified, but they were only thoughts in Afro-Asia. In the Black communities in major American cities it was a very different story. The United States abstention triggered some of the worst rioting since the Civil Rights flare up in the 1960's. But more worrying was the emergence of a new type of terrorism appropriate to the electronic society in which we live in the 21st century. The FBI's warning to Karl Nimitz that Black militants were planning a new campaign in support of M'Bundu proved to be well founded. Ten days after the American abstention in the Security Council, a little known group called *The Voice of Africa* was rocketed into world prominence with a feat more daring and better conceived than even the French action in Namibia. They managed to blow up several of the main computers controlling the New York Stock Exchange. For several days the world's financial markets were in chaos as engineers struggled to recover basic data from back up memory banks and to re-establish the main computer network, using data from London, Tokyo, Paris and other financial centres. No-one was hurt, but overnight the *Voice of Africa* became the most notorious and feared terrorist organisation in the world.

Though Britain, too, had abstained in the Namibia vote, the Black protests in London and elsewhere in the United Kingdom were in the form of relatively peaceful processions and mass-meetings. Britain's involvement in the struggle for Africa came about in a different way, which was described in Anatoli Pushkin's memoirs. In planning its Somali offensive into northern Kenya, the Kremlin made a close study of the 2002 crisis that had brought the Commonwealth Indian Ocean Task Force to the East African coast. The level of Commonwealth solidarity had surprised everyone, including Britain, it must be confessed. Since then the Black Homelander threat to East Africa had declined largely as a result of American pressure. The two brigades of 4th Indian Division had returned to India; the Indian Commander-in-Chief of the Task Force had left to take up another appointment; and the headquarters and logistic infra- structure of the Force had been disbanded. The first pre-requisite for success in Kenya, the Kremlin concluded, was to set the political stage in such a way as to pre-empt the mounting of another Commonwealth rescue operation. Indian attitudes would be crucial in this respect, so diplomatic efforts were to be made to subvert, or at least neutralize, Indian public opinion. The first step in this process was to be a clear and unequivocal statement made by M'Bundu, at Pushkin's bidding, that the Black Homelanders' ambitions did not include East African countries with whom M'Bundu was to claim that he was on the most cordial terms. M'Bundu made his statement in a speech at a dinner in Kinshasa to which most of the diplomatic corps had been invited. He was gratified to see that the Indian Ambassador nodded his appreciation of the gesture.

The world financial markets were barely functioning normally again after the Wall Street bombs when the second phase of the Kremlin's African offensive started to unfold in the Horn of Africa in August 2009. Such had been the world interest in the Namibia affair that a resurgence of bickering between Nairobi and Mogadiscio over the disputed districts of Northern Kenya had gone almost unnoticed in Western capitals. Not much attention was paid either when Kenya complained to the Security Council about Somali raids into its territory. The Kenyan delegation was advised that little was likely to be done about it as the Soviet Union was supporting the Somali claim and would certainly use its veto if pressed. The Kenya Government, therefore, turned to Britain and the United States for help.

The Kenyan request for help was a major embarrassment for the Foreign and Commonwealth office because it had supported the 2005 Defence Review reductions in Britain's ability to provide just the type of help for which Kenya was asking. The Army's reductions were complete; the Brigade of Gurkhas, which would have been ideal for operations in East Africa, was no more; and the Royal Navy and Royal Air Force were in no better shape to support operations outside the NATO area!

Whitehall's first reaction to the Kenyan request was to pass it smartly to the Commonwealth Secretariat. There was no Prime Ministers' Confer- ence in the offing so consultation had to be through High Commissions. India was the obvious starting point, but the Kremlin planners had done their homework properly. The Soviet Ambassador in Delhi had already called upon the Indian Foreign Minister and made it plain that Moscow believed the Somali claim to northern Kenya to be justified, although he appreciated that it broke the Organisation of African Unity's principle of the inviolability of African frontiers. The Somali claim should have been settled by the British before they gave independence to Kenya, but they had obstinately refused to do so. He hoped that the Indian Government would be more understanding. It would be a pity if anything were to come in the way of the Indo-Soviet agreement for the supply of the new MIG 42's to the Indian Air Force.

In replying to the Commonwealth Secretary General on 2nd September 2009, the Indian High Commissioner in London regretted that his Government could not help due to India's reductions in Defence expenditure, caused by the world economic recession. Similar answers came from the Canadian, Australian and New Zealand High Commissions. Only Zimbabwe and Tanzania agreed to help, but they could only provide lightly equipped infantry and not much else. The British Military Attaché in Nairobi stressed that the Kenyans were mainly interested in advanced anti-tank and anti-air equipments with the trained men to man them when dealing with the Soviet equipped Somalis.

I can remember the cynical 'we told you so' attitude in the Ministry of Defence when we were asked by Downing Street to recommend what could be done if the Government decided that help should be sent. Both the Ministry of Defence and the FCO were split internally on the issue. Some members of the Chiefs of Staff Committee wished to turn the request down out of hand. The Government had made their own bed by cutting Britain's overseas intervention capability, now they must lie on it. Wiser counsel prevailed. Defence would win a far better hearing in future battles for resources in Whitehall if it loyally supported whatever political decision was made. Moreover, the possibility of action against Soviet equipped forces would provide an ideal opportunity to try out, under battle conditions, some of the new ET (Emergent Technology) weapons that were just coming into service.

The political decision was not easy. If Britain did not go to Kenya's aid what little remained of the Commonwealth ethos would drain away. On the other hand, if Britain did intervene, she would be pilloried by Afro-Asia for interfering in African affairs. Moreover, in view of the obvious and growing instabilities on the African Continent, Britain might be taking on an open ended commitment that would draw more and more of her military resources into Africa at the expense of the defence of Western Europe.

No decision had been taken in the Defence and Overseas Policy Committee when the American Ambassador asked to call on the Foreign Secretary as a matter of urgency. With him he brought evidence of the Soviet plan to use the Somali claim to destabilise East Africa. The United States, he said, had its hands full with the Black Homelander issue, a growing Communist insurgency in Latin America, and the perennial crisis in the Middle East. He understood that Kenya had requested British military assistance. The Kenyan Government had also put a similar request to Washington. While the United States Ambassador appreciated British policy was to give priority to the defence of Western Europe, the British were historically better suited to helping Kenya than the Americans, who had little experience of East Africa. The President believed that it was essential to counter the Soviet move and so had authorised the Ambassador to offer Britain any military hardware she might need to undertake the commitment. The financial costs would, in theory, be subsumed in the Rock offset arrangements for the rental of United States bases in Britain but would, in practice, amount to a new lend-lease programme. This helpful arrangement, in fact, remained in operation until the end of the Third World War in 2035.

This generous American offer decided the issue, and the Ministry of Defence was directed to provide such help to Kenya as the British High Commissioner in Nairobi advised was necessary to give the Kenyan armed forces a fair chance of defeating a major Somali invasion. After much to-ing and fro-ing between London and Nairobi, it was agreed that the most useful British contribution would be a squadron of *Falcons*, a regiment of *Sabres* (the successor to the *Rapier* air defence missile system), a regiment of *Foil* (very recent replacement for the American MRLS surface to surface tactical missile system, which had the most advanced anti-armour and anti-personnel cannister war heads), a target acquisition battery, and an Army Air Corps squadron with a mixed fit of armed, reconnaissance and logistic helicopters. These units would need a firm base from which to operate and close protection in the battle area. It was, therefore, decided to send out the ubiquitous 5th Air-portable Brigade (lst Black Watch, 2nd Royal Anglians and lst Green Jackets) from Aldershot, which had survived the Defence cuts because of its role in reinforcing NATO's northern flank. The whole force would be commanded by Major General Colin Campbell with Air Commodore Dennis Wilson as his deputy. His small Force H.Q. would be established in Nairobi with the essential logistic backing that the force would need, and Brigadier Henry Baker, commander 5th Brigade, would be British Land Force Commander in northern Kenya. The RAF component would include fixed and rotary wing medium range aircraft in addition to their *Falcons*. No strike aircraft were to be sent out unless called for.

Apart from our small amphibious task force which went out to the Indian Ocean in 2002, we British had not mounted a major operation outside the NATO area since the Falklands campaign. I would not be telling the truth if I said that all went according to plan in the despatch of 'Eagle' Force to Kenya. It was a feat of improvisation of which, I suppose in retrospect, we should be proud. Few of the staffs had worked together before; half 5th Brigades' logistic units had to be scraped together from elsewhere; the *Sabre* and *Foil* regiments and the Army Air Corps units had to be brought back from Germany; and the Force Headquarters' com-

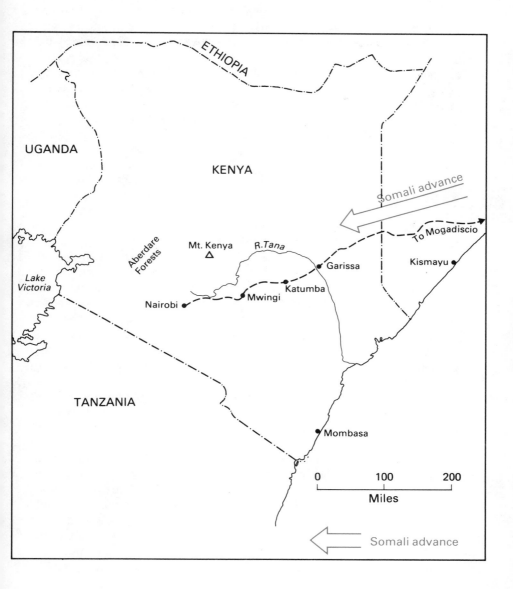

MAP 5: The Battle of the Tana River: 2nd November 2009

mand, control and communications systems had to be improvised from the Royal Corps of Signals training establishments at Catterick and Blandford. But in the end it all worked – just!

By mid-October Colin Campbell had shaken out his force which had arrived at Nairobi in chartered civil aircraft and some United States military transports for their heavier equipment. The Somali invasion, as opposed to cross frontier raiding, had already begun. The Kenyan Army had fallen back slowly in front of the main Somali thrust, which was being made on the direct route from Mogadiscio, the Somali capital, to Nairobi via Garissa on the Riva Tana. General Alan Cunningham had used this route in the reverse direction for his victorious offensive against the Italians in January 1941, which had ended in his triumphant entry into Addis Ababa in April and the surrender of the Italian Viceroy, the Duke of Aosta, at Amba Alagi a month later.

From the speed of the Somali advance it was calculated that the Tana River offered the best defensive position upon which to stand. Brigadier Baker flew up to Garissa, the small town that sprawls around the main road bridge over the Tana, to plan the defence of the Tana line with General Jacob N'jonjo, who was commanding the Kenyan force opposing the Somali advance. The Tana flows sluggishly through thick jungle which stretches a mile either side of the stream. Beyond the jungle the vegetation is sparse and thins out progressively as the ground rises gently to the watershed some five miles back from the river. There were only three recognised crossings over the Tana near Garissa that the Somalis might use; the main road bridge and two fords each about five miles up and down stream of the main road.

General N'jonjo had intended to hold the three crossings in strength with a thin line of observation posts on the river between them, and to hold about a third of his force in reserve well back from the river ready to counter attack. When Baker described the lethality of *Foil* to him and the need to clear killing grounds for it, N'jonjo agreed to deploy the bulk of his force on the higher ground west of the jungle belt with only battle patrols on the river itself. These would withdraw once the Somalis started to deploy to force a crossing. The bridge would be blown and the fords would be mined when the patrols were pulled back. N'jonjo and Baker would then depend upon a belt of electronic sensors positioned either side of the river by the British Target Acquisition Battery to locate the main Somali concentrations as they prepared to force the crossing. The Tana would be the *Foil* killing ground.

Leaving 2nd Royal Anglians in Nairobi, Baker moved the Black Watch at the end of October to the airfield at M'wing, 100 miles back from the Tana, where the *Falcons* were to be based, and took 1st Green Jackets on forward to Katumba to form the advanced British base from which he would support N'jonjo on the Tana. He was none too happy about the way the Kenyan troops were taking up their positions overlooking the Tana, but he had too many problems of his own to interfere in N'jonjo's affairs.

The Tana had been Cunningham's start point in 1941. On 2nd November 2009 the Battle of the Tana River was the first occasion on which the advanced British weapon systems *Falcon, Sabre* and *Foil* were to be used in anger. In reality it was little more than a skirmish or perhaps a major ambush, which ended in a horrible massacre. On 1st November the *Falcons* reported the advance of the Somalis in three columns, each containing about a dozen tanks and a large number of trucks carrying infantry and towing guns. They were heading, as expected, for the Tana bridge and the two fords. Attempts by the *Falcons* to close were met by missiles fired, fortunately, at extreme range, which the pilots were able to evade. It was late afternoon when the Somali columns nosed their way into the jungle belt. They were fired on by the Kenyan patrols and then shelled and mortared with the patrols directing fire. There was a minor disaster at the Tana bridge when the officer in charge of the demolition panicked and blew it too soon, forcing the platoon-sized battle patrol covering it to swim back, abandoning their vehicles and anti-tank weapons on the far side.

As darkness fell, N'jonjo successfully withdrew all his troops from the killing ground, and he and Baker watched the target acquisition plot. During the first half of the night remarkably little seemed to be happening – or the sensors were malfunctioning. Both commanders became increasingly anxious and Baker at last agreed to let N'jonjo send reconnaissance patrols forward to check both the demolished bridge and fords. Fortunately, there was just time to stop them before they had gone very far. The plot started to show activity around and stretching well back from the three targets. Both men agreed to wait until there was hostile movement on both sides of the river, indicating that crossings were being made.

Dawn was already breaking when Baker judged it was the moment to strike. There were some tanks across both fords, but none so far at the bridge. The plot suggested that the tanks in the bridge area were halted some way back waiting for re-bridging to be completed. With N'jonjo's agreement, Baker ordered *Foil* fire to be opened. It was still dark enough to see the flashes in the sky as the *Foil* cannisters opened to release their deadly cargos of various types of advanced munitions.[3] Then the jungle belt lit up with a myriad points of light as the weapons exploded; and, as daylight increased, the valley was seen to be shrouded in smoke and dust out of which several tell-tale spirals of black oily smoke were rising.

As no Somali force emerged from the jungle belt, N'jonjo ordered his battalions to push their battle patrols back down to the river to find out what had happened. The carnage in the target areas was gratifying but hideous. The dawn sortie by the *Falcon*'s reported scattered enemy vehicles driving back from the river in an easterly direction. The Battle of the Tana was over. During the day, N'jonjo's troops gathered in over a thousand shocked Somali prisoners, including their commander. *Foil*'s first engagement had been grimly successful.

But outside Africa, the news of the British military action, even though carried out with and at the request of an African government, created another storm of anti-Western hysteria. The Soviet Union was quick to call the Security Council into emergency session and this time Britain was forced to use the veto on an Ethiopian resolution branding Britain as the aggressor and demanding the withdrawal of British troops from Africa. The General Assembly was also in session which made matters worse. The anti-Western tirades were all too familiar, as was the vicious racial rioting that broke out in Brixton, Toxteth and other Black communities throughout the United Kingdom. It was three months before the hysteria died away.

Back in Africa the British Chiefs of Staffs' worst fears of an open ended military commitment were soon realised. Rebuffed by the French in Namibia and blocked by the British on the Tana, M'Bundu and his Soviet backers decided that the time had come to jettison all the assurances given about the Black Homelanders having no territorial ambitions in East Africa. American intelligence agencies were soon warning Washington, London and Nairobi that the Black Homelanders would soon open guerrilla campaigns against the British in East Africa and the French in Shaba. Any of the British Commonwealth countries in Africa that did not co-operate with M'Bundu's forces would be subverted and probably attacked by guerrilla forces. The time had come, M'Bundu himself declared, for all Africans to stand up and be counted. Those who were not for him, were against him and would be treated as hostile. Nevertheless, the logistic difficulties of opening a guerrilla campaign in East Africa would not be easy to solve. The distances alone were vast and the build up would take years rather than months.

The CIA's warning proved well founded. Fortunately, Baker's brigade had not been withdrawn to the United Kingdom, nor had General Campbell's force headquarters left Nairobi by the time the first Homelander guerrilla units were detected in the Aberdare forests north of Nairobi, which had been used as safe havens by the *Mau Mau* gangs in the 1950's. The Central African guerrilla campaign had begun. It was to smoulder for ten long years and would draw as many British units as the *Mau Mau* campaign had done half a century earlier.

By far the most worrying aspect of the situation was the apparent ease with which the guerrillas had crossed Uganda without check or even detection. There was clearly a measure of Homelander support in East Africa despite ethnic differences between the two sides of the Continent, but the question was, how much? The Homelander philosophy had been developed by Noah and M'Bundu as all embracing, anti-tribal, Black Nationalism. Most experienced African hands believed this to be impossible, at least in the short term, but it looked as though they were being proved wrong. The Intelligence view was that there must be the equivalent of the Ho Chi Minh Trail of the Vietnam War being developed across Africa.

The guerrilla war, which begun in East Africa in January 2010, brought personal tragedy to me and changed my whole life. I had intended to leave the Army early in the New Year. My husband had been posted back to his battalion and we both felt it right that I should return with him to become a real member of the regimental family and perhaps, God willing, to start a family of our own. Unfortunately, my husband's battalion, 1st Green Jackets, had gone with 'Eagle' Force to Kenya in October and had been closely involved in the battle of the Tana River. We decided that I should delay my resignation until he returned at the end of the battalion's emergency tour in Kenya. He never did come back: he was killed in one of the earliest Homelander ambushes in the Aberdares.

I thought of starting a new career outside the Army, which seemed to have destroyed my life. Wisely, as it turned out, both my Director in the Ministry of Defence and the Engineer-in-Chief persuaded me not to do so. They asked me where I would like to go if it could be arranged. I had had two Intelligence jobs and knew I should widen my experience if I was going to get anywhere in the Service, but, at that moment, I felt that I wanted interest rather than worry about career prospects. I also wished to get out of Whitehall and overseas if possible. 'Was there an Assistant Military Attaché's job coming up anywhere?' I asked. There was – in Colombia!

What could be more appropriate and exciting? I had the necessary Intelligence background, having sat at the Latin American desk in Defence Intelligence for over three years. I had a smattering of Spanish that I had acquired doing the job, and it was agreed that I should do a six months course at the Defence Language School at Beaconsfield before taking up my post. Incidentally, I and my late husband had decided that I should, like many other career women, keep my maiden name for professional purposes so I was still known in the Army as Major Catriona Reid RE. I allowed my married name to lapse.

And so it came about that I arrived in Bogota, the capital of Colombia, in time to see the opening of the Kremlin's offensive in Latin America. We knew much less about its planning because Pushkin was not directly involved and so there are only sketchy references to Latin America in his book. It does seem that the Kremlin did a better job in planning their renewed offensive in the mountainous regions of Colombia, Venezuala, Ecuador, and Peru than they had done in Africa. Though Fidel Castro had died some time ago, Cuba was still a pro-Moscow Marxist State and had strong working links with Communist guerrilla bands in all four countries and in the Central American states as well. The Kremlin decided to reinforce those links and to establish a sea and air bridge via Cuba, through which increased supplies of arms and equipment could be fed into the Communist controlled areas. Some Eastern Bloc arms were sent by sea to small ports, but the bulk of the equipment was landed by air at remote air strips, many of which were still being used for cocaine running, despite all the U.S. efforts over the years to proscribe the trade.

There is a tinge of envy in one of Pushkin's references to Latin America. He said Colombia was chosen as the starting point for the offensive because of the close clandestine links established between the Communists and the Church. He wished such a linkage could have been established in the Congo, where the Christian Church was neutral, if not actively hostile, to M'Bundu.

When I arrived in Bogota, there was a general nervousness that something unpleasant was about to happen. Domingo Garcia's bands had, in recent months, been able to claim a number of successes against the Army and Police in the provinces; and his leaflets, signed 'El Caudillo', were avidly read and often given greater prominence by publication in the Press as news items. It was generally and correctly assumed amongst the diplomatic corps that the Archbishop was involved, and the Government thought so too, but could not prove it. Like Makarios in Cyprus, he was too slippery a customer to be caught out in treasonable dealings with Domingo, and his well tuned ecclesiastical intelligence network gave him enough warning of incipient Government threats to his position.

Outwardly, Bogota was as normal as its altitude, the Latin temperament of its establishment, the poverty of its people and the guerrilla war in the countryside would allow. Life went on as it always had done since the Spaniards founded the city in 1538. Life for the Diplomatic Corps, however, was claustrophobic and incestuous. With large parts of the country classed as 'no-go' areas for the security forces, the Colombian authorities discouraged us from travelling except on special occasions when they could provide adequate escorts. In consequence, we were thrown very much in on ourselves, gleaning most of our local intelligence from the endless round of diplomatic functions at which the guest lists only varied marginally. We did our best to widen our contacts with the Colombians, but our own social lives tended to be confined, due to linguistic and cultural barriers, to the British and American communities.

The British military and diplomatic services, unlike the civilian professions, commerce and industry, are firm believers in what is best described as the British regimental system, whereby husbands and wives form an integral part of the team, be it an infantry battalion, a frigate flotilla, an air squadron or an embassy. My former director in the Ministry of Defence had written both to the Ambassador and to my immediate boss, the Military Attaché, alerting them to my personal tragedy and my wish to sink myself into a constructive job in order to start rebuilding my life. I will always be grateful to both men and their wives for all they did for me in the aftermath of my bereavement.

The Diplomatic Service abounds with unusual couples. Sir Douglas Kent and his wife, Helen, were no exception. He was a tall man with a high forehead, stretching up to a balding dome, who looked more like a university don than His Excellency, the British Ambassador. He had a keen sense of humour and was never at a loss for words, whereas Helen was a slight person, who was painfully shy and found being Lady Kent rather daunting. The Military Attaché, Colonel 'Jock' Cameron, was the antithesis of Sir Douglas. He was a stolid, practical Scottish infantryman and his wife, Kirsty, was an equally down to earth Highland lass. She had born him four sons, who kept her more than busy, though she always found time to accompany her husband on the diplomatic round.

The first job that Colonel Jock gave me was to update the profile sheets and dossiers held by the Embassy on all the principal military and militant personalities on the Colombian scene. These included not only the more important officers of the security services, but also politically active members of the priesthood and, of course, whatever we could glean about the guerrilla leaders. It was an ideal starting job because I could submerge myself in it, and it enabled me to get to know as much as there was to know about the actors in the Colombian drama quicker than I might have done otherwise.

Colonel Jock's decision to start me off on profiles was not entirely to keep me busy. He knew that, as a woman, I had a number of obvious advantages in gathering information in a Latin society. No Colombian male could resist trying to enhance his importance in my eyes by showing how much he knew about the internal intrigues that were going on behind the scenes. As the wine flowed at diplomatic receptions and dinner parties, so indiscretions increased and blanks in my profile sheets were filled in with only the slightest prompting from me.

There was also an intriguing James Bond element in the job. Beaconsfield had only given me a smattering of colloquial Spanish, which enabled me to converse at functions, but not necessarily to understand the nuances of what was being said. This was a disadvantage suffered by most British military officers attached to embassy staffs abroad, so electronic microrecorders were provided. Here, too, I had an advantage over my male colleagues: I carried a handbag, making a recorder easier to conceal. A lady's bag, however, is usually held too low down for recording conversations at a cocktail party, so our surveillance experts provided a 'bug' microphone, which, in my day uniform, was sown into my aiguillette. In formal evening mess dress, which was still the elegant Norman Hartnell cream brocade gown introduced for the WRAC in the 1960's, it was concealed in the epaulette on the shoulder, which supported my scarlet sash as a Royal Engineer Officer (the WRAC wore lovat green sashes).

For civilian day clothes or evening dresses I had a number of 'bugged' brooches.

My 'day' in Bogota really started when I left for whatever function I was due to attend that evening. When I got back to my flat I would write up my diary and set down any 'profile' information that I had gleaned while my memory was still fresh. Next morning, when I reached my office in the Embassy, I would hand my recorder to Sergeant Louise Strong WRAC, who was my clerk, computer operator and interpreter. Her father was a Gunner, who married a Gibraltarian girl when he was stationed on the Rock. After he retired, his wife, like all good Gibraltarian women, took him and Louise back to Gibraltar where she became a fluent, if ungrammatical, Spanish speaker. While I went through the latest Embassy press and intelligence reports on my office video, Louise would produce a type-script of my evening's activities from my recorder, and then we would update the profiles held on the Embassy computer with any new information that had come my way. All our inputs were automatically transmitted by satellite data-link to the Ministry of Defence Intelligence computer in Whitehall so that my successor on the Latin American desk had the information available to him if he needed it.

I found the whole exercise fascinating and it did much to restore my confidence. It also rekindled my ambition to make a success of my career in the Army. Our local intelligence work was supplemented by international information supplied to us from London by the same satellite data-link. Colonel Jock also encouraged me to develop close links with my opposite number in the American Embassy from whom I received a lot of helpful information on United States views and intentions. Kirsty, his wife, was less enthusiastic about the liaison. In her down to earth way she warned me: 'Beware of the rebound! Major Tommy Tomlinson is a pretty attractive chap, but my instincts say 'watch it'.

So did mine – at that time!

Tommy was not, in fact, my only admirer. There was Father Devlin, who was old enough to be my father and yet went out of his way to meet me as often as opportunities presented themselves. There was no lack of them because he was one of the Archbishop's secretaries and often accompanied him to major diplomatic functions and sometimes represented him at minor ones. He was a Dominican friar, who had been born in Dublin, and, as a young man, had volunteered to come to Colombia to help in the relief work after the volcanic eruption in 1985 which submerged the villages in the valleys below in a river of mud. He had stayed on and had been picked by Ignatius Bolivar as one of his assistants. While he obviously enjoyed the female company that his calling denied him, I was under no illusion that he was using me much as my colonel intended that I should use Tommy Tomlinson – as a useful channel of unofficial communication between the Archbishop and the British Embassy, and indirectly to the U.S. Embassy as well.

I was well settled into the rhythm of my new life when the Colombian revolution came to the boil. I am indebted to Tommy Tomlinson and Father Devlin for much of the colour – most of it previously unpublished – of this account of what happened. I met both men on many occasions throughout the crisis: Father Devlin when he had a political problem on his mind; and Tommy Tomlinson for more intimate reasons. I regret to say that I found myself ignoring Kirsty's advice as the weeks went by and my relationship with Tommy blossomed.

Thanks to Father Devlin, I was able to warn Sir Douglas Kent, and he to alert Silas P. Witzleben, the American Ambassador, to the possibility of an ecclesiastically inspired coup in Caracas, the capital of Venezuala. The Communist guerrilla leader there had appealed to Domingo Garcia for help. Though his men were being just as successful as Domingo's, they did not have the same *rapport* with the Church. The Archbishop of Caracas was getting on in years and was a firm supporter of the established order. Though the more junior members of the Venezualan priesthood were as disgusted as their Colombian colleagues with the inequalities of wealth and opportunity amongst their flocks, they had no charismatic leader like Ignatius Bolivar.

It was in trying to remedy this weakness in the Venezualan Church that Archbishop Bolivar prematurely triggered the Colombian revolution of October 2010. The course of events is tangled and obscure, but it seems that he made one of his few tactical mistakes. Hearing that the Archbishop of Caracas was ailing and was not expected to live more than a few months, Bolivar started an intrigue to ensure that his successor had the 'right political ideas and the ability to carry them through' – in other words, was a 'Bolivarist'. The agent whom he used in Caracas was surprisingly careless. The plot was uncovered and the Venezualan Government gave the Colombian Ambassador in Caracas the hard evidence that the Colombian Government needed to proceed against their own Archbishop.

Unlike the British Government, which, in similar circumstances in Cyprus, arrested Archbishop Makarios and deported him to the Seychelles, the Colombian Government botched its attempts to get rid of their 'turbulent priest'. Warned by his links within the Colombian Cabinet, Bolivar escaped arrest and let it be known through his Church network that an attempt had been made to remove him. It was the Colombian Government that fell and not the Archbishop. By popular acclaim and with the support of the Catholic officer Corps of the Army and Police, Ignatius Bolivar stepped into the President's shoes and nominated a caretaker 'Government of National Unity' to rule Colombia until 'free elections' could be held in three months time. Some of the members of the new Government were known Marxist sympathisers but the majority were Colombian Nationalists of various shades of opinion, but mostly drawn, it is true, from the Left.

The Kremlin may have been disappointed in that they would probably have liked to have seen Domingo Garcia in the new Government, holding the home affairs portfolio, but it was a good thing from their point of view that he refused to leave his mountain fastnesses. Instead he advised the Archbishop to give the post to a senior Army officer to ensure the Army's loyalty. Responsibility for security in the main cities and towns should remain with the Army and Police so that he could hold his guerrillas in reserve until the reaction of the United States and of Colombia's neighbours was revealed.

It was the Venezualan Government that reacted first, demanding an emergency meeting of the Organisation of American States, and claiming that the Colombian revolution was due to external forces alien to the security of the American Continent. In its view there had been blatant Soviet interference in the affairs of Latin America. Much of Colombia and Venezuala was in Communist guerrilla hands; Bogota had fallen; and Caracas would fall too if action were not taken at once to restore 'democracy'.

Karl Nimitz may have hesitated over intervention in Africa. He had no need to be so cautious over Latin America, 'the back-yard of the United States'. He had the precedents of past American military action there. He could expect the full support of the Republican majority in Congress. And his 'gut feeling' was that the American people would expect and back a renewal of the anti-Communist crusade to stop the conversion of Latin America to Eastern Bloc 'Democracy'. The Roman Catholic Church's links with the Communists in Colombia were embarrassing to the President, but his advisers suggested that the Church might be useful as a moderating influence in the crisis. It did not seem to dawn upon them that they were witnessing the birth of a new political philosophy more appropriate in Latin America than the American version of Anglo-Saxon democracy. It would, in due course, be dubbed 'Bolivarism', but this still lay in the future. For the present, Karl Nimitz was unconcerned with what it was. The salient fact was that it was Communist linked and this was enough for him and most Americans.

Once the decision to intervene had been taken, the only delay was to allow enough time for the White House staff to swamp the world media networks with supporting propaganda. The President himself came on Television to make the case personally, and at the end of his broadcast announced that two American airborne task forces were at that moment landing at Bogota and Caracas 'at the request of the Organisation of American States'. Most of his listeners in the United States applauded the application of the Monroe Doctrine: elsewhere there was much less support.

At Caracas airport the United States troops were welcomed by the Venezualan Government, the prime mover in the OAS request for intervention and, surprisingly enough, by the people of Venezuala, who had no wish to be engulfed in a civil war. All previous political change in

Venezuala had been bloodless and most of the population hoped it would stay that way.

At Bogota airport the reception was very different. No attempt was made to obstruct the landing as the Archbishop saw the intervention as legally authorised by the OAS, to which Colombia belonged. His plan was to make the United States Forces' stay in Bogota as politically, militarily and logistically as embarrassing as possible. Elaborate courtesy was to be adopted; military confinement to the airport area was to be imposed by Colombian Army road blocks; and no supplies of any kind were to be provided except enough aviation fuel for the departure of the force.

The only people at the airport to welcome Brigadier General George M. Gow, the United States Task Force Commander were the Air Port Manager representing the Colombian Government and Silas P. Witzleben the American Ambassador. The Air Port Manager made it clear to Gow, accompanied by Major Tomlinson as his military Aide, what the rules were. The Bogota Air Traffic Control would continue to ensure safety of air movements; the United States Forces had been allocated three large hangars with aircraft parking spaces in front where they could live during their 'short stay' in Bogota; no United States personnel were to move beyond the Airport perimeter – the Colombian Army was in position around it with orders to open fire without challenging first; and no supplies of any kind would be provided or purchased. The American Ambassador could only confirm to Gow that these were the Colombian Government's instructions. He had cabled them to Washington. Until fresh instructions were received, the General should comply with the Air Port Manager's instructions.

Gow was issuing instructions to his Chief of Staff when an immaculately dressed Colombian Colonel arrived with an invitation for the Ambassador and General to call upon the Archbishop at the Presidential Palace. Cars and escort were waiting to drive the General into Bogota. The Ambassador's car could join the convoy. There would be no objection if the General wished to travel with the Ambassador. Gow accepted and followed the Ambassador into the United States Embassy car.

During the drive into Bogota, Gow noted that the Colombian Army was indeed deployed around the Airport with tanks and artillery. The roadside was thronged with people who showed positive hostility towards the Ambassador's car with its stars and stripes fluttering from the flag poles on its front wings. Hostility grew worse as the convoy nosed its way into the centre of the city. It was more noisy than dangerous. The only thing thrown at the car was the usual epithet, 'Yankees go home'.

Archbishop Bolivar met his two guests with the elaborate courtesy that he had instructed his staff to show. It was, Gow realised, a courtesy of deliberate condescension. Archbishop Makarios could not have done better! As soon as the three men were seated in the Presidential Office, the mood changed. Archbishop Bolivar politely but firmly made it plain that Gow and his force were uninvited guests; and advised him not to unpack as his stay in Colombia would be short. The Archbishop admitted that, for the moment, his Government was only provisional, but it was the *de facto* Government of Colombia, having been ushered into office by popular acclaim. In three months' time its legitimacy would be established in a general election that was already being prepared. Then, turning to Gow, the Archbishop said with great dignity:

'While I appreciate the United States' Government's concern for democracy, that political commodity comes in many forms. On behalf of the Colombian people I, as their present representative, must formally ask you to withdraw your force back to the United States. Aviation fuel will be supplied by my Government for that purpose and no other'.

Silas Witzleben stepped in quickly before Gow could reply, fearing that the grim jawed soldier would use less than diplomatic language.

'Your Grace, I must remind you that the United States is acting on the instructions of the Organisation of American States. General Gow has instructions to take such measures as are necessary to restore the *de jure* Government of Colombia.'

The Archbishop bowed:

'If General Gow can re-establish such a Government that has the full support of the people of Colombia, he is at liberty to do so, but he will receive no support from the *de facto* Government or the Colombian Armed Forces which are loyal to it.'

A young priest, who was obviously one of the Archbishop's secretaries, entered the room and handed a note to the Archbishop.

'I see from this General that you have already acted. All the airport facilities, including air traffic control, have been taken over by your men. I cannot resist the power and might of the United States, but I will not co-operate with you.'

And turning to Silas Witzleben, he said:

'I must ask you to inform your Government accordingly. I hope Washington has calculated the cost of trying to re-impose a rejected regime upon the Colombian people. It will not be cheap.'

With the temperature of the conversation rising, the Ambassador took a conciliatory line.

'I think you will agree, your Grace, that we must do everything we can to avoid bloodshed whilst our two Governments seek a way out of this difficult situation by negotiation. I know that the President of the United States will hold you in the greatest esteem if you will instruct your troops to take no hostile action against the United States Force at the Airport so that negotiations can begin between us.'

'On two conditions: that no United States military personnel, except for authorised liaison officers, leave the Airport perimeter; and that the control of the Airport and Air Traffic Control are handed back to the Colombian authorities'.

Gow nodded and then said:

'I have not had time to see the area allocated to my troops. May I have your assurance that they will be provided with adequate accommodation if our stay is prolonged?'

It was the Archbishop's turn to nod assent, and at that moment Silas M. Witzleben's professional diplomatic training came to his aid. He could see a possible face-saving formula.

'I think my Government would consider its obligations to the OAS fully discharged if we could reach a mutually acceptable formula for the supervision of the elections that you propose to hold to give your provisional Government *de jure* as well as *de facto* status. OAS observers could be administered by General Gow's force. It could be used by them to ensure that there is no intimidation during the elections.'

The Archbishop paused before replying, no doubt calculating the acceptability of OAS observed elections to his Government ministers. A continued policy of dignified reasonableness seemed the right course. He stretched out his hand to the Ambassador, saying as their hands met:

'I hope our two Governments will agree. You may convey to Washington my acceptance of your idea. I will put it to my colleagues when you can confirm it is acceptable to President Nimitz.'

Silas M. Witzleben's success was short lived. While Archbishop Bolivar was prepared to comprise to achieve his ends, the Kremlin was not. The Soviet Union delegation to the United Nations demanded an emergency session of the Security Council, at which the usual resolution condemning the United States as the aggressor and demanding the withdrawal of American troops from Bogota and Caracas, was tabled. Ominously the Soviet delegate made it clear that the Soviet Union was not prepared to stand aside while the United States used its military power to deny the people of Latin America the right to chose the regimes under which they wished to live.

In the Security Council debate the American delegation found once more that it could only count on Western support and, on this occasion, even their NATO allies expressed doubts about the wisdom and morality of Nimitz's action in air-landing troops at Bogota and Caracas. Much to the annoyance of the Third World, the United States demonstrated, yet again, the impotence of the UN by using its veto to block the resolution.

Sensing that the United States had only marginal support for its action, Gorbachev decided to launch a coup, long contemplated by the Kremlin. In a strongly worded personal message to Karl Nimitz, he said that the people of the Soviet Union and of the German Democratic Republic found the continued presence of United States, British and French troops in Berlin sixty-five years after the ending of the Second World War just as intolerable as the United States Government found Socialist regimes in Latin America. The American argument that Colombia and Venezuela were in the United States 'backyard' could be applied with greater force to the situation in Berlin, which was far closer to the Soviet Union and actually within the Socialist state of East Germany. Unless United States forces were withdrawn from Bogota and Caracas within ten days, the Soviet Forces in the German Democratic Republic would escort all Western troops and their dependents out of Berlin, using force if need be.

I happened to be lunching with Tommy Tomlinson when the news of the Soviet ultimatum was being broadcast over the radio.

'Check mate', I muttered and he could only agree. This piece of successful brinkmanship placed the seal of Soviet approval on their long serving leader's career. Mikhail Gorbachev retired soon afterwards at the age of 80 when his reputation could not have been higher. Berlin retained its international status and the Western troops and their dependents stayed on. General Gow's troops did not stay in Bogota to help supervise the Colombian elections on behalf of the OAS. Nor did the American troops remain in Caracas: their mission there was said to have been successfully completed!

The main benefactor of Gorbachev's brilliant piece of brinkmanship was Archbishop Bolivar. There was no doubt about the outcome of the Colombian election, which took place on schedule. The 'Bolivarists', as his followers had now become, swept the poll, thanks largely to the world publicity surrounding the crisis. The Archbishop's Government could drop the word 'provisional' from its title and become the Government of National Unity *de jure* as well as *de facto*, and was recognised by the United States as such. Domingo Garcia deemed it safe to leave his mountain base and to join the Bolivarist Government as Minister of Defence. Within a year, Bolivarist supporters had also secured power in Caracas. The Kremlin had won a large 'liberated area', stretching across the whole of the northern part of the South American Continent.

The main loser in the fall-out from the crisis was Karl Nimitz. In the presidential election of 2012 he was unseated by the Democrat candidate, Robert Mackenzie, who condemned the Republican interventionist policies and promised to protect American interests around the world by political, economic and psychological means rather than through military confrontation. His arguments may have lacked reality, but while success breeds success, failure has its own rewards. Mackenzie became President because the American voters decided to penalise Nimitz for failure.

My personal affairs had gone no better. I had been swept along almost unwittingly by my frequent meetings with Tommy Tomlinson both officially and socially, and I was becoming more and more attracted to him. Kirsty Cameron said no more to me about my relations with him, but Lady Kent saw what was happening and decided she must intervene before it was too late. Unbeknownst to me, she invited Doris Witzleben, the American Ambassador's wife, to lunch to find out more about this Major Tomlinson. A few days later she asked me to morning coffee to discuss fund raising for the local Red Cross, in which she was interested. In her shy and sincere way she said:

'Kitty, my dear, you do know don't you that Major Tomlinson is married?'

'Of course, Helen,' I replied, feeling deeply hurt that the Ambassador's wife had been prying into my private affairs.

'He's quite open about it. He expects to get his divorce through in a matter of months.'

'I'm afraid not, Kitty,' Helen said, putting her hand on mine., 'His wife is a Roman Catholic and has steadfastly refused to divorce him in spite of his infidelities to her over a number of years.'

Helen paused to let the significance of her remarks sink in. Then she continued.

'You would have to give up your career to live with him, and it might be many years, if ever, before you would be able to marry him.'

My world seemed to be falling apart again. I don't think I really heard her saying:

'Doris Witzleben tells me that Tommy has been posted back to the States and will be leaving in three days time. Once he has gone, you will have time to think whether you want to follow him or not.'

Tommy and I had a farewell lunch before he left. Neither of us mentioned his wife's intentions. Both of us knew that Helen's intervention had been as decisive as it was right, and I was very grateful to her. I realised that constructive work in my chosen career was still more important to me than intimate companionship. I would continue to enjoy riding alone. The regimental spirit of the British Services has much to commend it. Without it Helen would never have intervened in what might have been a disastrous affair and the end of my career.

Notes

1. The Abyssinians had eventually won the War in the Ogaden in 1990 and Somaliland became a tributary Marxist State closely allied to the Marxist regime in Addis Ababa.
2. There had been several attempts in the 1990's to revise the composition of the Security Council so that the permanent membership of Britain and France, and hence their vetos, could be assumed by the representative of the European Community – possibly the President. Britain was inclined to acquiesce but France was not, and so the proposals ran into the sands of international indecision.
3. Each missile's warhead was a cannister out of which a shower of bomblets and minelets of various types were released over the target. There were two anti-tank versions: one with homing bomblets to attack the top of tanks and the other with minelets to be scattered in front of advancing vehicles. The anti-personnel versions had bomblets to inflict maximum casualties on men in the open, and another version which would penetrate deeply dug defences.

5

Impotence in Brussels (2013–2014)

'Western Europe has not yet grown into a political animal.
It is still a colony of mussels clinging to the same rock.
Most of the time their shells are open and their feeding tentacles
are in a sort of unison in the currents generated by the
superpowers. At the least sign of danger they clam shut and
look to their own interests. There is no corporate external vision.
no foreign policy and hence no military strategy.'
Diary entry for 30th November 2014

After the 2010 episode of superpower brinkmanship, there was a short period of calm in international affairs as the world digested the implications of Mikhail Gorbachev's resounding victory over Karl Nimitz. The Eastern Bloc was naturally jubilant. Western Europe should have been able to take comfort from the clear signs that the world economic recession had bottomed out: Middle East oil was flowing again, energy prices were dropping and so were interest rates.

But the scars of the recession were still open in the West: unemployment was higher than ever, national budgets were tight and internal unrest was endemic. The Berlin climb down by the United States rubbed salt into those wounds. Both EEC and NATO became more inward looking than ever and national self-interest had become the predominant influence in the corridors of power in Western capitals.

This phase of Western European introspection could not have come at a worse time for Britain and the United States whose policy makers were, in general, more aware of the Four Horsemen though, of course,they were not recognised as such at the time. In the NATO and EEC bureaucracies in Brussels balancing budgets rather than global strategy was the main concern.

In East Africa the guerrilla war, started by M'Bundu in 2010, had not flared up as quickly or as intensely as he had hoped. It had been relatively easy to infiltrate small guerrilla bands through Uganda into the Aberdare forests north of Nairobi, but the two obvious difficulties had arisen. The vast distances involved made re-supply a major problem; and ethnic differences between Eastern and Western Africans were so great, and xenophobia so deep seated, that building up clandestine bases was far from easy. Pushkin and other Soviet advisers became impatient with the lack of progress. M'Bundu, however, was no sycophant. He was determined not to suffer another Namibia style rebuff, this time at the hands of the British. He insisted on the careful build up of subversive cells in the main East African cities and the proper stocking of guerrilla bases in safe areas where dissident tribes were known to exist and could be relied upon to give adequate support.

While M'Bundu developed his subversion of East Africa more slowly than the Kremlin planners hoped, he did agree with their broad strategy. Uganda was to be undermined first. It was the least stable of the three Commonwealth countries comprising East Africa as it had been wracked by tribally based civil wars ever since gaining its independence in 1962. In recent years the causes of tension in Uganda had become more religious than tribal, as the frontiers of Islam were pushed slowly but remorselessly southwards into Sub-Sahara Africa. Senegal and Nigeria had already become Moslem states on the western side of the African continent and Uganda was now in the frontier zone on the eastern side. Thus M'Bundu could exploit not only tribal but also religious differences in subverting Uganda. From the Kremlin's point of view, a Homelander success in Uganda would provide the belt of Socialist states across the waist of Africa, linking the Congo to the Horn of Africa. After a pause to build up his resources in Uganda, M'Bundu could strike southward into Kenya or Tanzania – which it should be, could be decided later in the light of events. As a sweetener, Pushkin assured M'Bundu that the Soviet Union would exert maximum political pressure on the British Government in all international fora to compel with withdrawal of Eagle Force.

The three East African Governments should have been able to take effective measures to defeat M'Bundu, but 2011 and 2012 had been wasted years. The Homelander threat was recognised but belittled. The victory on the Tana River and a few successes in capturing Homelander gangs during 2010 had led to unwarranted over-confidence in East African military prowess.

'We won the Battle of the Tana River, didn't we?' expostulated a Kenyan Minister, talking to Major General Ralph Thornton, Colin Campbell's successor in command of Eagle Force, at a British High Commission reception in Nairobi.

Thornton had suggested that it was high time that the Kenyan Government enacted the necessary Emergency Regulations before the Homelander threat forced it to do so.

'Don't worry!' the Minister had continued, 'The Ugandans have M'Bundu's people taped. The Congolese are no match for us East Africans. There's no point in alarming people unnecessarily by declaring an Emergency. Our Security Forces can cope. *Business as usual* is our policy.'

Thornton was not so sanguine but it was none of his business to agitate for Emergency Regulations. Since the early ambushes in the Aberdares, in which my husband had been killed, the status and responsibilities of Eagle Force had been formalised by the Eight Power African Defence Understanding, negotiated in 2011 between Kenya, Uganda, Tanzania, Zimbabwe, Zambia, Malawi, Botswana and Britain. Eagle Force was to remain in Kenya as an air mobile strategic reserve, primarily for use against external aggression. Thornton's directive from London forbade Eagle Forces' deployment on internal security and his interference in local politics. He was in support of the three East African Governments and not in command.

Complacency reigned in Nairobi, Dodoma and Kampala as it had done in Kuala Lumpur and Singapore in the early years of the Malayan Emergency, and in Nairobi at the start of the *Mau Mau* rebellion, both in the 1950's. This time it was African Governments and not the British colonial administrators who were underestimating the threat and overestimating their own abilities. The police forces were being expanded it is true, but at a relatively leisurely pace. In the larger towns and cities the Police Special Branch cells still gave the political opposition parties more attention than Homelander subversion. And in the country districts tracking the Homelander gangs was left almost exclusively to the Army.

But the worst feature of 2011–2012 period was the depth of suspicion which existed between the three governments. In public there was wholehearted co-operation: behind the closed doors of ministerial offices there was none. The worst offender was Uganda, which refused to accept a contingent from Zimbabwe to help patrol its borders, and which kept Eagle Force at arms length.

It was the Uganda Government that had most cause to regret its narrow nationalistic attitude. Indeed, it was tribalism rather than nationalism or religion that was its undoing. On 5th July 2013 the predominantly Luo recruited units of the Uganda Army mutinied in Kampala and Entebbe and declared for the Homelanders. The Luo members of the Buganda dominated Government defected as well and Uganda sank once more into another bitter civil war in which tribal loyalties were paramount. The Luos were more intent on seizing power than supporting M'Bundu's cause. Nevertheless, within a couple of months Uganda had become the sixth state of the Black Homelander Union. Traditional African values were re-established and the Moslem advance was temporarily halted.

The Kremlin geo-politicians had succeeded in linking the Congo Basin to the Horn of Africa, and now had a base from which to undermine the anti-

Homelander governments of the other East African States. A decision had to be taken as to whether Kenya or Tanzania or perhaps both should be attacked next. Nairobi was the nearest and politically the most important prize, but the stability of the Kenyan Government and the presence of Eagle Force would make it the harder nut to crack. M'Bundu decided on a two handed strategy: he would overtly threaten Kenya first while building up his strength in Tanzania; and he would then launch a limited offensive against Tanzania before actually attacking Kenya. He would also threaten the French in Shaba every time he needed a diversion.

The shock of the collapse of the Ugandan Government reverberated through the corridors of Washington, Whitehall, Nairobi and Dodoma. In Washington there was a natural tendency for the Administration to blame the British for allowing the slide to disaster in East Africa to gain momentum. In London reactions were mixed. The pro-European Continental strategists took the line of 'I told you so. Eagle Force should never have been sent there in the first place. Africa will act as a suction pump drawing our military resources away from Europe which is against well established government policy.' The Maritime lobby, on the other hand, brushed this view aside as mere theory. The hard facts were, they claimed, that something had to be done quickly to stop the rot otherwise the Kremlin would be chalking up another victory which would do Western Europe no good at all. In the two East African capitals the complacency and nationalistic pride of 2012 was swept away in a surge of doubt with an accompanying loss of confidence. The two governments came together in a joint appeal to London and Washington for help.

Such was the concern of the new Democratic Administration in Washington about events in East Africa that President Mackenzie despatched his Secretary of State, John R. Chapell, on a fact finding mission to London, Nairobi and Dodoma. The upshot of his tour was the creation of a Joint War Council in Nairobi, chaired alternately by the Prime Ministers of Kenya and Tanzania, and the appointment of Jacob N'jonjo, the victor of the Battle of the Tana River, as Joint Director of Operations. Eagle Force was to be reinforced and would come under the command of N'jonjo for operations, but like Commonwealth contingents under British commanders in the Second World War, Thornton would have the right of appeal to the British Government if he considered his force was being put in jeopardy. In the first instance, he could appeal to the British High Commissioner in Nairobi who was to be a member of the Joint War Council. Thereafter he could appeal direct to London.

Placing a British force under an African Commander would have been unthinkable in the 20th century. In 2013 it was just as unthinkable for there to have been a British Director of Operations in two countries which had been independent for almost half a century. Co-operation between East African and British forces was eased by their common military background and traditions. Most of the Kenyan senior officers and some of the Tanzanians had been trained in British Military establishments and there had been a British Forces' training team in Kenya for many years. N'jonjo and Thornton had been at Sandhurst together as cadets and, being the same age group, had met again both at the British Army Staff College at Camberley and at the Royal College of Defence Studies (the old Imperial Defence College) in Belgrave Square in London as recently as 2011. They were firm friends and determined to make collaboration work.

Possibly the most important legacy of past Commonwealth collaboration in Military Training was the extensive study of British campaigns in the latter half of the 20th century. Nuclear weapons had made the study of the Second World War less relevant than the counter-insurgency operations undertaken during Britain's withdrawal from Empire. Gerald Templer's success in Malaya, Walter Walker's in Borneo and John Akehurst's in the Oman had become military folklore.

N'jonjo and Thornton in their preliminary discussions agreed that the situation in East Africa was more akin to the Borneo Confrontation with Indonesia than the Malayan conflict with the Chinese Terrorists. In Malaya the threat had been internal: in Borneo, and now in East Africa, the threat was mainly external, with some internal subversion. In both cases there was a thousand miles of open frontier to control.

N'jonjo's plan, which Thornton endorsed, was to create a defensive zone some fifty miles deep along the frontier in which to identify and, if possible, destroy Homelander gangs trying to infiltrate both countries. This zone would be manned and patrolled by East African Forces and contingents from Zimbabwe, Zambia and Malawi. Eagle Force would provide air mobile strike forces to encircle and destroy intruder gangs which could not be dealt with by the static framework battalions in the Defensive Zone. Both N'jonjo and Thornton would have liked full Malayan style Emergency Regulations to have been brought into force and for a start to have been made in building up village Home Guards, but they realised this was probably politically unacceptable at that time. They did, however, persuade the Joint War Council that the Police forces should be expanded in a crash programme in order to build up intelligence and security behind the Defensive Zone.

At the earlier meetings of the Joint War Council some of the 'business as usual' attitudes returned, and high cost defensive measures were relegated to the pending tray. The Police expansion was implemented and a network of Malayan style Provincial and District War Executive Committees was set up to co-ordinate the action of the Civil administration, Police and Army, but only minimal Emergency Regulations were asked for from the Kenyan and Tanzanian Houses of Assembly. All eyes in the War Council were on the British High Commissioner, who was expected to do more than honour the John R. Chapell agreement that Eagle Force would be reinforced. No specific figure had been set. It had been left to the War Council to send 'a shopping list' to London via the British High Commissioner of the reinforcements that were required.

Chapell had stressed that the lend-lease system, agreed in 2008, could be used to defray costs.

In Thornton's view three things were needed. First of all, he required a second brigade with supporting air forces for deployment in Tanzania. His original 5th Brigade of Eagle Force would stay as strike force in Kenya. Both these brigades could become closely involved backing up the Defensive Zone in the two countries, so his second requirement was a third brigade to form a central reserve and to underpin the defences of the base ports of Mombasa and Dar-es-Salaam. The third requirement was for the latest automated Command, Control and Communication (C^3) system, without which Eagle Force would not be able to operate at maximum efficiency. He could not rely on the local communications, which were neither secure nor reliable.

Thornton flew home with N'jonjo's Chief of Staff to present his shopping list to Whitehall. In preliminary meetings in the Ministry of Defence it was made quite clear to them that the most they could plan on was the despatch of one extra brigade. The provision of an adequate helicopter lift for it would take some months as the additional machines would have come from the United States. The possibility of providing the C^3 equipment in under a couple of years was remote.

The records of the Whitehall discussions are still secret under the thirty year rule, so I have had to depend upon the memoirs of the Chief of Defence Staff, Admiral of the Fleet, Sir James Trowbridge, and a few other published sources to reconstruct what happened.

If Sir James' recollections are correct, Thornton's pruned shopping list was put to the Defence and Overseas Policy Committee, chaired by the Prime Minister, in September 2013. The Chiefs of Staff's paper suggested that there were two options: find the additional brigade from forces assigned to the Northern Flank of NATO or from BAOR. They recommended the latter on the grounds that the Scandinavian countries were more vulnerable to a Soviet attack and a Soviet success there would present a more immediate threat to the security of the British Isles. They pointed out, however, that the Defence Review of 2005 had already reduced the three divisions of 1st (British) Corps to two brigades instead of three. The removal of another brigade would mean reducing the corps to two divisions only, and would be in breach of the Gibraltar Accord. In presenting the Chiefs of Staff paper, Sir James commented: 'The loss of this brigade will bring Britain very near the cliff-edge of having to withdraw 1st (British) Corps from its sector of the Central Front because it will no longer have the strength to fulfil the role assigned to it by the Supreme Allied Commander, Europe. The Gibraltar Accord would also have to be re-negotiated with the United States.'

Sir James called it a cliff-edge because of the far reaching consequences of such a withdrawal. The whole of the NATO deployment would have to be recast; our Continental allies would have to do much more; and the British would in all probability have to give up command of the Northern Army Group. There was a danger that the whole carefully woven fabric of the NATO Alliance would start to unravel as national self-interested intruded upon the re-building of the Central Front. Re-negotiating the Gibraltar Accord was seen as relatively easy because the United States were supporting the British effort in East Africa.

In summing up the discussion the Prime Minister agreed that the brigade should come from BAOR and that 1st (British) Corps should be reorganised on a two divisional basis. This had the advantage of releasing a divisional headquarters worth of the latest C^3 equipment and some badly needed helicopters. The withdrawal should be presented to Britain's NATO allies as *temporary* and they should not be asked to concur. With the United States Ambassador to NATO firmly behind the British decision, none of the other national delegations in Brussels were prepared to raise substantial objections. They knew they would risk increasing their own financial costs if they did not accept the word *temporary* and insisted upon redeployment to cover the gap. The slide towards the total withdrawal of 1st (British) Corps from its defensive sector on the Iron Curtain had begun virtually by default on the part of Britain's NATO partners.

In his memoirs, Sir James records his thoughts that evening as he wrote up his diary. He had only been in the Chief of Defence Staff's chair for six months and so he felt in no position to make a personal *démarche* in Whitehall just yet. He knew from his experience of being Chief of Naval Staff for three years that Whitehall never likes to be taken by surprise, even by one of its own mandarins. Its collective consciousness has to be in the right mood to accept a major change of policy, and changing its mood takes time and great patience. All he was prepared to do officially at this stage was to initiate an in-house study of the implications of withdrawing a further brigade from BAOR if, as he expected, the situation in East Africa continued to deteriorate.

But Sir James felt a deeper disquiet. Apart from the collapse of Uganda, three other important events had occurred in the first half of 2013. They were all political and involved national choices of leaders in elections of one kind or another around the world. Each had been given separate coverage in the Joint Intelligence Committee's summaries – the Red Books – but Sir James' instincts told him there must be some connection between them. He suspected they represented a rising tide of nationalism rather than a further surge of communist inspiration, but what the linkage was he could not, as yet, decide. His diary entries, however, suggest that he was probably the first senior officer to come near to sensing the presence of what I, with the full advantage of hindsight, have described as the Four Horsemen.

The first and most significant choice had been Nogi's landslide victory in the Japanese General Election of January 2013. Nogi was the direct legatee of the World economic recession that had undermined the old guard of Japanese political life and had made his message attractive to the Japanese people, who had seen their living standards eroded and the frightening disorders created by left wing extremists in most Japanese cities. His message was one of moderation and of national pride. In his election manifesto he declared:

> *'Since the Second World War, have we not trodden the wrong path? We have tried to join the Occident, but we belong to the Orient. In consequence, we are accepted by neither. Our true destiny lies in the leadership of the Third World through moderation and the excellence of the Japanese way of life. Let us first build a new Co-prosperity sphere in Asia in peaceful co-operation with all the people of Asia and for our mutual benefit. Let us export the Japanese way, the way of the Gods, to people who can appreciate its merits. We have already built up great commercial and industrial enterprises in Asia. Let us now provide the leadership.'*

To Sir James, Nogi's New Shintoist platform was little more than old fashioned Japanese Nationalism. He was prepared to accept Nogi's protestations of moderation in all things and to believe that Nogi would stand by his creed of leading through Japanese commercial and industrial excellence rather than Samurai valour. But, and it was a big but, would Nogi's followers be content with idealistic moderation?

The second electoral choice had occurred in Mexico in April 2013. The result had sent shivers down the spines of Sir James' American colleagues on the NATO Military Committee in Brussels. Since Archbishop Bolivar's triumph in Colombia and Venezuala in 2010, Bolivarism had become a self-generating political movement, which fired the imagination of most Latin Americans who did not belong to the ruling establishments. Although the Archbishop had exploited Soviet aid to achieve his breakthrough and his movement had been dubbed Christo-Communist, it was more Nationalist than Communist. Bolivar was doing for Spanish Latin America what Philipe Gonzalez had done for the Spanish Motherland in the 1980's. Gonzalez had been the first really successful Socialist Prime Minister of Spain and had shown that the old establishment no longer had a God-given right to rule. The circumstances in Latin America were more extreme and it had been Bolivar's good fortune to be the right man at the right time, who triggered the reaction that burst the Latin American political mould and released the pent up popular dynamic for fundamental change. Though Bolivar was more than a mere catalyst who made the movement possible, it was largely self-sustaining and generated a momentum of its own. It won enough seats in the Mexican General Election to frighten the Mexican establishment and the United States Government. Washington saw only the hand of Communism behind the Bolivarist successes in its own 'back yard' and not the socially inspired nationalism that was at the heart of the Bolivarist movement.

The third important choice did not come about through an election at all and can hardly be classed as popular. Since the assassination of his rival and superior by the women of the Revolutionary Guard in Tehran in 2005, the Ayatollah of Baghdad had consolidated his power in the *Shi'ite* world. He had successfully brought Iran, Iraq and Saudi Arabia together in the Federation of Islamic Republics. He had wisely decided to make no further attempt to consecrate the *Shari'a* of Kerbala until passions cooled. By 2013, however, he was beginning to believe what his closest and most sycophantic advisers had been hinting at for some time. His political successes had been so remarkable that they could only have been inspired by Allah. He must, in truth, be the *12th Imam* of the *Shi'a* succession. It was his duty to lead the Moslem world in a renewed *jihad* against the enemies of Islam. But first he needed the formal acceptance of the *Shari'a* of Kerbala, certainly by the *Shi'a Ulema* or theologians, and at least neutrality from the *Sunnis*.

In May 2013 a new conclave of the *Shi'a Ulema*, with observers from the main *Sunni* centres of learning like the al-Azhar University in Cairo, and from fanatical extremist groups such as the Moslem Brotherhood, met in the holy city of Qum under the Ayatollah's chairmanship. The business was in two parts: the acceptance of the *Shari'a* of Kerbala and the initiation of *Jihad*. The Ayatollah's supporters had done their political preparatory work well. The *Shari'a* was accepted by the Shi'a *Ulema* and not opposed by the *Sunni* observers. When it came to the debate on *Jihad*, the Ayatollah made the telling point:

> '*When the Israelis stole our lands in Palestine with American help in 1947, less than a million followers of Islam were dispossessed. Forty five million of our brethren in Central Asia live under the godless rule of the Politbureau in Moscow.*'

While he was second to none in his loathing of Israelis, sixty years of warfare with them had produced little return. It had absorbed resources and distracted attention from the much larger problem of the plight of the Soviet enslaved millions of believers. He then called upon all true followers of Islam to support him in *Jihad* to restore the Moslem way of life to Central Asia.

He received thunderous applause and a well rehearsed cry of:

> '*Show us Allah's way.*'

Without a moment's hesitation, he replied:

> '*With Allah's help, we will first restore the freedom of his believers in Afghanistan. Allah will reward with eternal bliss all who fall in this cause co-equally with the Martyrs of the struggle against Israel.*'

The first evidence of rhetoric being translated into action was an invitation to the Ayatollah from General Mohammed Khan, President of Pakistan, to visit Islamabad to discuss 'matters of mutual interest'. At press briefings in Tehran and Islamabad before the visit, officials made no secret of the fact that the unsatisfactory life being led by the Islamic majority in the Autonomous Soviet Socialist Republic of Afghanistan[1] was on the agenda. The powerful radio transmitters, set up by Ayatollah Khomeini and General Zia of Pakistan in the early days of the Afghan guerrilla war in the 1980's before the Russians managed to consolidate their hold on the country, began to step up pro-Islamic rather than anti-Communist broadcasts to the Central Asian Soviet Republics. Moscow could hardly protest because one of the planks of Soviet policy in Central Asia was religious tolerance: a Communist euphanism for religious discouragement without actual proscription.

The usual anodyne communique was issued after the Islamabad meeting which took place in June 2013. The harshest sentence was one which said that both leaders were personally committed to furthering the cause of Islam throughout the former Moslem lands of Central Asia. The diplomatic double talk was translated unusually quickly into deeds. After many years of undeclared peace, the guerrilla war in Afghanistan was rekindled and the *Mujahideen* – the Holy Warriors – took to the mountains once more with fresh supplies of arms reaching them from both Iran and Pakistan. The CIA's part in the rejuvenation of the *Mujahideen* should not be underestimated. Afghanistan began to merit headlines in the world media once more, as it had done in the 1980's.

Moscow was not slow to react. The Soviet Ambassador in Tehran warned the Ayatollah in a 'frank exchange' that interference in the internal affairs of the U.S.S.R. could place Soviet aid to the Federation of Islamic Republics (F.I.R.) in jeopardy. Furthermore, the Soviet Union would not hesitate to act if evidence came to light of direct Iranian support to the *Mujahideen* in Afghanistan. The Ayatollah is reported to have replied. 'Allah's will be done: we are but his servants.'

The Soviet Ambassador in Islamabad received a similarly curt reply from General Mohammed Khan. Diplomatic relations between Moscow and the two Islamic capitals were not served, but Soviet aid was abruptly cancelled and Soviet technicians working in the Federation of Islamic Republics and Pakistan packed their bags and left. The *Sunni* states of the Moslem world could but applaud the Ayatollah's audacity. Suspicion of

Shi'ite ambitions and uncertainty about the outcome of so brash a challenge to the Soviet Union checked any tendency there may have been amongst them to supply more than moral support.

While 12th Brigade and its supporting air component were being flown to Tanzania, the Chief of Defence Staff held a series of meetings with his advisers on whether British Defence policy should continue to be centred so exclusively on the defence of Western Europe in spite of the growing instability of the world outside the NATO area. His questioning of established policy seemed to have little effect at first, but the Ministry of Defence behaves like the iron filings in that first lesson in physics enjoyed by most school children. The filings are scattered on a white piece of paper. When a magnet is brought up underneath, all the filings turn towards it and create patterns showing the force lines of the magnetic field. As the minutes of Sir James' meetings were circulated, the subordinate staffs began almost imperceptibly to swivel towards the views inherent in Sir James Trowbridge's questions. The unthinkable became thinkable. The paramountcy of Western European defence in Britain's military policy was being questioned officially for the first time since the Falklands War of 1982, when it had been decreed in the Ministry of Defence that the Battle of the South Atlantic should be treated as an historical aberration that was unlikely to be repeated.

The first public glimpse of a change in Whitehall thinking came in the Defence White Paper published in February 2014. The build up of British forces in East Africa was no longer described as 'temporary'. On the contrary, it was held up as an example of Commonwealth solidarity and as a recognition of Britain's determination to go on helping in the creation of a multi-racial world through evolution rather than revolution. British policy in East Africa was a lineal descendant of her successful policy of moderation which had led to the second Lancaster House Settlement and the establishment of a multi-racial Azania in place of the former Union of South Africa in 1995. The continuation of this policy had necessitated reductions in Rhine Army and RAF Germany.

Deep in the verbiage and statistical data of the White Paper lay evidence of the first minimal change in British Defence policy. The Army had cancelled the re-equipment of the last two of its armoured regiments with the new *Conqueror* Main Battle Tank (*Challenger*'s replacement). The two regiments were 11th Hussars and 9th/12th Lancers, both of whom had won fame in Montgomery's Western Desert Campaign as reconnaissance units equipped withh armoured cars. The Army Board had decided to transfer them to the Army Air Corps for conversion into helicopter units. The Royal Air Force was making similar changes. The last buy of the European Fighter Aircraft was to be cut back in order to fund a new buy of larger helicopters and short range transport aircraft. Both moves were explained away as short term measures to meet specific requirements. It was far too early to acknowledge a radical change of policy, which was far from winning general acceptance in 2014.

Sir James Trowbridge could not have made the progress he did in softening Britain's over-commitment to Western European Defence had it not been for the support he received from the Secretary of State for Defence. After a series of Secretaries of State, who were only interested in financial control and, as they put it in Americanese, 'getting a bigger bang

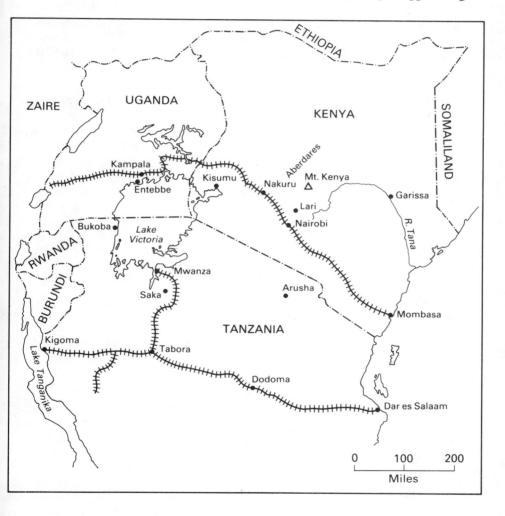

MAP 6: The Black Homelander Offensive in East Africa, 2013–2014

for the buck', it was refreshing to find that Alexander Clarkson, was more interested in strategy and Chiefs of Staff thinking than in the financial manoeuvres of the Permanent Under Secretary. His political instincts told him there were more votes to be won championing world-wide causes than the narrower interests of the European Community which bored and often antagonised the British electorate.

In East Africa there was an uneasy calm as M'Bundu consolidated his position in Uganda. He followed Hitler's technique of declaring at mass rallies in Kinshasa that he had no further territorial claims in Africa. The only enemy he had left in Africa, he maintained, was the 'illegal' government of Shaba and their French and Belgian supporters. Their time was running out. Although M'Bundu had no intention of attacking the French until he had absorbed Kenya and Tanzania, he gave substance to his deception plan by engineering a number of guerrilla attacks near the French military base at Kamina (*see Map 4*).

In Tanzania the deployment of 12th Brigade and its supporting air forces had been completed in October 2013. Their main base was in Dar-es-Salaam with forward operational bases at Dodoma and Tabora on the main railway to Kigoma on Lake Tanganyika and Mwanza on Lake Victoria. A rudimentary C^3 system had been established in both Kenya and Tanzania by the Royal Corps of Signals and the expansion of the Police Forces of the two countries was being pushed ahead.

But, by Christmas 2013, much of the shock of the Uganda collapse had worn off. Nothing had happened. Both governments and the local media began to take M'Bundu at his word. The French, they began to believe, really were the next Homelander target. The Emergency Regulations started to become irksome and the mounting cost of precautionary military measures seemed unwarranted. This was especially so in Tanzania which had only a relatively short common border with Uganda between the northern end of Lake Tanganika and the south western corner of Lake Victoria, and even this was partially blocked by the mountainous area of Rawanda and Burundi. These small states had, so far, shown surprisingly effective resistance to Homelander blandishments. Their fall would give Tanzania early warning of a Homelander offensive.

Almost exactly a year after the Homelander coup in Uganda, M'Bundu opened his feint offensive against Kenya in July 2014. Accusing the Kenyan Government of border violations he launched a surprise attack on Kisumu airfield at the north east corner of Lake Victoria. Some of his troops came by fast patrol craft and others were launched by helicopter. The small Kenyan garrison, which consisted of little more than a platoon from the local framework battalion responsible for the area, was quickly surrounded and forced to surrender. Fortunately, there were only two light aircraft on the field at the time. Both were destroyed and the raiders withdrew with their prisoners before a counter-attack could be mounted.

Kampala radio made the most of their success, describing it as a warning to unco-operative neighbours.

General N'jonjo came under immediate political pressure in Nairobi to avenge the insult to Kenya. Intelligence sources also warned him that the Homelanders were again infiltrating guerrilla gangs into the Aberdare forests north of Nairobi. This was confirmed by a relatively small but nasty ambush of a police patrol on the road north west of Nakuru. Several policemen had been killed and others wounded. As joint Director of Operations, N'jonjo decided to move the Zimbabwe contingent, which had been in the Mwanza sector of the Tanzanian defensive zone south of Lake Victoria, across to Kisumu. The move attracted a great deal of attention from the media as N'jonjo intended it should do. In retrospect it can now be seen to have been an unfortunate decision.

M'Bundu maintained his threat to Kenya with a series of guerrilla actions, accompanied by political propaganda, for about three months. N'Jonjo did not need to move more troops north from Tanzania as the Kenyan Security Forces themselves had one or two useful successes which gave him confidence that he had the situation well in hand. The Kenyan Government also had a reasonable hearing at the United Nations when it appealed to the Security Council to brand M'Bundu the aggressor at Kisumu.

In October 2014 M'Bundu sprung his trap in Tanzania. Two large car bombs exploded in Dar-es-Salaam's busiest shopping streets, killing over a hundred people and injuring several hundred more. Almost simultaneously, news reached Dodoma, the Tanzanian capital of a cold-blooded massacre of all the inhabitants of the village of Saka, near Mwanza on the southern shore of Lake Victoria in the sector previously occupied by the Zimbabwe contingent. The Saka atrocity was reminiscent of the Lari massacre in 1953 at the start of the *Mau Mau* campaign in Kenya. As at Lari, the village was surrounded in the early hours of the morning, the huts set on fire and, when the inhabitants rushed out to escape the flames, they were shot down – men, women and children. Those who did not die in the fusillade were hacked to death later with pangas. Over three hundred mutilated corpses were found by Tanzanian troops and police who reached the village too late to trap the gang.

Word was spread quickly by Homelander agents that the same thing would happen to other villages which did not support the Homelander cause. To reinforce the warning two more villages were razed to the ground over the next fortnight and, in a further show of Homelander strength, two bridges were blown up on the railway near Shinyanga, half way between Tabora and Mwanza.

Political recrimination was immediate and bitter between Dodoma and Nairobi. The very people who had found the Emergency Regulations most galling, were the first to scream loudest for better protection. N'jonjo and

Thornton were pilloried for failing to anticipate and prevent the Homelander atrocities. Thornton was fortunate in that 12th Brigade had some success in its follow-up operations. 1st Royal Anglians from Tabora trapped and killed most of the railway gang, but the Saka Gang escaped without any contact being made with it. It probably perpetrated the two other village atrocities. N'jonjo, on the other hand, was not so lucky and came in for quite unjustifiable denigration in Dodoma. He was *Joint* Director of Operations, but in Tanzanian eyes he was a Kenyan and partial to Kenya. Had he not moved the Zimbabwe contingent away from the very area that had been attacked in order to reinforce Kenya's defences? The fact that Kenya had only suffered some border skirmishes and that Nairobi itself was unscathed confirmed N'jonjo's partiality in the minds of Tanzanian Government ministers.

Though a good but unlucky soldier, N'jonjo was no politician. Knowing that the Tanzanian members of the Joint War Council were after his blood, he decided that attack was the best form of defence and there was much in the Tanzanian performance which was wide open to attack. He pointed out to the Council that the Tanzanian Police Special Branch had failed to penetrate the clandestine Homelander cells in Dar-es-Salaam and so could give no warning of the car bomb attacks; and slowness in creating a Police field force, due to financial constraints, had contributed to the Saka and the other massacres.These Tanzanian failings could not be denied, but he weakened his case by making a personal attack on the Tanzanian Commissioner of Police whose moderate performance lay at the root of these setbacks. If he had confined his remarks to the War Council, which always met behind closed doors, his reputation as victor of the Battle of the Tana River might have saved him.

Unfortunately, he did not. A television interviewer trapped him into unguarded remarks about the Tanzanian Police performance. Both Prime Ministers agreed that he must go. Selecting a successor was not so easy.

The political furore was not confined to East Africa, where there was a steady escalation of terrorism throughout Tanzania. In Westminster the consensus of opinion was that Britain should either reinforce to end the emergency quickly or get out. The usual 'troops out' marches took place and the *Voice of Africa* terrorist organisation, which had made itself felt in the United States with the bombing of the Wall Street computers, started issuing threats of a similar campaign in Britain if Eagle Force was not withdrawn.

I was just finishing three months leave in England after leaving Bogota when the *Voice of Africa* campaign started. I had been promoted lieutenant colonel in the half yearly list and was to take up the appointment of Military Assistant to the Commander-in-Chief of Northern Army Group at Rheindahlen in West Germany. The campaign began with riots in most British cities with large Black communities. They were shown in lurid close-up on our television screens every night for about a fortnight. They combined the viciousness of the sectarian riots in Belfast and mindless arson of the Toxteth and Brixton disturbances of the 1980's. At their height, the Black militants behind the *Voice of Africa* launched what must have been another long pre-meditated coup against the electronic society in which we live. There were no loud explosions as there had been in Wall Street. Only the startling announcement by the Department of Health and Social Security that the memory banks in their Manchester, Liverpool, Birmingham and Newcastle computer centres had been wiped clean. An attempt to do so in London had failed because there were too many back-up facilities available. No pensions or social security payments could be made in the Midlands or Northern England!

In the subsequent investigation it was discovered that the *Voice of Africa* had infiltrated 'sleepers' into the DHSS computer programming staff over a number of years. At a given signal, these 'sleepers' fed instructions to the machines to erase their memories. Very few of the culprits were identified and those who were, were both Black and White, the latter being Black activist supporters. The infiltration of the Black 'sleepers' was made relatively easy by the British Government's equal opportunities policy in which Government Departments were expected to set an example. The *Voice of Africa* made itself a household word in Britain as it had done in the United States. Unfortunately, so few of the 'sleepers' were identified that suspicion fell upon all Black employees in the Government's service, undoing many years of effort put into ending racial discrimination to which Britain was pledged.

Although opinion in the British Cabinet had been veering towards further reinforcement of Eagle Force before the riots began, the Government hesitated. The country was almost as deeply divided over the issue as it had been over the Suez intervention in 1956. The great difference between the two crises was the complexion of the Government in power. In 1956 a Conservative Administration was being led by a sick man, Anthony Eden. In 2014 the Social Democrat Government had no such impediment, but the crisis it faced was no easier to resolve. The vociferous 'Troops out' lobby of 2014 was an alliance between the usual pacifist elements, Black Nationalist supporters of M'Bundu, who looked upon Kenya and Tanzania as neo-colonialist states, and the 'Little Englanders', who believed that Britain should confine herself to Europe and eschew world wide military involvement.

Had it not been for the determined leadership of the Prime Minister, ably supported by the Foreign Secretary and Secretary for Defence, a decision might have been taken to withdraw Eagle Force, which had originally been sent to Africa by their Conservative predecessors. In Government's view, Britain was committed to the Lancaster House policy of achieving a multi-racial world by evolution rather than revolution. The

Homelander regime was bent upon the latter and should be opposed if it was practical to do so. Unlike Anthony Eden, who was at loggerheads with President Eisenhower over how to deal with Egypt's President Nasser, the Social Democrat Government had the full support of President Mackenzie in its effort to check M'Bundu. The international opposition to Eagle Force was coming from Britain's European Allies, who were still recovering from the economic recession and who had no wish to see more British military resources withdrawn from Europe. They would be faced with the cost of filling any gap that might be left in Western Europe's defences.

The Cabinet decided at the beginning of November 2014 to send out two ministerial missions before taking a final decision on whether to stay in or pull out. The Secretary of State for Defence and the Chief of Defence Staff would go to Brussels for consultations with NATO on further British withdrawals from BAOR and RAF Germany; and the Foreign and Commonwealth Secretary, accompanied by the Deputy Chief of Defence Staff (Intelligence) would fly to Nairobi and Dar-es-Salaam to assess the situation in East Africa and the reinforcements that would be required if Britain decided to stay.

Of the two missions, the East African team had the easiest row to hoe. Once in Nairobi, both men concluded very quickly that Britain could not withdraw without doing irreparable damage to the Commonwealth and without ruining all she had achieved with the Lancaster House Settlement of 1995. Withdrawal would be tantamount to handing East Africa to M'Bundu on a plate. This view was reinforced by a new and sinister development. In a frontier clash that occurred three days before the mission arrived, the Zimbabwe battalion in the Kisumu area captured an East German officer who admitted being part of a 'volunteer' force that had recently been landed by Soviet aircraft at Entebbe airport in Uganda.[2] His task was to train the Homelanders in Uganda to use the latest Eastern Block equivalent to the British *Foil* missile system, which had won the Battle of the Tana River for the Kenyans.

The question to be resolved by the East African team was no longer whether to stay or not: it became 'What do we need to win?' The answer they concluded was in three parts. First, a 'Supremo' of the General Templer mould was required to grip the situation and to develop and impose battle winning policies. Secondly, an experienced director general of Intelligence was essential, together with a fully automated C^3 system to replace the rudimentary improvisation set up by Thornton. And thirdly, Eagle Force must be reinforced to counter the appearance of the East Germans in Uganda. A third brigade, equipped with the most advanced weapon systems and substantial air reinforcements were both essential to counter the East German arrivals.

In a series of telegraphic exchanges between London, Washington and the East African capitals, a solution was hammered out. Neither East

African government could put forward a man of the Templer calibre. Even if they could neither government would accept a nominee of the other. Furthermore, they certainly had no-one with the experience to handle the weapon systems being introduced to counter the East German intervention. The only man known to both governments, who inspired mutual confidence, was Colin Campbell, the first Commander of Eagle Force and the real victor of the Tana River. He had been promoted to lieutenant general and knighted for his subsequent work as British Defence Adviser in Washington. Sir Colin was a strong personality and an able soldier, who had within his genes the ability to get on with Afro-Asian people: amongst his ancestors was Sir Colin Campbell of Indian Mutiny fame and several other British pro-consuls, who had served in political and military capacities East of Suez over the last two hundred years. London, Nairobi and Dodoma agreed that he should be appointed the new Joint Director of Operations, responsible to the Joint War Council. Unlike N'jonjo, he would have full powers over the military and police forces of both countries but, unlike Templer in Malaya, he could not be given political power as well.

There was no obvious choice available for Director of Intelligence. During discussions with the American Embassy in Nairobi the British Ambassador pointed out that the CIA had the best organised and most extensive Western Intelligence in Africa. Would Washington be prepared to second a suitable man for the post? And so it came about that a U.S. State Department Official, Edgar J. O'Hanlan, was proposed to and accepted by the Kenyan and Tanzanian Governments, who appreciated that his appointment would provide access to the very wide spectrum of United States Intelligence sources.

When it came to deciding what reinforcements should be asked for, both East African Governments showed some nervousness at the prospect of more British troops arriving in their countries. Would they ever be able to get rid of them once the war was over? Were they opening themselves up to some new form of 21st century colonalism? Their decision to accept General Thornton's recommendation that Eagle Force should be brought up to the strength of a full division of three brigades and that the RAF *Falcons* should be backed by the latest strike aircraft armed with advanced stand-off missiles, was made easier by reports coming in of a major cross-border raid. A strong column of Homelanders tried to occupy Bukoba just over the Uganda/Tanzania frontier on the western shore of Lake Victoria. The Tanzanian battalion called for help. 12th Brigade responded, flying 1st Black Watch by helicopter north from Tabora. A strike by *Falcons* was needed before the Homelanders decided that Bukoba was not as easy to take as they had expected. Most of them escaped back to Uganda, but the Black Watch trapped and captured one group of about twenty men, including another Eastern Bloc officer – this time a Czech.

In Brussels, the British team received one of the coolest receptions that Admiral Sir James Trowbridge could ever recall. It was not just a matter of 'going over the cliff edge' as he had previously described further British withdrawals from BAOR; it was like dropping head first into a deep-freeze and having the door shut over you! Only the Americans showed any warmth and that was only in private. In the Council Chamber of the NATO Headquarters they kept the British at arms length, hoping in due course to produce a compromise package of measures acceptable to the Europeans, whose delegations were all calculating the financial cost of themselves of a further withdrawal of British troops.

In the Military Committee, Trowbridge explained the British proposal to withdraw a further brigade from 1st (British) Corps which would make it militarily unsound for the rump of the Corps to go on holding a sector of the Central Front. Moreover, with the rotation of units between BAOR and East Africa which would be needed, if the crisis in Africa were prolonged, 1st Corps' training for European type operations was bound to suffer. There were two options: withdraw 1st (British) Corps into Northern Army Group Central Reserve, so that it could look after Western European interests outside the NATO area; or for Britain's allies to join her in establishing a European Rapid Reaction Force to undertake the task. It was Western interests and not just Anglo-America interests that were at stake. Nor was the threat confined to Africa: instability was growing in the Middle East, the Far East and Latin America. The withdrawal of 1st (British) Corps into reserve provided an opportunity to recast the NATO deployment so that Western Europe could face up to the challenge to its interests outside the NATO area.

Trowbridge might have been addressing a meeting of the deaf without the benefit of deaf and dumb sign language. The most the Committee would do was to accept the British decision to withdraw further troops and aircraft and to instruct the Supreme Allied Commander to fill the gap left in the front by side stepping formations. There was no demand that Britain should give up command of Northern Army Group. The Dutch and the Belgians were still loath to accept a German Commander of the Army Group, and the Germans themselves were unwilling to impose a candidate and were happy to leave the British Commander-in-Chief with the unenviable task of managing the re-deployment.

In the NATO Council, the Foreign and Commonwealth Secretary made just as little headway. His argument that it was just as important to check Moscow's ambitions in the world at large as it was to do so in Europe, carried no conviction amongst Britain's Continental allies. Even evidence of East European involvement in East Africa did not sway their view that they could not afford any increase in military expenditure. Their economies were still recovering from the recession, which the Warsaw pact countries had ridden with relative ease. First things first: countering the

Warsaw Pact threat absorbed all their available resources. The hard fact was, as Trowbridge remarked, that Western Europe still did not have the collective political will to play a world role.

I watched the debate from the Commander-in-Chief's office at Rhindahlen. The British staff at the Army Group Headquarters were naturally relieved that the British were not giving up the command, but international relations in the headquarters reflected the anti-British atmosphere in Brussels. We were looked upon once more as Perfidious Albion, pursuing our own national self-interest. Looking back as I write this book in 2040, it is clear to me that in 2014 our allies did not have the collective determination to face the challenges that the 21st century apocalypse would bring. Britain is often accused of being insular psychologically as well as topographically: Europe is far worse.

In Nairobi General Sir Colin Campbell took over as Joint Director of Operations just before Christmas 2014. He had three principal subordinates. Thornton remained as Commander of the reinforced Eagle Force. N'jonjo became Commander of the Kenyan Security Forces, and the Tanzanian Army Commander, Charles Lundu, took over operational direction in Tanzania.

2015 dawned in East Africa with a further deterioration in the guerrilla war. Sir Colin Campbell, like Templer in Malaya, had no magic wand he could wave. As in Malaya, the security situation became worse as more and more people re-insured with the Homelanders. Some tribal communities saw the chance of enhancing their own status and of paying off old scores with their neighbours by actively supporting the M'Bundu-ist cause. In short, 2015 was to be a difficult year for Sir Colin as he fought to re-establish confidence internally and to beat the Homelanders externally. The usual counter-insurgency vicious circle set in. Confidence would only be regained by Security Force successes; and their success required an increased flow of intelligence, which itself needed greater popular confidence. It was Campbell's task to find the formula which would break the circle.

During the first decade of the 21st century, while 'the mice and men' of the middle and lesser powers were concentrating upon human squabbles on earth, the two superpowers had gone on struggling for supremacy in space. Beam weapons had proved practical, but the problems of attenuation in the earth's atmosphere were still not solved so that such Star Wars systems as had been deployed depended upon intercepting incoming missiles in space, rather than in the boost phase while the missile was still in the earth's atmosphere and had not released its warheads. The estimated effectiveness of the most efficient system was still well below eighty per cent.

The first generation Anglo-Japanese *HOTOL* had proved itself far superior to the American space shuttle and *Ariane* as a satellite launcher: so superior, indeed, that both superpowers were developing their own version, while the Anglo-Japanese consortium was already building a second generation vehicle with larger engines and greater payload.

Both superpowers had become suspicious in 2010 that Anglo-Japanese *HOTOL* collaboration might result in 'third power' weapons in space, and both concluded that it was time to make another all out effort to negotiate a treaty prohibiting such weapons. Like all the previous disarmament negotiations, each side sought more concessions than the other could possibly concede. By 2014 President Mackenzie had decided reluctantly that his negotiators were wasting their time. He did not recall them but they received no directions from Washington to make any further concessions without which progress became impossible.

Notes

1. Despite the Soviet failure to conquer Afghanistan by military means in the 1980's, political pressure eventually triumphed and Afghanistan became the Autonomous Soviet Socialist Republic of Afghanistan in 1998, retaining a measure of independence. Its army was subject to operational direction by the Soviet High Command.
2. According to Pushkin, M'Bundu had asked for Cuban support but Moscow had decided that Cuba had enough to do supporting the Bolivarists in Latin America: hence the appearance of East German troops.

6

The Nationalist Surge in Asia (2015–2017)

> '2017 has been the year of the Veto. It has been
> used three times in quick succession in the Security
> Council and has given the Third World
> a *caçus belli*.'
>
> Diary entry for 10th October 2017

During Britain's withdrawal from empire in the latter half of the 20th century, it had often been hard to distinguish whether it was Communism or Nationalism that was the primary driving force behind the various anti-British liberation movements that waxed as Britain's power and will to rule waned. The mix was always different, but it was rare for one to succeed without the other. Even when the Communist philosophy was anathema to particular nationalist movements, Soviet financial aid and supplies of Eastern Bloc weapons were usually welcome, provided they were offered without blatant political strings.

In the first decade of the 21st century there was no difficulty in disentangling Communist from Nationalist influences. There was little doubt that Communism, fattened by the world economic depression, used African and Latin American Nationalism to rejuvenate its cherished ideal of world revolution. In the second decade, however, the dynamic of Nationalism began to re-assert itself and Soviet aid became less important to the World's militants since an alternative and more attractive source had begun to emerge with the election of Nogi as Japanese Prime Minister in January 2013. By the end of the second decade, Communism was to become as embattled as Colonialism had been in the 20th century.

Nogi lost no time in exploiting the political contacts he had made in China and South East Asia during his eight long years as leader of the

Japanese parliamentary opposition. Admiral Trowbridge's analogy of the iron filings of the British bureaucracy in Whitehall turning towards the most powerful magnet is even more apt in Tokyo where corporate consensus is the foundation of Japanese decision making. The surface of the paper on which the Japanese iron filings lie is stickier than the Whitehall version and it takes longer and more powerful magnetic forces to change political direction in Tokyo. Nogi had the drive and political charisma to induce change.

Within six months of taking office, Nogi broke through the inflexibilities of Japanese bureaucratic thought by appointing one of his nominees as Japanese Ambassador to Peking. Through him he engineered an invitation from the Chinese Government to pay a formal visit to China in 2014. China was still nominally a Communist state, but has been aptly described as more Confucian than Communist. Chinese traditional values had reasserted themselves, and the Confucian ideals of good government had brought a return of the profit motive in Chinese society and the acceptance of private enterprise alongside state ownership. In the resulting mixed economy major Japanese firms, working strictly on commercial lines, were playing an important role in building up the technological infra-structure of China and in helping to bridge the wide gap between Chinese and Japanese standards of living.

By the time Nogi came to power, with his political philosophy of peacefully generated Asian Co-prosperity, Chinese international confidence had risen in step with improved living standards. Nevertheless, the Chinese and Japanese Governments and their peoples still held each other at arms length for reasons rooted deep in Sino-Japanese history. There was even less warmth in Sino-Soviet relations when Nogi arrived in Peking in June 2014. Moscow was accusing Peking of aiding and abetting the Islamic *Jihad* in Central Asia, pointing out that the *Shi'ite* virus could infect the ten million Moslems living in northern and western China. The Chinese Government had countered by accusing the Soviets of incubating a vicious strain of anti-Chinese bacteria in Vietnam by building up Russian Naval and Air strength at the former American bases in Cam Ranh Bay and Dahnang. Furthermore, the complimentary modernisation and strengthening of Russian forces in Eastern Sibera did nothing to foster amicable Sino-Soviet relations.

Nogi found in Chu Cheng, the Chinese leader, a kindred spirit. They both envisaged what Western journalists had written about and feared for years: the development of an East Asian political and economic community that could face up to both the existing superpowers. The community that they envisaged would be based upon their common historical traditions and cultural values, and their relationship to one another would be analogous to the Anglo-American special relationship with only the narrow China Sea instead of the wide Atlantic Ocean between them. China and Japan were so obviously complimentary to each other in the shrunken world of the 21st century that a determined mutual effort should, in their view, be made to soften old rivalries and the causes of Sino-Japanese hostility. Both Chinese Communism and Japanese Democracy were moving away from their original Soviet and United States models and towards an oriental system more in keeping with their traditions and psychology. The process should be encouraged and deliberately guided in a way which would reduce Sino-Japanese differences in political approach.

Nogi and Chu were practical men as well as idealists. They knew that the rise of an East-Asian superpower would be unwelcome in Washington and Moscow. Nor would their Asian neighbours look favourably upon such an accretion of power by two countries that they had always feared. Both men agreed that it was essential to emphasise the 'peaceful co-prosperity' theme in their collaboration, and to play down any suggestion of missionary zeal. Expansion would come through neighbouring states wishing to jump on a successful bandwagon, as had happened with the European Economic Community.

But, while success breeds success, both men appreciated that it also attracts predators. Political and economic success could be short lived without military collaboration as well. United States forces in the Pacific area had been drastically reduced over the last twenty years to maintain the primary American commitment to the defence of Western Europe. Those that remained were neither a bulwark against Soviet aggression nor a threat to the countries of Eastern Asia. The Soviet forces in Eastern Siberia and Vietnam, on the other hand, were the menace that had to be countered, and this could best be done by arming Chinese manpower with Japanese technology.

The discussion on military strategy led logically to space programmes. Both China and Japan had their own rocket systems, and the Japanese had their major stake in *HOTOL*, but there was still a wide gap between Sino-Japanese space capabilities and those of the two superpowers. Neither leader was a space technologist or even a graduate in scientific subjects, but both appreciated that, in lay terms, three breakthroughs were needed to snatch superiority in Space: much greater payloads which might be provided by *HOTOL* technology; a step advance in computer power, which Japanese computer firms were confident they could provide; and a new source of power capable of overcoming the attenuation of beam weapons by the earth's atmosphere. The last would be needed if an agreement was reached to prohibit weapons in space. They would have to be operated instead from earth: a much more difficult proposition. Chu thought he might have a solution. Would Nogi consider a joint project for the development of hydro-electric power in the Yangtze Gorge? The project could purport to be aimed at meeting China's domestic power requirements and need have no apparent connection with weapon development. Nogi agreed to consider Chu's proposal with his experts.

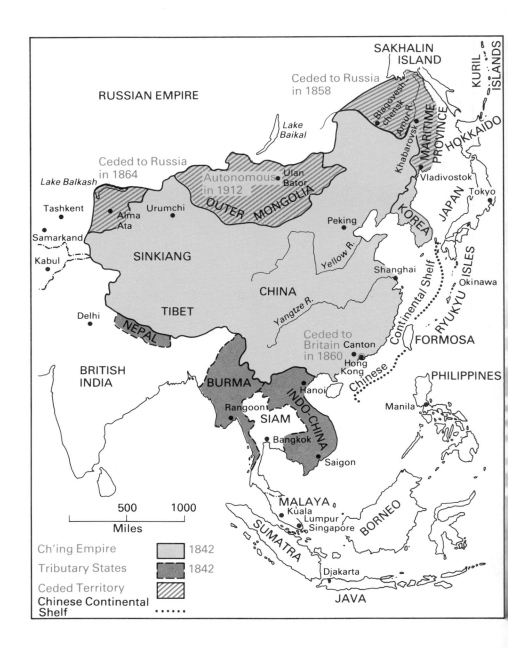

MAP 7: The Ch'ing Frontiers of China in 1842 and
the Chinese Continental Shelf in 2014

There remained the awkward question of Sino-Japanese territorial rivalry. Towards the end of the Nogi-Chu meetings, Nogi grasped the nettle nestling in the garden of their ideals:

'Our political and economic collaboration could pay great dividends for our peoples,' he said tenatively. Then, with even greater diffidence, he asked 'What are your territorial ambitions on land and on the sea bed?'

Chu did not hesitate. 'The Ch'ing frontiers of 1842 on land,' he replied, 'and the edge of the Continental shelf at sea.'

That reply came as no surprise to Nogi. The Chinese empire in the days of the Ch'ing or Manchu dynasty was at its zenith by 1760. In its decline it did not lose territory until the Opium Wars (1839–42) with the British, which led to the ceding of Hong Kong to Britain and the five Treaty Ports to European jurisdiction. Subsequently, Russia seized the province of Alma Ata in Central Asia and the Maritime Provinces of Eastern Siberia astride the Amur River; Outer Mongolia became autonomous under Russian protection; Tibet became autonomous too under British influence rather than protection; Japan annexed Taiwan and Korea; and the Chinese tributary States of Nepal, Burma, Siam, and Indo-China ceased paying any further allegiance to the Dragon Throne in Peking.

Regaining what had been lost since 1842 seemed to Nogi a reasonable ambition on land. Agreement would not be so easy at sea. The Chinese claim to all the Continental Shelf in the China Seas rather than up to the Median line between the Chinese and Japanese shores was hard for Nogi to stomach. The Chinese Continental shelf came very close to the Japanese and Ryukyu island chain, and gave the Chinese a grossly unfair advantage, but Nogi appreciated that acceptance of this long standing demand of Peking's was the price Japan had to pay for Chinese friendship and he was prepared to pay it.

The meetings ended with an agreement to set in hand the drafting of a formal treaty establishing 'a Sino-Japanese co-prosperity Alliance'. The work was to be carried out in Peking and Tokyo by a special joint planning staff under the co-chairmanship of a Chinese and Japanese senior career diplomat, each with ambassadorial status. If they were successful in drafting a treaty acceptable to the Chinese and Japanese Governments, the two ambassadors and their staffs would be charged with supervising its implementation. In the final communiqué they were referred to as 'The Co-prosperity Planning Staff' which was soon corrupted by the Western media into COPPS and then the Copps.

No secret was made of the establishment of the Copps. Their terms of reference stressed the political and economic aspects of future Sino-Japanese collaboration which included a major effort in space. What was not revealed, and was to become one of the best kept international secrets of all time, was the existence within the Copps of a small planning cell of able military officers, defence scientists and weapon technologists under the Chinese General Tzu Te and the Japanese General Woa Oyama, whose task it was to give the Co-prosperity ideal the sharp teeth it would need in the practical world and in vastness of space.

Drafting the treaty took almost a year. With a nice sense of history, Chu invited Nogi to meet him in Hong Kong on 20th May 2015 to sign it. Most of the Western press took the choice of Hong Kong to symbolise China's success in developing a mixed economy. Since Hong Kong's reversion to Chinese sovereignty in 1997, China had scrupulously honoured her 1985 agreement with Britain. Hong Kong had been allowed to retain its British codes of practice; its prosperity had continued; and the Chinese Government took a pride in showing off the former British colony as an example of its responsible attitude towards the wishes of the Hong Kong people and to the merits of their way of making a prosperous living. None of the world's most erudite commentators noticed the neat historical allusion to the part played by the cession of Hong Kong in 1842 that began the collapse of the Ch'ing Empire. Chu looked upon the signing of the Sino-Japanese Co-prosperity Treaty of Hong Kong as the starting point of the recovery of the Ch'ing frontiers. Only Nogi and the members of the Copps appreciated the innuendo behind the choice of Hong Kong for the formal ceremony.

The Treaty of Hong Kong received a cautious welcome in the major capitals of the world. There were obvious parallels with the Treaty of Rome which had established the EEC. Its political and economic provisions were unexceptional apart from an agreement for the joint financing of the Yangtze Gorge hydro-electric plan which had been discussed for years but had, so far, lain beyond China's economic resources and technological capabilities. There were equally obvious dangers of a new 'ganging-up' process that could generate further international conflict. On balance, most commentators were prepared to take Nogi's slogan of 'peaceful co-prosperity' at its face value; at least until it was shown to have other less desirable traits.

The Treaty's reception would have been very different if the existence of three secret protocols had become known: the first was geo-political, the second military, and the third concerned space.

The secret geo-political protocol set out, in the broadest terms, the steps to be taken by both powers to restore the Ch'ing frontiers and to delinate their respective spheres of influence in the proposed Asian Co-prosperity Sphere. China would lead in policy affecting the recovery of the Province of Alma Ata in Central Asia, Outer Mongolia and the Siberian Maritime Provinces. Japan would lead in drawing the countries of her Second World War Co-prosperity Sphere back into the newly fashioned fold (i.e. Burma, Thailand, Malaysia, Indonesia and the Philippines). The one exception would be Vietnam, which Chi insisted should be a Chinese responsibility.

The secret military protocol was more detailed and reflected the close study made by the military cell in the Copps of Russo-German military collaboration after the First World War, which had enabled the Germans to circumvent the military restrictions imposed upon them by the Treaty of Versailles. The basic experimental work, which gave Hitler's *Wehrmacht* its decisive superiority over the victor powers of 1918, had been carried out in Russia in the 1920's. Sino-Japanese military collaboration was to be based on the simple philosophy of using Japanese technology to equip Chinese manpower with battle winning weapon systems, using remote areas of China for secret experimental work. In practice the bargain was not quite so clear cut or one sided. China could contribute her nuclear weapons and missile know-how to the technological pool; and Japan could provide Maritime experimental areas to augment the secret land/air weapon development and training areas in the Chinese hinterland.

In one important area of negotiation there was a clash between the civil and military members of the Copps. The Ambassadors wanted to insert a date into the military protocol by which warlike preparations were to be completed. They suggested a five year time span and proposed 2020 as the target date. The military and technological members objected. They accepted the need for the discipline of a target date, but they argued for a ten year period. The German General Staff had advised Hitler in 1932 that his rearmament programme would take ten years. The Copps military cell estimated that they could not do the job any quicker. The politicians, however, pointed out that Hitler, in fact, went to War in 1939 instead of on the target date of 1942, and did not do too badly, certainly at first. A compromise was reached. In the Military Protocol the target date was set for 2025 with the proviso that Sino-Japanese forces must be ready for limited engagement by 2020.

The Space protocol inevitably had a Star Wars ring about it. The Copps assumed that the superpowers would eventually agree upon banning the permanent stationing of weapons in space, and the lesser space powers like Britain, France, Japan and China would be forced by public opinion to acquiesce. The emphasis in the Sino-Japanese military space effort would, therefore, be directed to overcoming the attenuation of the earth's atmosphere on beam weapons so that they could be earth rather than space based. The primary reason for collaboration in the immensely expensive Yangtze Gorge hydro-electric project was to provide the power source for a Sino-Japanese space weapon centre, which was to be built simultaneously with and under cover of the construction of the series of massive dams on the Yangtze envisaged in the scheme. No target date was set for the completion of the civil or military sides of the project. It could certainly take more than ten years.

During the Copps deliberations on the Space protocol, the Chinese members pressed their Japanese colleagues for agreement to share, clandestinely if need be, the fruits of Anglo-Japanese collaboration on

HOTOL. General Oyama, however, was adamant that Japan could not break faith with Britain. If the proposed Sino-Japanese beam weapon system needed reflectors in space which could be provided by *HOTOL*, then Japan would provide the necessary vehicles for the purpose. The Chinese accepted the wisdom of Japanese refusal to break their agreements with Britain: they might need London's help if Washington and Moscow started to gang-up against Peking and Tokyo. The British were adept at using the balance of power for their own purposes. They could be useful one day.

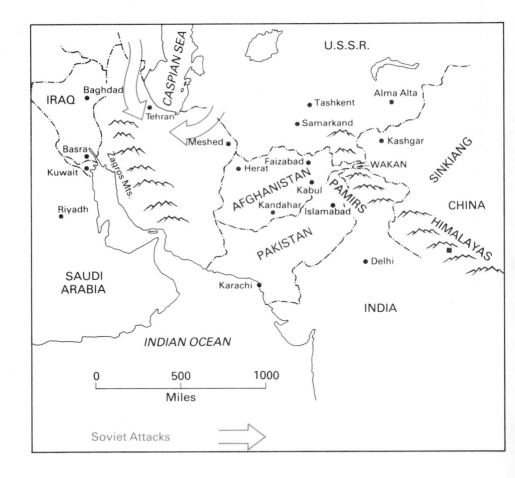

MAP 8: The Afghan Guerrilla War and Russian Occupation of Tehran: 2013 – 2017

If the Ayatollah of Baghdad and General Mohammed Khan had known anything of the secret protocols attached to the Treaty of Hong Kong, they would have deemed the time scale too long for their purposes. Reading between the lines of the published main section of the treaty, the two Moslem leaders saw that it would lead to increased Sino-Soviet tension, which they should be able to exploit. The first essential was to ensure that the Chinese Moslems gave Peking absolutely no cause for alarm. In due course they might be encouraged to join the *Shi'ite Jihad* to free their fellow Moslems from Soviet thraldom, but for the time being it was not in Islam's interest to court Chinese as well as Russian hostility. Tehran and Islamabad had enough on their hands re-energising the Afghan rebellion and making preparations to fend off any stab in the back by the American backed *Sunni* states led by Cairo, or a Soviet supported Indian attempt to settle old scores with Pakistan.

It was not until the winter of 2016/2017 that the *Jihad* in Afghanistan burst into flames. It had smouldered for three years. Then quite unexpectedly the *Mujahideen* recaptured the world headlines by two surprising successes: one in the west and the other in the east. In the west, the guerrilla bands supplied from Iran managed to encircle Herat. They came close enough to do considerable damage to the city before the Soviet equipped Afghan Army managed to break through their cordon and raised the siege. In the fighting, the Government of the Soviet Socialist Republic of Afghanistan obtained undeniable evidence of Iranian involvement.

In the East, Pakistan-backed *Mujahideen* surrounded Kandahar and on 16th January 2017 surprised and massacred the Afghan Army garrison. The attack took place in a blinding snow storm which enabled the *Mujahideen* to catch the majority of the Afghan troops sheltering in their barracks. Amongst those killed and mutilated were two Russian officers and twenty of their men manning the Russian Communication centre in Kandahar. The fat was in the fire as far as the Soviet Union was concerned.

Moscow's reaction was sharp and clearly pre-planned. Without any preliminary diplomatic orchestration two Russian armoured columns crossed the Iranian frontier east and west of the Caspian Sea heading for Tehran, and a Russian air-mobile force attempted to land at Tehran's international airport. The Iranians were not taken by surprise. The long Iran/Iraq war had given them a generation of senior commanders who knew their business. The Russians, on the other hand, had not been in action since the crushing of the Hungarian revolt in 1956, apart from their anti-guerrilla operations in Afghanistan and the bloodless invasion of Rumania in 1995 after the collapse of the Caecescu regime. In the David and Goliath contest of February 2017, the Iranian David had battle experience and Shi'ite fanaticism to sustain him: the Soviet Goliath depended upon the awe that his ponderous might inspired.

David did not slay Goliath this time, but his initial successes did show that Goliath was not as fit nor as well armed as he was thought to be. The first attacks by the Soviet Air Force to suppress the Iranian radars were only partially successful. The approach of the helicopters and transport aircraft of their air-mobile force was detected by the Iranians early enough for Tehran's air defences to go into action with optimum effect. The Soviet landing force suffered crippling losses. Those troops, who were not killed in aircraft shot down by Iranian SAMs, fought hard but were eventually rounded up by the Iranian Army. The two armoured columns fared no better in their early encounters with the Iranian defenders of the two roads leading to Tehran from east and west. Both were decisively checked.

It was some ten days before the Soviet High Command managed to recover from these set backs and to bring overwhelming force to bear. Soviet reinforcements were poured in and the Iranian defenders were forced southwards uncovering Tehran. Inside the Iranian capital there was a patriotic upsurge, led by *Shi'ite* fanatics, calling for resistance to the death. The Ayatollah deemed Fabian tactics more appropriate. He withdrew his government to Baghdad and ordered his forces to withdraw south west into the Zagros Mountains from which they were to wage a guerrilla war against the puppet government that he anticipated the Russians would install in Tehran.

The Russian occupation of Tehran was doubly counter-productive as far as the Soviet Government was concerned. It united the Arab world behind the Ayatollah; and it revealed that there were weaknesses in the Soviet military establishment. Within a few days of the fall of Tehran, all the Moslem States of the Middle East and Northern Africa, without exception, sent emissaries to Baghdad offering support. What had been a *Shi'ite Jihad* so far became *Jihad* for the whole Moslem world. Such was the spirit of the times that when the Israelis, as fellow Semites, offered their support as well, it was not rejected by the Ayatollah.

The United States was not slow to seize the opportunities presented by the anti-Soviet clamour. The State Department judged correctly that the situation was ripe for a fresh attempt to build a new Baghdad Pact to bring all the countries of the Middle East into an anti-Communist alliance. The Baghdad Pact of the 1950's, engineered by John Foster Dulles and Anthony Eden, had failed, due to the rivalry between Nasser's Cairo and Hashemite Baghdad. In 2017, the Russians had brought all the Arab world and Israel onto the same side: no mean achievement.

The flaws in the Soviet Goliath's performance were not very obvious to the world at large. The Iranian David had put up a sterling performance, but he had been crushed in under three weeks. Within the inner conclaves of Western Intelligence a very different picture emerged. Nowhere was the Russian performance more critically analysed than in the major NATO headquarters in Europe. As Military Assistant to the Commander-in-Chief, Northern Army Group, I was privy to most of the studies undertaken. The general conclusion was that the Soviet Armed Forces were paying the price for their system of selecting their senior officers. Age, experience and Party acceptability counted more than the drive of youth and military efficiency. In the 1980's some of the Second World War Commanders had still been in office. Old Father Time and the election of Mikhail Gorbachev had cleared them away, but the younger men promoted by Gorbachev were still in command in 2017. A stultifying orthodoxy had consequently gripped the Russian military establishment and lack of recent battle experience ensured that the steam roller methods used by the victorious Soviet armies in the Second World War were still in vogue. In planning the invasion of Iran, Soviet military and political Intelligence had been faulty; in execution, the methods used had been cumbersome; subsequent flexibility and speed of reaction to the initial set backs had been slower than expected; and the performance of some of the much vaunted Soviet weapon systems had been disappointing.

My Commander-in-Chief, when discussing the Intelligence reports at one of his routine morning television conferences, remarked: 'It looks like the Russo-Japanese War of 1904 all over again.'

The Head of the Northern Army Group Intelligence Staff, *Bundeswehr* General Hans Schmidt, was quick to press his microphone switch and his face appeared on the large, life-size TV monitor in the C-in-C's office as he said: 'No, Sir; they are a long way off that as yet, but seeds of decay may be beginning to germinate. It is too early and far too dangerous to draw analogies with 1904. Tsarism was rotten to the core: that cannot be said of the Soviet Union – Communism is still a dynamic force.'

Headquarters Northern Army Group was the first headquarters that I had worked in which had the latest C^3 system, code named *Cyclops*, installed and fully operational. Indeed, before I took over as Military Assistant to the C-in-C, I had to do a three months' course at the Royal Corps of Signals Training Centre at Blandford in Dorset to learn how to handle the equipment in his private office. It was the equivalent of the Spanish language course, which I had been sent on before going to Bogota. The language, however, was the latest 21st century communications and computer jargon.

In my grandfather's day, a Military Assistant to a Commander-in-Chief was his principal private secretary, who handled his papers and ordered his day. I soon found when I took over at Rheindahlen, that the MA had become the C-in-C's television director and producer as well as his secretary and personal adviser. My office would have been a credit to the control room of a major television network. Ranged along the walls were banks of monitors, connecting us to all our subordinate formations, to other Army Groups and Air Headquarters at our own level, and to SACEUR'S Headquarters and the Ministry of Defence above us. My desk was the control console through which I could feed the screen in the C-in-C's personal office. Gone were the days when commanders and staff officers had to make long and tedious helicopter trips to Rheindahlen to discuss important issues with the Commander-in-Chief. They could speak to him or any other senior officer by video phone. Conferences could be called and attended without the commanders, who were often hundreds of miles apart, ever leaving their own headquarters. The personal touch, which is so important in assessing what can or cannot be achieved, was not lost because they could all see as well as hear each other. The only thing they could not do was to share a drink together when arguments became over-heated and the balm of a gin and tonic or a Schnapps would have been helpful.

While the use of secure fibre optical and data links had great advantages in speeding up decision making, in improving co-ordination, and in saving commanders' and staff's time, it had some perverse side-effects. For instance, officers had come to realise that their reputations, and hence their promotion prospects, depended upon their television charisma almost as much as their military ability. The inevitable 'one-upmanship' produced an over emphasis on presentation at the expense of substance. Moreover, good television personalities could run circles round much abler but less extrovert rivals, sometimes with unfortunate results.

From my personal point of view, the days of taking endless minutes of meetings at conferences were over. Arguments deployed and decisions taken were all available for recall from the Command computer memory banks. Paper, like cash, was almost a thing of the past. Dexterity in handling the latest advances in command, control and communication technology had replaced literary clarity as the measure of a staff officer's competence and efficiency.

In the real world beyond the NATO command system, life went on in its repetitively tiresome way. The Federation of Islamic Republics wasted no time in appealing to the Security Council, accusing the Soviet Union of wanton aggression and demanding the withdrawal of Soviet troops from its territory. The Russian delegate countered, arguing that the Soviet Union had acted in self-defence to end the blatant Iranian interference in the internal affairs of the Afghan SSR. He took the opportunity to warn Pakistan of the advisability of pondering the consequences of Iranian bravado. In the debate that followed, both Japan and China sided with Iran, as did all the Third World delegations. Iran had a substantial majority when the vote was taken on the final resolution, which branded the Soviet Union as the aggressor. It demanded the withdrawal of Soviet troops from Iran and the establishment of a United Nations Peace Keeping Force on the Soviet-Iranian frontiers. Acute and understandable Soviet embarrassment led to the inevitable Soviet veto, and to a feeling of frustration amongst the Asian delegations.

While the Security Council debate had been in progress during March 2017, the United States found itself similarly embarrassed in Latin

America. The Bolivarists of Panama had just won a closely contested general election in Panama City, and had been prevented by the Army from taking power on the grounds, probably well founded, that the Bolivarists had used corruption and intimidation to unseat the Government. The Bolivarist leaders appealed to Domingo Garcia for Colombian military support. When Domingo passed this request to the Colombian Cabinet, Archbishop Bolivar hesitated. Interference in an area so strategically sensitive to the United States would be asking for trouble. Bolivarist movements throughout Latin America were winning power successfully, using the ballot box rather than the bomb and bullet. It would be unwise to court United States hostility by military action in Panama. On the other hand, failure to support his own emulators in Panama could have an adverse affect on the Bolivarist movement which was snowballing so nicely. Domingo was, therefore, authorised to help the Panama Bolivarists, but he was to avoid an outright clash with the Panama Army, if it could be avoided. Enough cash was placed at his disposal to encourage the Panamanian Generals to see the situation through Bolivarist spectacles.

Domingo might have succeeded with a mix of military threat, bribery and strong local Bolivarist support amongst the people, had it not been for the counter-activities of the CIA, which was determined to keep the Bolivarists out of power in Panama because of their Communist connections. Indeed, the CIA had been largely responsible for the Panama Army's refusal to accept the verdict of the original general election. Domingo managed to infiltrate a large force of Colombians across the frontier disguised as Panama guerrillas, and he bought the loyalty and acquiescence of the military commander of the La Palma military district, which is less than one hundred miles south of Panama City (*see Map 3*). Then the alarm bells began to ring in Washington, alerting President Mackenzie to the Bolivarist threat to the Canal.

President Mackenzie's room for manoeuvre was quickly reduced by an official request from the Panama Government for American military assistance. Under the United States/Panama Defence Agreement, which was signed when the United States forces finally withdrew from their bases in the Canal Zone, the United States Government was pledged to go to Panama's assistance if requested to do so, or if, in the United States President's judgement, the security of the Canal was endangered. The President was in no stronger position to refuse support than Archbishop Bolivar had been. In fact, he was considerably weaker because he had only just won his second term as President by an uncomfortably narrow margin in the 2016 Presidential Election. The American political pendulum was swinging strongly towards the Republican end of the spectrum and so he could not take unnecessary political risks. In the characteristically simplistic terms in which complex issues are articulated in the United States, Communism was seen to be mounting a renewed offensive in Central

America as well as in Iran. A line must be drawn somewhere and what better place to do so than in Panama where the Canal had always been deemed vital to American interests?

And so it came about that in May 2017 the United States once again went to the support of a reactionary regime because it appeared to be the only alternative to a supposedly Communist backed Bolivarist take over. With speed and precision, that contrasted sharply with the Soviet intervention in Iran, a U.S. Amphibious Task Force reoccupied the former U.S. bases in the Panama Canal Zone. The professional ease with which the operation was carried out masked the weakness of the American's position. The regime they were trying to underpin lacked popular support. Their intervention rekindled the Central American Civil War of the 1980's and '90's, which was seen locally as a struggle between progressive and reactionary forces, and in the United States as an anti-Communist crusade. Domingo Garcia joined men like Cuba's Fidel Castro and Vietnam's General Giap in the American public's rogues gallery.

Arguments used in the Security Council about the United States intervention in Panama mirrored the recent debate on the Soviet action in Iran. The surprising thing about it was that Japan rather than the Soviet Union put the case for the prosecution. The Japanese delegate launched a scathing attack on American foreign policy. He accused the United States Administration of assuming the same role that the British had played in the great American Rebellion of 1776. In opposing the Bolivarist movement the Americans were failing to understand, as the British had done, the true aspirations of the Latin American peoples. The Bolivarist movement was as nationalist as the American colonists had been. They were worthy of support from rather than repression by the leaders of the non-Communist world – the United States. In his final peroration the Japanese delegate made his now famous plea:

> '*Japan, will be giving up her rotational seat on the Security Council to Malaysia at the end of this debate.*[1] **I wish, therefore, to take this opportunity to express my country's disgust at the emasculation of the Security Council's powers through the over-use of the veto by its permanent members, who owe their privileged position to the outcome of a war fought and won over seventy years ago. Some new way must be found to manage the world's affairs before it is too late. Japan is pledged to find that way**.
>
> '*As an old friend of the United States, Japan asks her to ponder carefully the further use of the veto and to accept the spirit of the resolution before the Council. It is understanding and not condemnatory of the U.S. position. The reputation of the United States would be enhanced by its acceptance and by agreement to allow the replacement of her forces in Central America by a United Nations force tasked to supervise fresh elections in Panama.*'

The emphasis marked in this quotation is mine. I believe those words are the key to all that was to happen in the last twenty years of the Third World War. They provided the clarion call, which eventually brought the Four Horsemen together in the 21st century Apocalypse.

The Japanese delegate had made his closing speech late in the evening of 2nd June 2017. The Chairman adjourned the debate until the following day to allow time for delegations to consult their governments before the vote was taken. The lights of the White House, State Department and Pentagon blazed most of the night as the President and his advisers sought a worthy answer to the Japanese challenge. At the start of the consultations President Mackenzie, in true Democratic Party tradition, argued for acceptance of the resolution, provided adequate safeguards could be devised to protect United States vital interests in Central America. As the night wore on, the tide began to turn against him as satellite and other sources of Intelligence confirmed the Pentagon's worst fears. A major Soviet airlift of equipment, and possibly troops, had begun across the Atlantic to Cuba, and there was evidence of the re-establishment of the old air bridge from Cuba and Colombia which had enabled Archbishop Bolivar and Domingo Garcia to win power back in 2010. By dawn the American veto had become as inevitable as the Russian veto had been in the debate on Iran two months earlier.

Britain abstained in the final vote taken on 3rd June 2017 for a variety of reasons. There was, of course, no point in reinforcing the American veto. But Britain had also much sympathy for the Japanese position. She recognised that her own situation had certainly changed since 1945. At that time she was not only one of the victors; she could also speak with authority for about a quarter of the world's population. In 2017 she had less right, in terms of world power, to exercise the veto than the Japanese. Furthermore, she had doubts about the American landings in Panama. Over the centuries she had been hostile to Spain. In her view, it was the legacy of the Spanish political system which had created the inequalities of wealth and opportunity in Latin America. There was much to be said in favour of the Bolivarist movement: it was Christian and Socialist, and its only connections with Communism were those common to most left wing revolutionary movements – financial aid and arms supplies from Moscow. It was, indeed, embarrassing that her close American ally should be so wedded to supporting reactionary regimes simply because they were anti-Communist.

Britain was soon to be embarrassed herself. It was two and a half years since General Sir Colin Campbell had taken over as Joint Director of Operations in Nairobi and the third British brigade group had been flown out to Mombasa. They had been difficult years. In 2015 Campbell had felt at times that he was losing the race to build up a sound security framework before the Homelanders managed to disrupt the political stability of either Kenya or Tanzania. He had a much more difficult task than Templer in malaya because M'Bundu had at his disposal Eastern Bloc helicopters, supply dropping aircraft and advanced communication and surveillance equipment which Chin Peng, the Communist Terrorist leader in Malaya, did not. Although the East Germans were not allowed by their Government to cross into Kenya or Tanzania in order to avoid any unfortunate confrontations with British forces, M'Bundu had enough capable Black American expatriates to man those equipments. Campbell was, therefore, faced with creating a favourable air environment as well as security on the ground. For that he needed the latest radars and communications equipment, all of which took time to provide, establish and man.

In the first half of 2015 the Homelander gangs were being landed and supplied in remote areas by helicopter. The distances were so vast and the expanse of country to be watched so great that the RAF *Falcons* had few opportunities to intercept. Gradually, the establishment of more advanced detection and communication equipment improved their chances and they made a number of successful kills. Nevertheless, throughout 2015 the graph of terrorist incidents rose remorselessly as M'Bundu developed his campaign. If Campbell has not been an able politician as well as a good general, he would not have been able to ride the political in-fighting that flowed from the sense of imminent failure created in Government circles by those statistics. Although he was aware of a gradual improvement in Police efficiency, in the flow of intelligence and in the military speed of reaction, the general public and the politicians could only see the dark side of the security coin: the remorseless rise in the casualty figures.

At the beginning of 2016, Campbell was able to report to the Joint War Council that he believed a plateau had been reached. The curve on the incident graph, he admitted, had not turned down, but it had not gone up either. The Police and Army expansion programmes were nearing completion and the security framework was now well established and working satisfactorily. He had introduced Templer's system of 'Black', 'Grey' and 'White' districts. In the 'Black' districts the full rigours of the Emergency Regulations were applied because the Homelanders were active in them and were probably being supported by the local tribes. 'Black' districts could be promoted to 'Grey' and eventually 'White' as the rate of elimination of hostile gangs and the co-operation of the local people improved. There were as yet no 'White' districts, but Emergency Regulations had been relaxed in the six districts that had achieved 'Grey' status.

Campbell's optimistic assessment was seconded by the Director General of Intelligence, Edgar O'Hanlon. He reported that M'Bundu was in some difficulty. It had not been easy to establish satisfactory operational bases in Uganda. East and West Africans distrust each other as much as, say, the Germans dislike the Slavs. There was also friction between the Black American expatriates and the East German advisers. Supply and reinforcement of Homelander units operating in Kenya and Tanzania by air had become very costly and could only be used sparingly. In short, O'Hanlon believed the turning point had come and that the Joint War Council should start considering the type of counter-offensive which should be prepared and launched to bring the Homelander challenge to an end.

So matters rested until the end of 2016. Campbell, in the meantime, had been maturing plans for the offensive action O'Hanlon had suggested. He had in mind General Walter Walker's successful actions in Borneo that brought the Indonesian Confrontation with Malaysia to an end in the 1960's. Walker's solution to the problems of a thousand mile frontier was clandestine cross-border operations to ambush the Indonesian reinforcement and supply trails near their base camps. President Sukarno's Nationalist pride had prevented him from admitting publically that British troops were operating inside Indonesia. O'Hanlon confirmed that he expected a similar reaction from M'Bundu, who, like Sukarno, was claiming that he was merely supporting Kenyan and Tanzanian internal liberation movements.

In March 2017, Campbell proposed to go further than Walker had done. His offensive, which he called 'Challenger', would be in two phases. In the first, he would ambush Homelander supply routes inside Uganda without acknowledging that the troops under his control were operating across the border, having been lifted into ambush positions by helicopter. In the second phase, a deliberate attempt would be made to over-run M'Bundu's supply bases and to raise Uganda in rebellion against the Homelander Union.

Kenyan and Tanzanian Ministers accepted the concept behind 'Challenger', but the British High Commissioner insisted that to reduce the risks of an international outcry, British troops should not cross the frontier. All cross-border operations should be carried out by East African troops supported by East African piloted aircraft. Much to Campbell's annoyance, the High Commissioner's restrictions were upheld by Whitehall, although he did manage to extract reluctant agreement to two exceptions. British troops could cross 'in hot pursuit' of Homelander gangs, and they could go to the rescue of East African troops if they got into trouble in Uganda. That was the least the British could do to help their East African allies.

The actual go-ahead for 'Challenger' was not given by the Joint War Council until July 2017, when the incident graph had shown a marked decline in Homelander activity and O'Hanlon had reported that conditions were right for the start of the counter-offensive. At first all went well. Three successful cross-border ambushes were staged and considerable casualties inflicted on the Homelanders without any public recognition by M'Bundu that his losses had been sustained inside Uganda.

Then N'jonjo, who was commanding operations across the Kenya/Uganda frontier, became over-confident and over-ambitious. There were security lapses in Nairobi and the Homelanders were able to anticipate a raid in the Entebbe area. 2nd Kenya Rifles, who had been landed by helicopter near their proposed ambush positions, were themselves ambushed and encircled. Campbell had no alternative but to order 5th Brigade to intervene and extract N'jonjo's men.

There was no disguising the clash which followed in September 2017. 2nd Light Infantry were flown in to secure an airhead at Entebbe through which the Kenyans could be flown out. RAF *Falcon*'s were concentrated to give air cover and to provide close support. Their appearance over Uganda gave the East Germans the excuse they needed to intervene as well. Losses mounted on both sides as 2nd Light Infantry and the Kenyan Rifles fought their way out of the Homelander trap and were eventually flown out. Two *Falcons* and three British helicopters were lost and there were ninety British casualties, mostly sustained in the loss of the helicopters. There were over three hundred Kenyan casualties.

At Lake Success, the Eastern Bloc mounted a fully orchestrated attack on Britain in the Security Council. It was Britain's turn to use the veto. This generated protest marches in London and some arson in areas with militant Black communities. The *Voice of Africa* was unable to launch another of its sophisticated attacks on our modern electronic way of life because it was not forewarned of the Battle of Entebbe and could not mount a terrorist effort quickly enough to exploit the situation. Their failure, however, was amply made up for by the chorus of left wing 'Troops out' organisations, protesting at the tops of their voices about the iniquity of British troops operating in Africa at all. The *New Statesman* referred to Eagle Force as 'the British Cubans in Africa' and the epithet was echoed by other left wing journals.

But it was not the merits or de-merits of British military action in Africa that was significant. It was the further demonstration of the impotence of the United Nations, caused by the veto, that rankled in Afro-Asia and the Third World generally. The superpowers vetoes were understandable, though hardly acceptable: a veto by a middle power like Britain was humiliating.

Looking back over the first thirty two years of the Third World War it is now apparent that the relatively insignificant skirmish at Entebbe was the catalyst which brought the Four Horsemen together and made the Apocalypse of the 21st century inevitable. 2017 had been the Year of the Veto. Its use three times in quick succession was more than the deep-seated nationalism of Afro-Asian and Latin America could tolerate. A new way forward to more effective World government would have to be found.

Note

1. Japanese reluctance to return to power politics, and the failure to re-negotiate the Security council permanent membership, intended to incorporate a European Community representative in the 1990's, had resulted in Japan continuing to accept temporary membership.

PART II

Convergent Courses

'Then I saw another mighty angel
coming down from Heaven. He was wrapped
in cloud, with the rainbow round his
head; his face shone like the sun
and his legs were like pillars of fire.
In his hand he held a little scroll unrolled.'

Revelations of St John, Chapter 10
(New English Bible)

7

The Collapse of the United Nations (2018)

'Resolution 7555 (LXXI)
. . . the Secretary General is directed to negotiate
the withdrawal of foreign troops from Panama,
Iran, Kenya and Tanzania by the end
of 2018 and to report the results of his
negotiations at the 72nd Meeting of the General
Assembly.'
United Nations General Assembly Record for 23rd January 2018

It was the British veto in the Security Council rather than the skirmish at Entebbe that brought the Four Horsemen together in 2018. Entebbe was only the trigger which started the reaction. They were not uniting against Britain, nor had Britain the power to play more than a catalytic role in the crucial events of 2018. In truth the British people had always had some sympathy for the growing ambitions of the Third World. The Four Horsemen's vision of the world, to which they were riding, was not far removed from the British tradition, symbolised by *Magna Carta*: a world free from over-concentration of political power, in which the voice of the majority was decisive and yet the legitimate rights of minorities were safe-guarded.

History is made up of the random coincidence of events, most of them unexpected. The British veto of the Eastern Bloc resolution on East Africa would not have changed the course of history had it not coincided with a minor heart flutter suffered by Nogi in the Autumn of 2017. Only Nogi and his personal doctors knew about it. They advised him to take things more easily. Their warning impressed him, but not in the way they intended. Cecil Rhodes' words became his spur:

'So much to do, so little time to do it.'

127

It might be too early for Japan to sever her ties with the West and to seize the leadership of the Third World, but he knew that he could not wait until the Copps target date of 2025. His challenge to the superpowers must begin at once. He saw the British veto in the Security Council as the ideal opportunity to start his 'end-run', to use American football slang.

Japan has the equivalent of the British thirty year rule for the release of confidential government documents, but is more liberal in the interpretation of confidentiality. I have been privileged to read the draft of Nogi's ghosted autobiography which was not to be published in his life time, and I have a copy of General Oyama's book, *'The Sword of Co-Prosperity'*, which gives a lucid account of the work of the Copps, including that of its secret military cell. My account of the United Nations crisis of 2018 is based upon these two books and my own diaries.

On hearing that Security Council action had been aborted for a third time in six months by a veto and that the third was applied by a middle power, colonial 'has been', Nogi summoned the Japanese members of the Copps. He told them that, in his view, the time had come to bring the United Nations to its senses or to get rid of it as a useless 20th century anachronism.

> *'Was the United Nations, as it stands today, a help or a hindrance to our co-prosperity plans?' he asked. 'If you conclude that it is an obstacle to progress, what should be done about it? Do we attempt to re-model it to the needs of this century or do we walk out? Please discuss our options with your Chinese colleagues.'*

The Copps report to both governments concluded that it was the power politics of the superpowers rather than the United Nations organisation that was at fault. There were three options: modification of the Charter; living with the Charter by manipulating it; or walking out. The superpowers would defeat the first. Although Japan had not pressed for permament membership of the Security Council, as was her undoubted right, the Hong Kong powers could live with the system, as suggested in the second option, by using the Chinese veto. If the third option was to be seriously contemplated, the walk out must be staged on an issue that would attract Third World support. It had to be realised that the Hong Kong Treaty and the Sino-Japanese concept of Co-prosperity were seen by many Afro-Asian states as a cloak for the revival of both Japanese and Chinese imperialism: in their eyes, a most dangerous combination. The Copps, therefore, recommended pursing the second option until a suitable opportunity occurred for an effective walk out.

Chu was prepared to accept this advice: Nogi was not – he knew he could not wait. In his view, three vetoes in six months, all on Third World issues, compelled action if the Hong Kong Treaty powers were ever to gain a world following. Nevertheless, he was prepared to go cautiously, as the Copps recommended. The first step should be to place the superpowers on trial at the next session of the General Assembly which was due in November 2018. This should be done by launching a 'Uniting for Peace' resolution under Sino-Japanese co-sponsorship, demanding the withdrawal of American, Soviet and British troops from Panama, Iran and East Africa and their replacement, if need be, by United Nations peace keeping forces. The threat of a Sino-Japanese walk out, if the superpowers failed to comply, would be hinted at in public, but should be given more substance amongst the Third World delegations in the lobbying behind the scenes in New York.

Chu accepted Nogi's proposal with one important proviso. A decision to walk out should depend upon the degree of Third World support likely to be forthcoming. He and Nogi would make a considered judgement at the time as to whether a walk out would enhance or reduce the attractiveness to the Third World of Sino-Japanese leadership as an alternative to domination by the existing superpowers. In anticipation of the judgement going in favour of action, the Copps were to plan a walk-out and recommend changes in Sino-Japanese policies that would be needed in its aftermath.

Chu's caution and Nogi's impatience did create stresses within the Hong Kong Alliance and no more so than within the military staff of the Copps. Having reached agreement with Chu on the 'Uniting for Peace' resolution, Nogi summoned General Oyama to brief him on progress made so far in Sino-Japanese rearmament. 'When will it be possible,' he asked, 'to begin offering "clients" alternative sources of military equipment to wean them away from their present superpower suppliers?' 'That depends upon what class of weapons our future clients will want: *Sparrows*, *Crows* or *Hawks*?' was Oyama's cryptic reply.

Oyama went on to explain that the supra-technology (ST) weapon systems being developed under Copps' direction were far in advance of the ET systems in service with the superpowers. They fell into three groups, named after birds. The *Sparrow* class comprised a number of light 'fire and forget' anti-tank, anti-air and anti-personnel missiles, named after small birds, which would 'lock' onto whatever target was being engaged when the firer pulled the trigger. Having a much higher velocity than the comparable ET weapons of the superpowers, they were much more difficult to decoy. They also had a markedly higher lethality and hit probability. The *Crows* were a family of larger medium range 'maids of all work', which were replacing almost all the conventional mortars and artillery in the field armies. And *Hawks* were the long range killers that Oyama described as the creators of nuclear scale destruction by non-nuclear means, hence with no radiation side effects. Naval and air weapons were modifications of the same three basic families.

'We could supply *Sparrows* now for use by guerrilla forces,' Oyama advised Nogi, 'but at a price that our Chinese colleagues are reluctant to pay. It would mean delay in the re-equipment of their forces, which they believe should be completed before any export is allowed.'

Since Nogi's medical warning, he was becoming increasingly impatient at any hint of delay to his plans and irritated by the least sign of over-caution in Peking. 'You must persuade Tzu Te that decision to export should be treated on the merits of each case. Training schools and a supply organisation for clients should be set up now.'

Oyama noted this direction on his pad and then gave 2020 as the estimated date for the start of *Crow* issues to the Japanese and Chinese forces. Not many would be available for export much before 2025. Paradoxically, the *Hawk* family would be available earlier because, though larger, they had been developed first. As decisive battlefield weapons they had had the greatest effort lavished on them. They were already coming into service, but Oyama stressed:

'*Hawks* must never leave our hands; nor must their actual performance become known. It is impracticable to keep their existence secret now that they are coming into service with our own troops, so they are being presented as relatively innocuous Japanese improvements on existing conventional systems already in service in most countries. Only a very few selected Japanese and Chinese officers are aware of the capabilities of the actual warheads. For training purposes conventional war heads are being used, except on the secret trial range in Sinkiang.'

Nogi took Oyama's points in quickly and said:.

'So its *Sparrows* now, *Crows* 2025, *Hawks* never!'

'That is my considered view: General Tzu is reluctant to recommend any *Hawk* issues until we have used them in action.'

'Co-prosperity means close and willing co-operation with our clients as well as with China. Such caution may not be possible,' replied Nogi, gesturing as if to close the interview.

Oyama had one more point to make before he bowed out of the Prime Minister's office. 'None of these weapons will give us the decisive tactical superiority that we seek unless we have the capability to acquire targets for them with sufficient accuracy to make full use of their lethality. The short range *Sparrows* are no problem as we have the necessary optical sights for day and image intensifiers for night use. The very long range *Hawks* are also well covered by satellite systems. It is the mundane, medium range *Crows* that present the problem and, as they will be the most used battlefield weapons, solving their target acquisition problems is crucial. We have directed more resources to beating the problem than we planned, but I am happy to report that it seems to have paid off. We are testing the system we have evolved in Sinkiang. Keeping the technology used and its performance securely in our hands is just as important as keeping the secret of the *Hawk* warheads. The *Crow* target acquisition system is code named *The Eye of Heaven*.'[1]

Nogi smiled, 'What about the superpowers? Have they anything comparable?'

Oyama said that he thought not, but assured the Prime Minister as he took his leave that the Copps would be watching for any evidence that they were on the same trail.

Nogi had not discussed two important military programmes with Oyama because he had been recently briefed on them by Tzu Te. They were the Chinese nuclear weapon updating and joint Sino-Japanese Space programmes, both of which were on schedule. Japanese scientists and technologists were playing a major, though subordinate, role in the former, and were leading in the latter. Chu had promised Nogi that he would be able to announce Sino-Japanese 'nuclear sufficiency' by 2020. By that he meant a deterrent capability that could not be ignored by either superpower during periods of international tension.

'Nuclear deterrence,' he had said to Nogi when they last met, 'will become a three legged stool: much more stable and difficult to upset than the Washington/Moscow two legged version. Conventional forces will become ever more important. Men will repossess the earth! We have plenty of men – and women!'

The Secretary General of the United Nations was Karl Tell, an eminent Swiss international jurist who, for obvious reasons, had earned the nickname of William Tell or Willie for short. He accepted the Hong Kong Powers' 'Uniting for Peace' resolution for the 71st Session of the General Assembly, but was not prepared to inscribe it on the Agenda until January 2018 because, in his view, enough time should be allowed for careful presentation. If the truth be told, he was hoping for an out of court settlement in the lobbies of the Assembly rather than a superpower clash in a plenary session which could do no-one any good.

November and December were months of intense, behind the scenes, political and economic blackmail and horse trading, which was vicious even by United Nations standards. Third World disgust at the triple use of the veto in 2017 was matched by superpower determination not to be pushed around by the world's pygmies. The British Ambassador, Sir John Godwin, was heard to remark: 'This is the real Star Wars. The superpowers are trying to hold their satellites in orbit and to stop them flying off to circle the Rising Sun!'

John Godwin was nearer the mark than he either realised or intended. A true Star Wars battle was, in fact, going on, not in the United Nations, but on the hot line between Moscow and Washington. The Soviets had placed an unmanned military space station in fixed orbit above the Panama area. Washington was protesting that this was in breach of the 1999 Space Understanding under which both superpowers, together with the Europeans, Chinese and Japanese had agreed to treat space like airspace with international boundaries projected vertically upwards. Panama was part of the Americas and the Soviets had no right, the Americans claimed, to abuse Central American space. The Russians did not agree, claiming with equal validity that Central American 'space-space' was nothing to do with the United States. Nevertheless, the Soviet Government was willing to place the issue before the Space Tribunal, which had been established in Geneva to adjudicate problems arising from the 1999 Understanding. No publicity had been given to the argument, which was pursued in closed diplomatic channels, as neither superpower wished to heighten tension between them at a time when they were being drawn together by the growing threat to their interests posed by the Hong Kong Powers.

Both Chu and Nogi attended the January meetings of the General Assembly personally as the co-sponsors of the 'Uniting for Peace' resolution. Chu, as the representative of a permanent member of the Security Council, proposed the resolution rather than Nogi, who was to reserve his speech for summing up the debate. When stripped of its United Nations verbiage 'recalling' this and that resolution, and 'bearing in mind' various high flown moral principles, the draft Sino-Japanese resolution called for an immediate withdrawal of foreign troops from Panama, Iran, Tanzania, Uganda and Kenya, and their substitution, if required, by United Nations' peace keeping forces. Chu, however, made it as clear as diplomatic language would allow that it was the United Nations which was on trial. Failure to resolve the three current disputes which threatened world peace, might have unfortunate consequences for the United Nations and the world.

John R. Chapell, still the American Secretary of State, replied first with a carefully reasoned and unemotional speech. The United Nations policy in the Western Hemisphere he said, had remained constant since the days of President James Monroe. In 1832 the wording of the two fundamental principles of his famous doctrine had been:

'I quote', he said,

> '1. *The American Continents are henceforth not to be considered as subjects of future colonisation by any European power.*
>
> 2. *The United States should consider any attempt on their part to extend their system to any portion of this hemisphere as dangerous to our peace and safety.*'

'The only difference today is that the threat to the Western Hemisphere comes from an Eastern rather than a Western European power. If the representatives of the international community assembled here today wish to keep the peace in the Americas, they must address themselves to causes rather than symptoms. The United States will not support the resolution as it is currently drafted. Continuing interference by the Old World in the affairs of the New cannot be allowed today any more than in the days of President Monroe.'

The Soviet Foreign Minister, Vasily Kutuzov, in a correspondingly flat but hostile reply, poured scorn on the outdated concepts of the Monroe Doctrine. Marxist-Leninism was universal and could be excluded from the Western Hemisphere by artificial means. The Central and South American people were free to choose the political philosophy which suited them best, and to seek economic and military aid from whatever source they found served them best.

'But,' he continued, 'the Soviet Union was at one with the United States in opposing the resolution. The presence of Soviet forces in Iran was based on a far more ancient and fundamental doctrine than Monroe's: the right of self-defence. The actions of the *Shi'a* Moslem Fundamentalists of Baghdad, aided and abetted by the United States and its Arab allies in the so-called Baghdad Pact, constituted blatantly hostile interference in the internal affairs of the Soviet Union. There would be no withdrawal from Iran until the Soviet Government was satisfied that Moslem *Jihad* in Central Asia had been renounced by Baghdad and Islamabad.

Most of the national delegations had already committed themselves to one or other of the two superpowers, and so the rejection of the Chu/Nogi resolution looked a foregone conclusion, until Sir John Godwin rose to present Britain's case.

'The British Government,' he said in a firm clear voice, 'accepts the spirit, if not the letter, of the resolution and will vote for it.'

He then recalled that Britain too was guided by historically based doctrines and had proved it most recently in her responsible withdrawal from her empire and its conversion into the multi-racial British Commonwealth. Her actions in East Africa were guided by the Balfour Declaration of 1926 which defined all members of that Commonwealth as:

> '. . . *equal in status, in no way subordinate one to another in any aspect of their domestic or external affairs, though United by common allegiance to the crown and freely associated as members of the British Commonwealth . . .*'

As with the Monroe Doctrine, times had changed and the British Monarch had become Head of the Commonwealth rather than its Sovereign. Nevertheless, the principles of equality of status enshrined in the Balfour Declaration and the subsequent Treaty of Westminster remained unchanged. In East Africa Britain had gone to the help of her Commonwealth partners *at their request*. It was axiomatic, therefore, that she could only withdraw her forces with their agreement.

Sir John ended his speech with a trend-setting conclusion:

'Britain has considerable sympathy for the aims and aspirations of the sponsors of the resolution, which are not far removed from the principles enshrined in the Balfour Declaration. Co-prosperity is the goal of us all.

We have to find practical ways of achieving it. Britain will not herself stand in the way of changes in the organisation or working of the United Nations if such changes have the support of the majority and will lead to greater world co-prosperity. The Security Council system is far from perfect and is perhaps outdated. There is room for constructive change.'

It was left to the Indian Foreign Minister, Krishna Patel, to capitalise upon the flexibility of the British position. The Indian Government, he announced, would be prepared to provide the lion's share of a United Nations Force to replace the British Eagle Force in East Africa if requested to do so. But British support for the resolution, though helpful, solved nothing. As drafted, the resolution had little chance of success. Nevertheless, the antagonistic positions of the two superpowers were not as far apart as appeared at first sight. Both feared external interference in areas of supreme concern to themselves.

'Surely a way can be found,' he said, raising his voice to a shrill pitch of incredulity 'of balancing these fears through the good offices of a skilled and impartial negotiator?'

He then proposed the alternative resolution, which is set out at the head of this chapter with the easily recognised reference number of 7,555 (LXXI), and which was to become deeply engraved on the memories of most delegates in the weeks and months that lay ahead. It was to be the task of the Secretary General, Karl Tell, to find the mutually acceptable formula that would enable both superpowers to withdraw from their entrenched positions without loss of face. As a goal, the date by which the withdrawal of their troops from Panama and Iran was to be completed, was set for 31st December 2018. The Secretary General was, however, to report progress at the beginning of the next session of the General Assembly that was due to start in mid November. Karl Tell, therefore, had nine months to complete his challenging task.

Nogi as co-sponsor of the original 'Uniting for Peace' resolution demanded the last word. Grim faced and inscrutable, he thanked the Indian delegate for the helpful alternative draft and formally withdrew the original version. Then in measured tones he warned:

'The United Nations Organisation must prove itself. The Japanese and Chinese people hope that they will have good reason to continue their membership when the General Assembly meets again in November. Time is running out for the resolution of the World's difficulties in this august forum.'

The vote affected me personally. My time as Military Assistant to the Commander-in-Chief, BAOR was up and I had already received my posting order to become the next commandant of the WRAC Training Centre in March 2018. I had packed and was about to return to England when the Commander-in-Chief invited me round to his house for what I took to be a farewell drink. It was nothing of the sort. He handed me a sheet of crisp blue Ministry of Defence note paper with the Royal cypher at the top. It was a letter from the Military Secretary asking him whether he thought I would be the right choice for a new appointment that had just come up and whether I would be prepared to give up my command to take it? The Secretary General of the United Nations had been so impressed by the British stance on 'Resolution seven, triple five', as the 'Uniting for Peace' resolution was now known, that he had asked for a British military aide to be appointed to his personal staff at the U.N. in New York. Would I be prepared to go?

I was faced with a difficult decision. In the British Army successful command at regimental level is one of the qualifications for promotion to the higher ranks. I realised that it was not quite so important for female officers. Nevertheless, it was wiser in normal circumstances to jump rather than ride round the command obstacle. But were these circumstances normal? The request had come from the Military Secretary himself to the Commander-in-Chief, which in itself was unusual in a lieutenant colonel's posting.

The General read my mind. He had phoned the Military Secretary, who was a personal friend of his, and had been assured that missing command would not affect my future career. On the contrary, success in this representational job would enhance it. He then added: 'I asked him about rank. You see, in my experience of working in the States, anyone below the rank of "Eagle Colonel", as they call full colonels, is treated as a clerk. The Military Secretary has assured me that you will be given the acting rank of local full colonel for the job. You never know, it might stick!' he said with an encouraging pat on my shoulder.

I arrived in New York just before Easter 2018 and entered the Alice in Wonderland world of Lake Success where myth is reality and reality belongs to another planet. The inhabitants have, over the years, indulged in so much special pleading that they have begun to believe that black really is white and vice versa.

As so often happens when taking up a new job that has not existed in the Army before, I was given no directive and my briefing in Whitehall was of the sketchiest. It was clear to me that as far as the Foreign Office and Ministry of Defence were concerned, I would be a great help to them in providing early warning of Karl Tell's ideas and intentions, particularly on the replacement of Eagle Force in East Africa. I was to keep in close touch with the British delegation to the United Nations and with the British Defence Adviser's Staff at our embassy in Washington.

'But,' I was warned, 'you are to be part of the Secretary General's personal staff so your first loyalty must be to him. We will be grateful for any help you can give us, but do not risk compromising your neutrality. We value this post very highly and don't want to lose it!'

What other country, I wondered, would take up such an altruistic stance? I soon found out. None of my new colleagues had any doubt that their national loyalties came first. I was looked upon, as they were, as just another spy in the heart of the organisation through which information, more often false than true, could be fed unofficially and unobtrusively to our respective governments. As a female officer I had one asset that the male aides could not match. I soon found I was a godsend to the wives of heads of delegations as an unattached girl who could help balance their dinner parties, since many ministers and senior officials visiting the Lake Success came without their wives. And at diplomatic dinner tables it was always tempting for male guests, however eminent, to confide in me – *in vino veritas*!

At my first interview with Karl Tell he made the point very strongly that I was part of *his* personal staff and must think and act internationally. He appreciated how difficult it was to do so, and he had no illusions about how few of his staff succeeded in being neutral. He was a big man in every sense of the word and looked the part. He had a commanding personality of the type which turned heads when he entered a crowded cocktail party, and a quick wit which enlivened the dreariest of meetings. His wife, Ingrid, whom I got to know very well indeed, was a small vivacious Austrian woman with closely cropped raven black hair. The most startling feature of her appearance was a quiff, or what North Country people aptly call a 'calf-lick', of silver grey hair which swept up from the left side of her forehead. Coupled with the brightness of her brown eyes, it gave her coquettish appearance which belied her true character and abilities. She was, in fact, an excellent foil for her husband, and an intelligent and able hostess.

Karl and Ingrid had one great sadness in their lives: they had no children. Soon after I arrived, Ingrid invited me to their flat as Karl had told her that I was bound to be lonely as a single woman in the concrete canyons of New York. Before long they took to me and I to them. They treated me as the daughter they had never had, and I found no difficulty in reciprocating their friendship. I was totally at ease with them and they made my time in New York one of the happiest periods of my life. I had a challenging job, working for Karl, and Ingrid gave me a home from home.

I cannot be so complimentary about Lady Godwin. To her, I was one of those extraordinary career women, who had entered the male world and should be treated accordingly. To me, she was a self-centred, ambitious woman without the ability or charm to be a successful ambassador's wife. She was not beyond using me to balance her guest lists, and she irked me by assuming that, as a British United Nations official, it was my duty to do so. We never actually fell out because I was determined that nothing should mar my relations with the British Delegation.

Karl Tell – I never used his nickname, Willie, which he detested – started his negotiations to implement Resolution 7555 (LXXI) by requesting each of the three powers involved to present to him their conditions for withdrawing their troops. He hoped thereby to find a common denominator on which to base his negotiations. The United States Government reacted quickest, determined to get in the first word; the Russians held back until they had assessed the American position; and the British were slowest because they had to consult their Commonwealth partners.

The American tongue-in-cheek opener, in what everyone knew was going to be a very tough game of poker, was still based on the Monroe Doctrine, but owed much to the British ploy in the Falklands war of 1982. They demanded an exclusion zone drawn along the American Continental Shelf, through which no non-American arms were to be shipped or flown. It was to be the task of the Organisation of American States to provide regional forces to patrol the zone on behalf of the United Nations. They knew, of course, that the Soviet Government could never accept the inclusion of Cuba within the Zone, if indeed they were willing to accept the principle of exclusion zones at all. They had, however, given the Secretary General an easy opening gambit of being able to propose that the exclusion line might be drawn 200 miles from the mainland rather than along the Continental Shelf, thereby leaving most of the Caribbean Islands outside it.

The Russian opening bid was to demand the dismantling of the Baghdad Pact and a similar exclusion zone in the Middle East drawn along the Levant coast, Suez Canal, Red Sea, Indian Ocean Coast of Arabia and the Persian Gulf. They, too, knew that the inclusion of the American client state of Israel would make the bid unacceptable.

The Commonwealth Heads of Government met in Delhi at a specially summoned conference in June 2018 to advise on the British response. Karl Tell arranged with the Commonwealth Secretariat that I should attend as an observer amongst the officials since it would be my job to advise him on the arrangements for replacing Eagle Force. The Indian Prime Minister, as host and Chairman, asked the Kenyan and Tanzanian presidents to put their views first. Both men were quite categoric. There could be no peace in East Africa until the Homelander occupation of Uganda was brought to an end. The replacement of Eagle Force was irrelevant. The British Government must make it plain to the Secretary General that the sole condition for its replacement or withdrawal was the liberation of Uganda from alien Homelander rule. There was ample evidence to show that the former Ugandan Government in exile in Nairobi would be welcomed back if the Ugandan people were allowed a free vote. A United Nations force was needed, not to replace Eagle Force, but to supervise a plebiscite in Uganda.

Then the debate widened and even Uganda became irrelevant. There was much more interest in the attitude the Commonwealth should take towards the Hong Kong Treaty powers. There was a clear division of opinion between those who welcomed the Sino-Japanese initiative in the United Nations and those who saw the hand of a new imperialism inside the silken glove of Co-prosperity. As a generalisation the nearer to Peking and Tokyo the speaker's country lay, the less generous were his views. Malaysia and Singapore were positively hostile; India was ambivalent; and the Africans and Caribbeans were pro. The old Dominions reserved judgement. Though no vote was taken, I gained the impression that the Hong Kong powers were being given the benefit of the doubt, if only because their intervention was a welcome way of weakening the hegemony of the two existing superpowers.

The upshot of the Commonwealth meeting was a clear mandate for Britain to negotiate the future of Eagle Force on the basis of no withdrawal without a corresponding withdrawal of Homelander and Eastern Bloc forces from Uganda and acceptance of United Nations supervision of a plebiscite in Uganda. What none of us knew at the time was that M'Bundu was on his way to Tokyo as we all left Delhi at the end of the Conference.

The General Assembly debate had made Nogi the hero of the Third World's media. Here, at last, was someone willing and able to champion its cause. They were less happy about Chu due to an instinctive fear of China, and it was generally held that Japan was preferable as the leader of the Third World in the struggle for more equitable international relations. The simplistic theme, that the marriage between Japanese technology and Chinese manpower would produce a most potent force for the change, had become the talking point in the souks and bazaars of Afro-Asia and the slums of Latin American cities. Tokyo became a new Mecca, to which Third World leaders began to travel to touch the 'black stone' of Nogi's new Shinto-ism.

M'Bundu was the first to make the pilgrimage. He was becoming disillusioned with his Kremlin inspired campaign in East Africa. He could see no possibility of achieving a favourable decision and the cost of the campaign was crippling the economy of his Black Homelander Union. Invidious comparisons were being drawn between the economic success of the break away province of Shaba under French tutelage and the lack of progress being made in the Union. To make matters worse, there was some evidence of collusion between the French in Shaba and the Afrikaners in Azania to destablise the Congo Basin and Angola. His instincts were to cut his losses in East Africa and to concentrate upon making a success of the original five states of the Union. To do so he would have to find a way of reducing this dependence on the Soviet Union.

M'Bundu's meeting with Nogi helped him to change course. Nogi warned him that the Japanese Embassy in Delhi had reported that the British terms for the departure of Eagle Force were based upon a plebiscite in Uganda after the withdrawal of Homelander and Eastern Bloc forces. M'Bundu showed no surprise and replied that Uganda was a hopeless case from his point of view and not worth fighting for. It would become a Moslem state anyway before long. He had been forced into the war by the Kremlin.

M'Bundu's reference to the Kremlin gave Nogi the opportunity that he had been waiting for. 'Rest assured,' he said, 'if you wish to find an alternative source of financial aid and military supply, we have much to offer you. But in conformity with our no strings Co-prosperity policy, any change of sponsorship must be your decision. Chu and I will not attempt to influence you at all. I only hope you will join us in due course in creating an Afro-Asian co-prosperity sphere.'

And so matters were left with M'Bundu. Archbishop Bolivar and the Ayatollah of Baghdad, as spiritual as well as temporal leaders of their people, did not make the journey to Tokyo, but let it be known through diplomatic channels that their hearts were with Nogi and that he could count on their support in any show-down with the superpowers in the coming United Nations debate on Resolution 7555(LXXI).

During these preliminary skirmishes I was invited to several important dinner parties. Two have stuck in my memory, though their full significance only emerged much later. The first was at the British Ambassador's house. I was seated at dinner next to a relatively junior official of the United States delegation, who enjoyed his wine. As he mellowed and the threshold of his discretion was lowered, he began to discuss the thing uppermost in his mind.

'Don't be surprised,' he said in a confidential whisper, 'if Washington and Moscow forget their differences. They're both scared stiff of the Tokyo/Peking axis. I don't blame them, do you?'

I nodded assent and before I could reply he went on: 'We suspect that there is a secret agreement behind the facade of the Hong Kong Treaty. I wouldn't be surprised if they hadn't divided the world between them!'

'What makes you think that?' I asked.

'Oh, circumstantial evidence linked to common sense. This Co-prosperity nonsense is only window dressing for the Third World's benefit.'

I got no further because Lady Godwin 'caught our eyes' and we, ladies, got up and left the men to enjoy their own company and the Ambassador's port.

It must have been about a week later when Karl Tell asked me to accompany him to a Soviet Embassy function because Ingrid was away at the time. I had a mirror image conversation with a Czech diplomat. He quite unashamedly asked me, as a member of Tell's staff, whether we believed the nonsense about co-prosperity in the Hong Kong Treaty. He was sure, he told me, that Moscow and Washington would find a *modus vivendi* so that they could face 'the rising sun' together.

These remarks by American and Eastern Bloc junior negotiators were but straws in the wind. More substantial evidence of superpower collusion came at Karl Tell's morning conference with his personal staff at the beginning of June. He started his 'morning prayers' by telling us he had high hopes of negotiating a successful package deal between Moscow and Washington. The Russian delegation had told him informally that if he could bring about a secret understanding with the Americans that they would limit their support to the Baghdad Pact in return for similar restraint by the Soviet Union in Latin America, then Moscow would agree to the Secretary General announcing at the November session of the General Assembly that he had succeeded in negotiating the withdrawal of Soviet and United States forces from Iran and Panama. There was certainly something in suggestions I had heard that there was a superpower deal afoot to isolate the Hong Kong Treaty powers without loss of face in Moscow and Washington.

By the beginning of November, Karl Tell was certain he had pulled it off, and that he would go down in history as one of the great Secretary Generals. The Soviet and United States withdrawals would start in December, and M'Bundu had accepted a British Commonwealth monitoring force composed of Afro-Asian contingents to supervise the Uganda plebiscite in January. Eagle Force would stay in East Africa until the Governments of Kenya and Tanzania requested its withdrawal.

Poor Karl! His hopes were to be shattered two days before the 72nd Session of the General Assembly opened. I was watching the CBS News when the newscaster was handed a hot news item which he read with incredulity:

'Moscow has announced that one of its unmanned space stations has disintegrated. The Kremlin is accusing the United States of space piracy.'

If Nogi had wanted to break up the growing superpower *entente* he could not have chosen a better way of doing so. It seemed almost incredible that the United States should choose this very moment to test out their latest Star Wars break-through and to select the Russian Space Station over Central America, which they had been protesting about, as their target. But, as one of my colleagues in Tell's office reminded me, such inexplicable actions were not without precedent. In the 1960's the Eisenhower-Kruschev-Macmillan summit meeting had been aborted when Gary Power's U2 spy plane was shot down over the Soviet Union; in the early 1980's the Russians probably committed the still unsolved mystery of the shooting down of the Korean Airways Jumbo Jet just to the north of Japan; and in the mid-1980's there was the crass bungling of the arms to Iran scandal that almost unseated President Reagan.

The Americans quickly denied any responsibility and suggested that a fundamental design fault in the Soviet space vehicle had been responsible for its disintegration. Their denials fooled no-one, least of all the Kremlin, which was set the difficult task of assessing why it had happened at this extraordinarily ill-chosen moment. If it was a deliberate act, what was it meant to signal? Or was it one of those cases where the military left hand of the American Administration was unsighted by the massive complexity of its governmental bureaucracy and did not see what the diplomatic right hand was doing. Co-ordination within the tangled web of the vast American Administration and in the jungle of its numerous agencies was never easy; and there were always those extremists within them, who believed that any supping with Moscow was treachery.

Moscow did not give Washington the benefit of the doubt. The Kremlin concluded that the destruction of its space station was not a left hand/right hand nonsense. It was a deliberate act by the United States Government to demonstrate continuing American technological superiority at a time when their acceptance of Karl Tell's mutual withdrawal package could have been construed as weakness on their part. As such it had been well stage-managed. Those in the international community, who suspected that an American beam weapon had been used, admired the United States technical achievement; and those, who believed it was a structural failure in the Soviet space station, saw it as Soviet technological inferiority. The Americans won either way!

Despite this grave and unexpected set back, the 72nd Session of the General Assembly started on schedule. The atmosphere in the debating chamber was tense when Karl Tell made the formal announcement of the success of his negotiations on Resolution 7,555 (LXXI) and asked the three named powers to confirm their acceptance of the agreement. They gave their replies in alphabetical order – U.K., U.S.A., U.S.S.R. Sir John Godwin congratulated the Secretary General on his negotiating skill; thanked the superpowers for their co-operation; and confirmed Britain's acceptance of the agreement.

All eyes then turned on John Chapell as he walked to the rostrum. His speech was defensive and he, himself, was clearly ill at ease, but he did give the Assembly the assurance it needed that United States forces would start withdrawing from Panama on 1st December and would all be away by the 31st.

'Provided', he concluded, 'our withdrawals are matched by the phased evacuation of Iran by Soviet forces.'

When a smiling Vasily Kutuzov mounted the podium and began his speech by seconding Sir John Godwin's praise for the Secretary General, tension in the hall relaxed. All seemed to be over bar the shouting. The United Nations had survived the test set for it by the Hong Kong powers.

But then Kutuzov's mood changed as he reached the substance of his speech:

'It is not the Secretary General's fault that the Soviet Union is now compelled to withdraw herewith its acceptance of the agreement. Nor has the Soviet decision been taken entirely in response to the destruction of its space station by indisciplined militarists in the Pentagon. The reasons are much more serious . . .'

Kutuzov paused and looked round the stunned Assembly, and then continued in a slow, dramatic way, punching out his words as only the Russians can do:

'The Soviet Union has unimpeachable evidence of a secret protocol attached to the Hong Kong Treaty between Japan and China, which commits them to support the Islamic Fundamentalist *Jihad* against the Central Asian Republics of the Soviet Union. The protocol also compromises the United States, which is stated categorically therein to be supporting this programme of subversion amongst the peace loving people of the Soviet Union. This is intolerable, and a threat to world peace.'

Kutuzov was not finished. He went on to embarrass the United States and the Secretary General by revealing the American proposals for the 200 mile exclusion zone, which would have put Cuba under siege, and the American agreement to let the Baghdad Pact 'wither on the vine' in exchange for a Soviet withdrawal from Iran.

As Kutuzov left the rostrum, having sown as many seeds of suspicion as the Kremlin planners could devise in the short time available since the space station disintegrated, bedlam engulfed the chamber. Nogi demanded the right to reply, but Karl Tell, though crestfallen by this unexpected turn of events, was able and quick witted enough to realise that the debate must be adjourned to allow tempers to cool. Calling for order above the hubbub he announced that the debate would be resumed the following afternoon.

The Japanese and Chinese delegations recognised at once that, though the Russians might have evidence of the existence of the secret protocols, they were clearly unaware of their actual contents. The mention of American involvement was clearly fictitious. Kutuzov's attack was most probably based upon circumstantial evidence and guesswork by Soviet Intelligence. Nogi, with Chu's agreement, decided to brazen it out by taking the offensive. Working together for most of the night, the officials of the two delegations hammered out an agreed speech for him to deliver next day. He could, in all honesty, deny the existence of the protocol described by Kutuzov because the Russians had got the contents totally wrong. The suggestion that such a protocol could exist was, in the Sino-Japanese view, nothing more than an ingenious diversion to mask the failure of the United Nations to preserve the peace of the world. Resolution 7,555 (LXXI) had been a test case. It had failed. Japan and China would leave the organisation until it was reformed in a way that would restore its usefulness to the middle and lesser powers of the world.

And so it was that on 16th November 2018 the Japanese and Chinese delegations walked out of the United Nations, followed by the delegations of Colombia, India, the Islamic Federation and the Black Homelander Union. The League of Nations never recovered from the walk-out by Mussolini and Hitler in the 1930's; there were grave doubts about the survival of the United Nations. Poor Karl Tell, instead of going down in history as the greatest Secretary General of the organisation, might be its last. All would depend on whether Nogi and Chu adopted constructive or destructive attitudes during 2019. I felt desperately sorry for Karl. He had not deserved this unexpected turn of events.

In the office of the Copps military staff there was the same consternation over the disintegration of the Soviet space station as there had been in the General Assembly, but none of the bedlam. Tzu Te and Oyama set in train a careful assessment of the new United States space capability that had been revealed. Sino-Japanese close surveillance of space made them confident that the Americans must have used a beam weapon from earth, because there was no United States space vehicle in orbit at the time which could have been armed. It was, therefore, clear that the American scientists had succeeded in concentrating enough energy to enable earth-based beam weapons to break through the world's atmosphere with sufficient power left to destroy targets in space. The question was how long it would be before they devised ways of reflecting those beams back through the atmosphere to vapourise missiles in their boost phase or targets on the ground?

The Copps scientists' report, when it was completed, doubted whether the Americans would ever manage to do so using their existing technology. Once the Yangtze project was complete, China would have the immense energy generating source needed, but the Sino-Japanese team would still have to solve the problems of accurate reflection from space. The third generation *HOTOL* might provide the solution. The year 2035 was the earliest that the Hong Kong Powers could expect to be able to attack strategic targets, using earth based beam weapons via space. It was unlikely that either superpower would solve the technological problems any earlier. It would, however, be a 'close run thing' with no certainty about who would be the winner.

Note

1. *The Eye of Heaven* was based upon an advanced and powerful battlefield computer system. This resolved target acquisition data from a wide spectrum of strategic and tactical sources, stretching from satellite surveillance at one end through electronic intelligence gathering to battlefield sensors and pilotless air vehicles at the other.

8

The Charter of the China Seas (2019–2020)

*'The Atlantic Charter did not shorten the
Second World War. My guess is that
The Charter of the China Seas will sharpen and
lengthen the Third.'*

Diary entry for 13th August 2020

According to Nogi's autobiography, he returned from New York in a sombre and despondent mood, which the warmth of his reception in Tokyo did little to dispel. He had genuinely hoped that Karl Tell would succeed in his negotiations with the superpowers and thereby prove that the United Nations was an effective instrument for keeping world peace. Tell had failed and so Nogi's and Chu's bluff had been called. They had no alternative but to walk out, and this Nogi regretted. With hindsight he realised that they had nailed the Hong Kong powers' colours too firmly to the mast and had unwisely reduced their room for manoeuvre.

But what worried Nogi more than anything else was the negative figure he had cut. He had been destructive, quite contrary to the principles of his New Shinto-ism, which was rooted in creativity by corporate consensus. He had undermined and had probably destroyed an organisation which, for all its faults, had proved itself to be more effective and longer lasting than the two previous attempts at World Government: Tsar Alexander's Holy Alliance of the 19th century and the League of Nations of the first half of the 20th. The whole basis of his political philosophy was the construction of co-prosperity in the world through Japanese-style leadership. And yet, if the pessimistic prognosis of his doctors was proved to be correct, he might go down in history as a destroyer rather than a creator: a Kali rather than a Vishnu.

The dust of the New York fiasco was allowed to settle in most of the world's capitals over Christmas and New Year. It was not until the end of January 2019 that Nogi summoned General Oyama to discuss the future with him. The two men were old friends, and when Nogi felt the need for independent advice he often turned to Oyama, particularly when he was brooding over some intractable international problem. Oyama had a well trained military mind which, though simplistic in political terms, had a useful clarity of vision. Oyama, like Field Marshal Montgomery, could reduce the most complex problems to their bare essentials from which battle winning policies could be developed. As a member of the Copps, he was aware of all the forward planning being done to implement the secret protocols of the Treaty of Hong Kong, but he was not inhibited by policies being pursued by the political departments in Tokyo and Peking. Nogi prized his advice for its impartiality and, to some extent, for its orginality because his thinking was not influenced by political lore.

Nogi started their discussion with a *tour d'horizon*. He deplored the inexplicable action of the United States in destroying the Soviet space station at the worst possible moment. He appreciated that there was hard evidence from the Sino-Japanese space surveillance centre that the Americans had achieved a major breakthrough in beam weapon technology. They were probably determined to teach the Soviet Union two lessons: that they had the weapon, and that they were prepared to use it to defend their national boundaries in space. Whether it was a deliberate attempt to break up Karl Tell's negotiated settlement, he did not know, but, whatever the United States intention, the hard facts were that the guerrilla war in Central America would go on and the Islamic *Jihad* against the U.S.S.R. would be intensified. Only in Africa had anything useful flowed from his 'Uniting for Peace' resolution. M'Bundu had accepted his advice and co-operated fully with the Indian based British Commonwealth monitoring force in the Uganda plebiscite. The anti-Homelanders had won a decisive victory and Uganda was on its way to becoming an independent East African State again. The British Eagle Force was being withdrawn in phases corresponding to an agreed programme for dismantling Eastern Bloc bases in Uganda. Both sides should be out of East Africa by June 2019. The next crisis point in Africa, Nogi concluded, would probably be Shaba.

'Where do we go from here?' he asked.

'Whether you like it or not you are now the leader of the Third World,' Oyama replied, 'and the Third World is expecting leadership from you.'

'In my view,' he continued after a slight pause to allow Nogi to grasp the import of his words, 'you must make your policies known to your new followers.'

As he said this he walked across to the book shelves behind Nogi's desk and pulled down Volume III of Winston Churchill's *The Second World*

War, entitled *The Grand Alliance*. Thumbing through the pages he reached Chapter XXIV, *The Atlantic Charter*:

'This is the sort of thing you want,' Oyama said thoughtfully and began to read:

> '*The President of the United States of America and the Prime Minister, representing His Majesty's Government in the United Kingdom, being met together, deem it right to make known certain common principles on which they base their hopes for a better future for the world.*
>
> *First, . . .*'

Oyama handed the book to Nogi to read the eight principles set out by Roosevelt and Churchill in their famous *Joint Declaration*: no territorial aggrandisement; changes only in accord with freely expressed wishes of people concerned; the right of all people to choose their form of government; equality in economic opportunity; economic collaboration; collective security; freedom of the seas; and abandonment of the use of force.

Nogi looked up.

'That's it,' he said, 'I will cable Chu suggesting that the Copps should draft a joint declaration for us.'

Nogi's telegram reached Peking before Chu had made up his own mind what to do next. The events in New York had elated rather than depressed him. At one time he had feared that the two superpowers would unite to oppose the growing influence of the Sino-Japanese alliance. He was, however, sufficient of an old fashioned Communist still to believe in Mao Tse Tung's dictum that power grows from the barrel of a gun. With the superpowers again at each other's throats he saw that risks could be taken and that the time had come to start using the 'gun' that he and Nogi had been developing in secret.

The arrival of Nogi's cable in Peking highlighted the reversal of Chu's and Nogi's earlier attitudes. Before New York, it had been Nogi who had been leading the offensive because he knew his days might be numbered; since New York, it was Chu who was elated by the United Nations walk-out and who was bent on profiting from the situation as quickly as possible. In discussing Nogi's cable with the Chinese members of the Copps, Chu was elaborately polite about his colleague's idea, calling it wise statesmanship. Misreading Chu's mood, the Chinese Co-chairman suggested using Nogi's charter of Sino-Japanese political aims as the carrot in a carrot and stick strategy: the carrot of policies attractive to the Third World, backed by the stick of Sino-Japanese military power.

'No,' snapped Chu, 'use it as foreplay before seduction or rape: which it will be depends on our victims' reactions.'

'M'Bundu, Bolívar and the Ayatollah can prove their virility first with our help,' he continued, warming to his own crude analogy. 'We will conserve our strength for the final orgy. Moscow and Washington will be flat on their backs by then!'

Replying to Nogi's cable, Chu accepted the idea of an Atlantic Charter style declaration and suggested the point should be made by calling it *The Charter of the China Seas*. He also recommended inviting M'Bundu, Bolivar and the Ayatollah to a preliminary Hong Kong Powers Summit to discuss the way ahead and to provide the setting for the public promulgation of the Charter.

Nogi liked the summit idea and started to gild the lily. He wanted the Indian Prime Minister, Jawal Gandhi, to attend as well because discussion of Afro-Asian or Third World co-prosperity without India would be like eating curry without rice. Jawal Gandhi's presence should strengthen the altruistic image of the summit. He suggested two other points of symbolism. The Sino-Japanese Treaty of Alliance had been signed in Hong Kong to mark the end of the European epoch of world history. The Charter of the China Seas should be proclaimed at a place and time that would symbolise the beginning of the new multi-racial era which was already dawning. Why not use the opening of the joint Sino-Japanese oil production platform in the new oilfield on the edge of the Chinese continental shelf, 100 miles west of Okinawa, as the occasion for the announcement? It was, after all, one of the first fruits of Sino-Japanese co-prosperity. The Summit itself could take place at the Naha airbase on Okinawa, which had been handed back to Japan by the Americans in 1999. The choice of 12th August 2019 might add another symbolic touch as it was the anniversary of the signing of the Atlantic Charter. It was a pity it was not 2021 which would have made it the 80th anniversary. Fixing August as the date for the Summit would give adequate time for thorough preparation.

Oyama's account of the Copp's debates on drafting the Charter and agenda for the Summit itself is illuminating. Both teams appreciated that the declaration they were to draw up must 'mean all things to all men', but it must also offer something special to each of their potential clients – the Black Nationalists, the Islamic Fundamentalists and the Christo-Communists of Latin America. They agreed unanimously that they should only allude to the well worn principles of Roosevelt's four freedoms – of speech, of worship, from want and from fear – and the eight tenets of the Atlantic Charter, all of which could be taken as read and, in any case, had a dated ring about them in 2019. Instead they would highlight the changes that the Hong Kong Powers and their allies wished to make to bring about more equitable and democratic world governance. They did not wish, at that stage, to abolish the United Nations. Reforms should be made that would make it more effective and, therefore, worth rejoining.

With the field narrowed in this way, it was not difficult to produce the bare bones of the first draft which ran:

'The Chairman of the People's Republic of China and the Prime Minister of Japan, being met together, deem it right to make known the changes they seek in the United Nations to bring about greater justice, equality, peace and prosperity through better world governance.

First, all members must honour the principles of majority rule and respect for the legitimate rights of minorities;

Second, voting must reflect size of populations of member states;

And Third, permanent membership of the Security Council, together with the right of veto, must be abolished. All fifteen members must be elected by the General Assembly on a regional basis.'

When the Summit started at Okinawa in August 2019 this draft did not go unscathed. Nogi was disappointed that there was no reference to his policy of Co-prosperity. At his insistence the opening paragraph was changed to:

'The Chairman of the People's Republic of China and the Prime Minister of Japan, being met together, *are resolved to continue their joint policy of co-prosperity enshrined in the Treaty of Hong Kong.* They also deem it right to make known the changes . . .'

The Ayatollah objected to lack of specific reference to freedom of religion, and Jawal Gandhi advocated some reference to nuclear weapons and the unbridled use of space. M'Bundu and Archbishop Bolivar were satisfied by the highlighting of majority rule in the draft text. After some wrangling a final catch-all paragraph was added.

'They accept the four Freedoms enunciated by President Franklyn D. Roosevelt and the eight provisions of the Atlantic Charter upon which the United Nations was based; and they look forward to the eventual abolition of nuclear weapons and the demilitarisation of space.'

Chu paid little attention to the finalisation of the Charter, which he felt was Nogi's idea and hence his responsibility. Chu concentrated instead, both in the conference and during the lobbying outside, on plans for mutual assistance in sustaining unending guerrilla war in Latin America to rape the United States and in Central Asia to do the same thing to the Soviet Union. If M'Bundu decided to sever his links with Moscow, Sino-Japanese aid would be available to him.

Chu was disappointed by the response. The Archbishop saw no point in changing his supplier. The Eastern Bloc was doing him well and Domingo Garcia's guerrillas had confidence in the Soviet weapons fed to them via

Cuba. Moreover, most members of the Bolivarist Movement knew little of the Chinese version of Marxism and even less about Nogi's New Shinto-ism. The Archbishop, though grateful for the political support of the Hong Kong powers, was categoric in stating that the struggle to make Latin American society more equitable was for Latin Americans to pursue and no one else.

M'Bundu took much the same line though he expressed it with less vehemence. The chances of him changing his supplier were higher but, in his view, the time was not yet ripe for doing so. Since the New York walk-out, Moscow had redoubled its efforts to support him. He would prefer to take advantage of their largesse while it lasted.

Only the Ayatollah showed much enthusiasm for Chu's offer of help. He confessed that, since the Russian occupation of Tehran and the establish-ment of the new Baghdad Pact, the floodgates of United States aid had opened. Chu could, however, help with the supply of arms to the *Mujahi-deen* in Afghanistan. The Soviet presence in northern Iran was making supply from the west more difficult and so the Afghan SSR's army was able to concentrate its efforts on sealing up the eastern supply routes from Pakistan. The front could be widened if Chu would develop new routes through the Pamirs from China. The Wakan valley (*see Map 8*) was an obvious possibility.

Chu accepted the force of the Ayatollah's argument, and went on to suggest that the Ayatollah should attempt to persuade General Moham-med Khan to accept Chinese help as well. This was far from the liking of India's Jawal Gandhi, who protested violently when he heard about it. Any friend of Pakistan was an enemy of India! For the sake of Afro-Asian solidarity Chu and the Ayatollah dropped that idea.

The public announcement of the Charter of the China Seas took place as planned at the opening ceremony of the Okinawa oil production platform on the last day of the Summit. Nogi, in his speech, referred to the happy coincidence of the Atlantic and China Seas Charters both being signed on 12th August, though seventy eight years apart. Incidentally, the British Ambassador in Tokyo, who attended the opening, could take some pride in both events. In 1941 Britain had played a leading role in drafting the Charter: in 2019 the Okinawa oil production platform owed much to British North Sea technology and British firms had won a major share in the contracts to build it.

The reaction of the World press to the new Charter was unusually favourable. The *New York Times* headed its leader with 'Commonsense by Uncommon People'; the *London Times* used 'The Right Time for Change'; and the *Frankfurt Zeitung* commended the courage of Nogi and Chu for attacking the privileges of the victors of a war fought against Germany and Japan eighty years ago. Only Moscow's *Pravda* was scathing. It used a cartoon showing Japanese and Chinese Lilliputians trying to rope down Uncle Sam and the Russian bear. The periodical, however, which added a new word to international language was *Time* magazine. Its cover displayed a flattering portrait of a thoughtful Nogi with the caption 'The High Priest of Nogi-ism'. Thereafter the ponderous words 'Hong Kong Treaty Powers' was replaced in everyday jargon by 'Nogi-ists' and 'Nogi-ism'; an unwritten acknowledgement by the Western media that it was Nogi, rather than Chu, who was the driving force of the new world power that was emerging, and that the dynamic propelling it was Nogi's New Shinto-ism – the Japanese path to excellence – rather than old fashioned Chinese Communism.

Most political leaders of any importance in the world echoed the media and gave the Charter a favourable gloss in public. Behind closed doors in the world's capital cities very different views were being expressed. Few issues have divided governments so deeply as the question of how to deal with Nogi-ism. The re-emergence of a virile Japan after seventy-four years as a political eunuch was not unexpected, and yet few of the world's leaders had any clear idea how to handle the changes that were occurring in the balance of power. Was Nogi-ism a paternally benevolent force as Nogi claimed it to be, or was it the malignly malevolent threat, which the Victorians and Edwardians of Britain's imperial heyday used to refer to as 'the Yellow Peril'? Was Nogi-ist Co-prosperity to be applauded or decried? Should Nogi be befriended or held at arms length? Should attempts be made to drive a wedge betwen Nogi and Chu, or should the emergence of a third superpower be welcomed as a way of achieving greater world stability on the principle of the three legged stool? The list of questions was endless and there was a spectrum of answers to most of them.

In Washington division of opinion was all the starker because 2020 was presidential election year. Events of 2017–18 had not been flattering to President Mackenzie in his second term, and the Democratic Party caucus was in the midst of seeking a luckier, if not better, general to lead them in the 2020 election. The natural swing of the political pendulum was given added impetus by the failure of the Karl Tell negotiations and the inept handling of the space station incident by the Mackenzie Administration. The Republican's traditional battle cry of 'Negotiation from strength' fell on many ready ears; and within the great departments of state in Washington most officials were already trimming their sails to the Republican wind.

In the embattled offices of the President's Security Adviser no-one was under any illusion that a new superpower was emerging around the shores of the China Seas. Some pride could be taken in the thought that the Japanese half of the Hong Kong alliance was a United States creation, born of American idealism after the Second World War and possessing many filial links with the United States in particular and to the West in general. Nogi-ism had a laudible ring of moderation about it. The same could not be said of Chu's China. Would the two together produce a new Frankenstein or, indeed, provide the useful third leg for the world's security stool? The only firm conclusion the President's men could come to was that it was too early to formulate longer term plans. Time itself would reveal the true complexion of Nogi-ism.

In the meantime, immediate pragmatic considerations dominated American thinking. There was, as yet, no evidence of Sino-Japanese infiltration or intrigue in the United States' Latin American backyard. On the other hand, the same could not be said of the Soviet's equivalent in Central Asia. The American Ambassador in Islamabad was reporting growing Chinese diplomatic activity in Pakistan and his colleague in Delhi was noting mounting Indian anxiety about Chinese support for Islam. At the same time, the CIA reports were pointing to the development of new Chinese arms supply routes through the Pamirs to the *Mujahideen* in north eastern Afghanistan. The President's advisers concluded that American interests were not being placed at risk by the rise of Nogi-ism, whereas the Soviet's were: a good enough reason to recommend the maintenance of friendly relations with Tokyo and Peking.

One CIA paper did not receive as much attention as later events suggest that it should have done. It looked too far ahead for it to be of much concern to the dying Mackenzie Administration. It reviewed the chances of success of the Ayatollah's *Jihad* in Central Asia. It concluded that they were not very high, certainly in the short term, but that the Kremlin would blame United States' intrigue within the Baghdad Pact for any successes that the *Mujahideen* did have. The most likely Soviet counter-ploy would probably be a threat to, if not actual occupation of, the Iranian and Iraqi oil fields upon which the Western European and Japanese economies were still heavily dependent. Alternative sources of supply, like the North Sea fields, were in decline and the new fields in the China Seas could only help in a marginal way. Contingency plans should, therefore, be drawn up to forestall a renewed Soviet thrust towards the Persian Gulf. As Western Europe's oil supplies would be worst hit, it would be appropriate for NATO to take the lead in planning and providing the bulk of the forces needed for any counter-measures that were decided upon. Unfortunately, NATO had no equivalent of the United States or French Rapid Deployment Forces, apart from Britain's small Strategic Reserve, and the European Allies were reluctant to build one. The CIA suggested that the time was ripe and the cause right for the United States to bring pressure to bear on the Europeans to start carrying more of the burden of the defence of Western interests outside the NATO area. However, the time was neither ripe nor right in terms of the American presidential election process for any action to be taken. The paper was forwarded to the United States NATO delegation in Brussels without the strong endorsement from the President that it would have needed to make any impact in Europe.

In Moscow, Islamic Fundamentalism and Nogi-ism were co-equal at the top of the Kremlin's list of anathema. Both presented a threat to Soviet interests and to the advance of international communism. The Islamic threat was the most immediate and so attracted most attention. While there was a general agreement that the canker of Moslem religious revival must be cauterised, there was less unanimity about how it should be done. The traditional Muskovite hard-liners advocated ruthless repression: the more understanding non-Russians in the Politbureau argued that such policies would only create Islamic martyrs and aggravate the endemic rift between the Russian and Asiatic people of the Soviet Union. Neither side won an outright victory. A two track approach was adopted: conciliatory policies were to be pursued initially, while preparations were made by the Soviet Security Services and the Red Army to deal with any Islamic rebellion that might occur if, as the hard-liners confidently predicted, the conciliatory approach failed.

It was not long before Western Intelligence agencies were reporting to their governments a significant redeployment of Soviet forces. A number of highly reliable Soviet Guard divisions, manned almost exclusively by Russians, were observed leaving Eastern Europe. Their places were taken by divisions with a higher Asiatic content. There were also well corroborated reports from within the Soviet Union that KGB reinforcements had been sent to historic Moslem cities like Bukhara, Samarkand and Tashkent.

There was much less ambivolence within the Politbureau about how to deal with Nogi-ism, which was seen as a deadlier threat to Marxist/Leninism than Western style democracy. There was solid support for a policy aimed at discrediting Nogi's co-prosperity concept and New Shinto-ist ideas amongst Soviet client states. Anti-Nogi propaganda was to be stepped up and every means was to be exploited for denigrating the Charter of the China Seas. Discreet feelers were to be extended to Washington to see if the United States would collaborate in opposing the ideas of Nogi and Chu, particularly in the rebuilding of the United Nations.

I had a glimpse of the concurrent debate in London, because after the Sino-Japanese walk-out there was little point in my staying on in Karl Tell's office. Though there were high hopes in New York that the wounds inflicted would not prove fatal to the United Nations, it would be years rather than months before the Organisation's credibility and usefulness could be restored. I was, therefore, posted temporarily to Defence Intelligence within the Ministry of Defence where my New York experience, it was thought, might be useful. I was told by the Military Secretary's people that it would be several months before my next appointment would be decided. In the meanwhile, I would represent the Deputy Chief of Defence Staff (Intelligence) on the Cabinet Office Intelligence Assessment Team.

I flew back from New York to London by *Golden Arrow*. It was the first time I had flown in the civilian transport version of *HOTOL II*. The trip took just under the hour with only enough time for a couple of glasses of champagne as we enjoyed the astronauts' view of the world. In fact, we had just half an hour gazing out of the port holes because they were covered by heat shields during ascent and descent phases of the flight. We landed at the new fourth London airport, which had been built, at long last, on Maplin sands off the Essex Coast. Though we were whisked into London by high speed mono-rail train, the journey took as long as the flight across the Atlantic!

I experienced another first soon after getting back to London. The first electronic General Election took place. All electors were issued with plastic voters' cards in which their constituency code was implanted together with a 'one use only' cancellation device. On election day you fed your card into the voting machine and pressed the button for the candidate of your choice. Your vote was recorded electronically and fed to the central election computer. Your now useless card was ejected into a bin for disposal. It would have been possible to display running totals of the votes cast throughout the day, but it was realised that this would lead to tactical voting. As soon as polling ended at 10 p.m., the constituency results were displayed in alphabetical order on all the television channels, holding everyone in suspense until the end when the overall national result was displayed, and we knew which party would form the next government. I, and, I think, most people, missed the old fashioned election night with the results dribbling out and party fortunes swinging to and fro. In its place came an analysis by the media of the voting patterns, which continued into the early hours of the morning. I, personally, went to bed and left them to it after I had heard the final result at about 11 o'clock.

Before recording the result of the 2019 election it is perhaps worth while recalling the pattern of British politics since the turn of the century because, though Britain played only a small part in the final apocalyptic phase of the Third World War, she did have a major influence in the final international settlement. The Labour Party was unlucky enough to be in power when the world recession started in 2003. By 2005 the British electorate decided to give the Conservatives a doctor's mandate to use Tory remedies to get the economy back on its feet. Both the Labour and Trades Unions splintered as the militant Left tried to impose extremist policies on the moderate majority. The crunch came at the 2007 Labour Party Conference when the militants managed to force through a resolution calling on the Party to abolish the Monarchy and to establish a republic when returned to power. The moderates voted with their feet and joined the Social Democrats in disgust and the TUC ended its affiliation to the Labour Party, becoming politically independent for the first time in its existence. The surge of new members enabled the SDP to unseat the Conservatives in 2011, but it also killed the Liberal Party, which lost all relevance. The militant rump of the Labour Party replaced the Liberals as the 'has beens' of British politics in the 21st century.

The 2019 election was a straight fight between the SDP Government and the Conservative Opposition in which Labour did not even hold the balance of power. The Conservatives won a comfortable overall majority, not on policies but because the voters decided that the Social Democrats were tired and devoid of new ideas, and that it was time for a change in national management. Apart from the electoral view of the competence of the two ministerial teams, the only real difference between the parties was that the Social Democrats were to left of centre and the Conservatives just to the right of it. Both had fought to win the middle ground during the election.

In foreign affairs, which naturally interested me most, both parties embraced within their ranks pro- and anti-Europeans, pro- and anti-Americans, Continental and Maritime strategists, World-widers and Little Englanders and so forth. Both parties were also on the side of the angels purporting to believe in multi-racialism, freedom of the individual, liberal morality, Western style democracy etc. . . . Indeed, Britain's foreign policy could still be defined as the pragmatic pursuit of her own enlightened self-interest. The Conservatives had a vision of Britain becoming the Venice of the 21st century, thriving in her geographical security through financial and mercantile expertise, backed by the military ability to defend her own limited interests world-wide. Venice had grown rich manipulating the superpowers of the day to her own advantage: first, playing off the Holy Roman Empire against Byzantium, and then Spain and France against the Ottoman Turks. The SDP saw Britain as the Switzerland of the 21st century, looking after her own interests and determined to maintain her neutrality in the unstable world: a friend to all and an enemy to none.

Bearing this political background in mind, it is not surprising that I found just as much uncertainty in Whitehall as there was in Washington and Moscow about how to face up to the ambitions of Nogi and Chu. The Charter of the China Seas fitted logically into the evolutionary pattern of world history, and it appeared to reflect a continuation of Harold Macmillan's 'Wind of Change', to which Britain had bowed in the 1960's and 1970's as she withdrew from her empire. On the other hand, memories of similar complacency over Hitler's National Socialism in the 1930's, and of Anthony Eden's subsequent over-dramatisation of President Nasser's rise to power in the 1950's, still lingered and haunted the British corridors of power as ministers and officials contemplated the rise of a new 'ism' in world affairs. Frequent references were also made to the success of the pre-First World War Anglo-Japanese Alliance and the dire consequences that had flowed from failure to renew that alliance due to American pressure in the 1920's. Although the dark clouds of anti-Japanese sentiment, caused by our defeats at their hands in 1942 and their subsequent treatment of British prisoners of war, had thinned, a mist of uncertainty remained. As Sir John Godwin had shown during the last difficult debate in the United Nations before the walk-out, Britain was not opposed to Nogi-ism, but she was worried about its possible consequences. At the 2019 Commonwealth Conference, Jawal Gandhi neatly paraphrased Robert Mugabe's quip about the Black Homelanders during the 1999 conference:

'China Seas Charter, probably *Yes*; Sino-Japanese hegemony, definitely *NO!*'

In the NATO Council in Brussels, the debate on the impact of Nogi-ism took a different twist. The British and American delegations argued that Russian embarrassment in the Middle East and Central Asia and their current interest in supplying the Bolivarists in Latin America and Homelanders in Africa meant that the threat to Western Europe, posed by the Eastern Bloc conventional forces, had declined, though the nuclear threat remained as high as ever. In these circumstances they proposed that their European partners should begin to play a larger role in maintaining stability and protecting Western interests outside the NATO area. Britain offered to assign the units of Eagle Force as a nucleus around which a NATO Strategic Reserve or Rapid Deployment Force could be formed. The Americans, using the CIA paper on the possibility of a flare up in Central Asia and a threat to European oil supplies in the Middle East, offered to provide a lion's share of the strategic air transport that the force would need.

The Continental members of the Alliance took a diametrically opposite view. The events in New York had increased rather than decreased East-West tension and hence the threat to Western Europe, which remained the prime target of the Soviet Union. Sheer frustration in the world at large could lead to Soviet adventurism in Europe. The changes in Soviet military deployment might not be associated entirely with countering Islamic Fundamentalism. Some of the Mongolian manned divisions that had arrived in Poland were some of the best and most ruthless in the Soviet order of battle. Berlin still lay as a Western hostage to fortune, and could once again provide the scenario for another round of strategic blackmail and nuclear brinkmanship. The return of Eagle Force was a godsend. Its units should be used to bring BAOR back up to its original Brussels Treaty strength of four divisions.

The gap between the two views was too wide to be bridged in the debate in the NATO Council, which took place in April 2020. The usual compromise was reached by instructing SACEUR to put in hand a study to advise the Council upon the implications of the two more obvious options for the use of Eagle Force units: the creation of a NATO air mobile reserve for use world wide, or their re-assignment to 1st (British) Corps in North West Europe. He was at liberty to recommend other courses of action if they could be justified. One cycnic was heard to remark as the meeting closed:

'That will run into the sand.'

And it did.

None of the strategic debates in Washington, London, Brussels or Moscow was helped by an announcement by Chu in a major trend-setting speech during the 'Double Tenth' festival in Peking on 10th October 2020 that the Hong Kong powers had achieved what he termed 'Nuclear and Space Sufficiency'. China's latest generation of strategic nuclear delivery systems and space vehicles were in service, giving the Sino-Japanese alliance a credible deterrent capability and a foothold in space. China and Japan, he claimed, need no longer fear nuclear blackmail by either superpower or threats from the middle power members of the nuclear club.

'But,' he added, 'the Hong Kong powers would use their strength responsibly to further the aims set out in their joint declaration, the Charter of the China Seas.'

The November issue of *Time* had Chu's face on the cover with the caption:

Nogi's shield and buckler

If I had been writing this history in the style of *The Revelations of St John*, my account of the world situation at the end of 2020 might have read:

> '*And I saw before me the battle array of the forces of the new Jerusalem with the Four Horsemen at the heads of their hordes.*
>
> *The Japanese horse of New Shinto-ism with Prime Minister Nogi on his back stood before the largest horde, its ranks swollen by the infantry masses of his Chinese colleague, Chairman, Chu Cheng.*
>
> *On his left under the great green banner of Islam rode the Ayatollah of Baghdad, leading his Shi'ite horsemen.*
>
> *And on the flanks were the lesser hordes of Archbishop Bolivar, holding aloft the emblem of the 'Cross and Sickle' and of Victor M'Bundu, whose men were all black.*
>
> *Then I raised my eyes to the horizon and I saw the battle arrays of the two superpowers stretching as far as my eyes could see to east and the west.*
>
> *But their troops were not drawn up to oppose the advance of the Four Horsemen: they were facing each other.*
>
> *And I heard a voice from heaven calling to the Four Horsemen:*
> '*Now is the time. Advance and a third share of the wealth of the earth shall be yours.*'
>
> *And as I watched two flank guards were thrown out from the armies of the superpowers, but their main bodies remained glowering at each other.*'

The result of the 2020 U.S. Presidential Election was a foregone conclusion. The Democrats put up John Roosevelt, hoping to make capital out of the Roosevelt name. To some extent their ploy succeeded in that the Republican, Julius Hoffmeyer, did not win a land slide victory. Indeed, the result was uncomfortably close. Analysis of the voting showed that Hoffmeyer failed to attract the support of most ethnic minorities who remained pro-Democrat and pro-Nogi.

PART III

The Apocalypse

*'Then war broke out in Heaven. Michael
and his angels waged war upon the dragon.
The dragon and his angels fought, but
they had not the strength to win, and
no foothold was left them in Heaven.'*

Revelations of St John, Chapter 12
(New English Version)

9

Mutiny in Samarkand: (2020–2023)

*'The superpowers looked oblivion in the face
and stepped back from the nuclear brink.'*
Diary entry for 8th July 2022

Newspapers and journals of the 2020's, re-read today in 2040, show that no-one had yet identified the struggle, which had been waged continuously since 1985, as the Third World War. With the benefit of hindsight, it is now easy to see that it had been smouldering like a fire under moorland peat for thirty five years, coming to the surface and bursting into flames only intermittently and then being doused with relative ease, but never actually put out. The words *Third World War* were not associated in men's minds with a smouldering process: they conjured up a nuclear conflagration and the end of civilisation. The third decade of the 21st century – the start of the Apocalypse of my analogy of the Four Horsemen – was to bring the world terrifyingly near to its own vision of the Third World War, but fortunately for us all the nuclear brink was never crossed.

The early '20s were dramatic years by any standards. They could perhaps be called 'the years of the Ayatollah' because it was he who did most of the leg-work on behalf of Nogi and Chu, and he was the first of the Four Horsemen to draw superpower blood. After the proclamation of the Charter of the China Seas in August 2019, he stayed on in Tokyo for further discussions with Nogi and then went on to Peking to negotiate with Chu. In his meetings with Nogi he offered to align Islamic Fundamentalist policies with Nogi-ism, and, according to Oyama, went as far as asking to accede to the Treaty of Hong Kong, which he saw as the Asian equivalent of the Treaty of Rome. Nogi could not accept his request because, as he explained to the Ayatollah, the Treaty enshrined bi-lateral provisions, which would be difficult to extend to other powers. There was, however, an alternative. The Ayatollah had endorsed the China Seas Charter and

161

had thereby become part of the Afro-Asian Co-prosperity partnership that Chu and he were developing. They would both welcome, Nogi was sure, an Islamic Fundamentalist liaison team which would be attached to the Copps. No mention was made of the secret protocols attached to the Treaty of Hong Kong or to Oyama's and Tzu Te's military cell. Nogi, however, took the precaution of discussing special security measures with Oyama to prevent any leaks or embarrassments when the Islamic liaison team arrived. It was to be housed in the FIR embassy and not in the Copps offices.

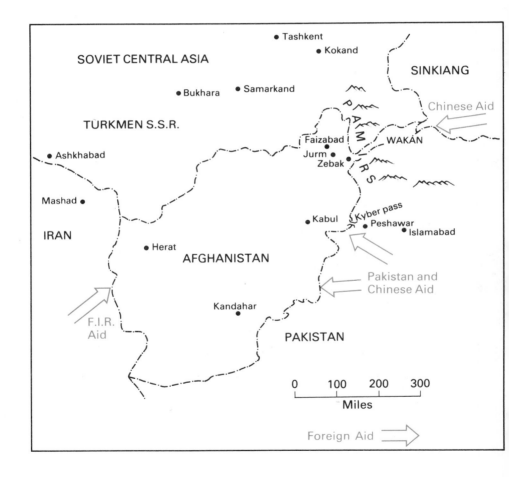

MAP 9: Jihad in Afghanistan in 2021

The Chinese and Japanese officials in the Copps were uncertain how to handle this intrusion into their carefully balanced and well oiled decision making machinery. The Moslem team had to be made welcome and yet kept at arms length. The problem was resolved by Nogi, who asked the Ayatollah to undertake the negotiations to bring about the first extension of the Asian Co-prosperity sphere beyond the Japanese and Chinese boundaries. The Copps had advised him that there was a ground swell of opinion in Malaysia, Singapore, Indonesia and the Philippines in favour of a South East Asia Co-prosperity Sphere or Common Market, affiliated to the main Sino-Japanese Co-prosperity Sphere. They were all states of Malay origin and, apart from Singapore, Islamic in religion. Who could be better chosen than the Ayatollah to bring them together? The Copps Islamic Liaison Team could master-mind the project which should give them a sense of fulfilment.

The idea of a South East Asia Co-prosperity Sphere was not new. The Japanese themselves had tried to form one during their occupation of the area during the Second World War, but the Japanese Army had alienated the local people and failed to respond to the spirit of nationalism that they themselves had aroused. In the 1960's Doctor Sukarno of Indonesia and President Macapagel of the Philippines had tried to coerce Malaya's Prime Minister, the Tunku Abdul Rahman, into joining a Union, which they called 'Maphilindo', but neither he nor the Malaysian people had any wish to exchange British colonial tutelage for Indonesian or Philippine domination. The British victory in the North Borneo campaign put an end to 'Maphilindo'. The time was not ripe for it. Each new nation in South East Asia wished to enjoy its own political freedom in the aftermath of colonial rule.

But times had changed, as the Ayatollah found out during his four capitals tour which took him to Djakarta, Singapore, Kuala Lumpur and Manila. He soon discovered that he was pushing at open doors. National feeling was still strong, but a new pride in being Asian as well had been triggered by Nogi's leadership and by the undeniable success of the 'Japanese Way' that had become synonymous with the 'Asian Way' throughout most of Asia. The Japanese capital and know-how, which had been poured into all the countries of the region over the past half century, had been used in such a way that local people had identified themselves with the resulting economic success and had gained a deeply moving sense of Asian achievement, upon which they wanted to build a new Asian world. Fear of China still lingered, but was assuaged by confidence in Nogi and by dreams of Japanese-style success flowing from their willing accept-ance of Nogi-ism. It was not just the sentiment of *Asia for the Asians*, but *Asia über alles* as well.

The Ayatollah arrived back in Tokyo elated by what he had seen and heard. He was convinced that Nogi-ism was catching and that a new spirit of corporate solidarity was sweeping Asia, which he felt that he should be able to exploit for Islamic purposes. He reported to Nogi that he believed the Treaty of Hong Kong should be revised in such a way as to open it to a wider Asian or perhaps Afro-Asian membership so that it could, indeed, become the equivalent of the Treaty of Rome and lead to an Asian or Afro-Asian Common Market. It was possible to envisage an Asian version of NATO with the Copps acting as its permanent staff. But Nogi, even with Cecil Rhodes' words still ringing in his ears, felt the Ayatollah was trying to move too fast and too far. The first thing, he insisted, was the consolidation of the Islamic Co-prosperity Sphere of South East Asia. The rest might follow if the Ayatollah, Chu and Nogi himself were interpreting the trends in world history correctly.

The Ayatollah had been flattered when Nogi had asked him to undertake the South East Asia mission and he had been engulfed by Nogi-ist enthusiasm during his tour, but, in truth, this was all a diversion as far as he was concerned. He was much more interested in meeting Chu in Peking to find out what practical help Chu could offer the Islamic Fundamentalist cause in Central Asia. He intended to call again upon General Mohammed Khan in Islamabad on his way back to Baghdad and hoped that he would have assurances of Chinese military support for *Jihad* in his pocket.

The Ayatollah was not disappointed in Peking, though the results of his meetings with Chu and subsequently with General Khan were not immediately apparent to the outside world since the three men agreed that 2020 and 2021 should be used for careful planning and preparation for a major *Mujahideen* offensive in Afghanistan during the autumn and winter of 2021/2022. The plan, which emerged from these consultations, was to encourage the *Mujahideen* to launch four widely separated offensives in successive months to force Dost Mohammed, the Afghan Army's commander, to shuttle his reserves to and fro 'like a headless chicken', as Chu put it. The four targets were to be Faizabad in the north east, the Soviet supply routes to Kabul in the centre, Kandahar in the south and Herat in the west. China would supply the Faizabad offensive, using the Wakan route through the Pamirs; the Kabul and Kandahar efforts would be Pakistan's responsibility; and Baghdad would support operations in the Herat area. The offensives were to start in October 2021 when the crops were in, freeing men for battle, and the autumn weather was closing in, making Soviet air support to the Afghan Army more difficult. As the passes through the Pamirs would be blocked by December, the Faizabad offensive would start first in October; followed by Kandahar in November; Kabul in December; and Herat, the most difficult target of all, under cover of winter weather in January.

Chu made one important proviso. The *Sparrow* anti-air and anti-tank weapons, which he and Nogi agreed should be tried out during the Faizabad operations, were to be manned by Mongolian troops of the Chinese

Army, disguised as *Mujahideen*. A careful balance would have to be struck between using them offensively and not risking their capture unnecessarily. They were to be withdrawn before the winter closed the passes.

The guerrilla war had been going on for so long in Afghanistan that the flare up in October 2021 went almost unnoticed by the outside world. In Kabul, Dost Mohammed, who was an able and energetic commander, soon realised something unusual was afoot. As reports reached him of the loss of two helicopter gun-ships sent to investigate reports of *Mujahideen* activity around Jurm, only thirty miles south east of Faizabad, he suspected Chinese involvement. He started to move reserves towards Faizabad and reported his suspicions to the Soviet Commander of the Turkestan Military District at Tashkent, who was his immediate military superior in the Soviet hierarchy.[1]

In the Kremlin the report of Chinese activity in Wakan was not unexpected, but before reacting publically the Soviet Government needed hard evidence. Dost Mohammed was given authority to use the 105th Guards Airborne Division, stationed in Kabul in Soviet strategic reserve, to trap the hostile forces in Wakan to prove or disprove Chinese interference in the internal affairs of the Soviet Union.

Dost Mohammed's operations to trap the Wakan force nearly succeeded. He decided to advance with an armoured force from Faizabad towards Jurm to hold the *Mujahideen* frontally and then to land part of the 105th Guards Division at Zebak to encircle them and sever their withdrawal routes back to China, if that was where they came from. The *Sparrows* brought the armoured thrust to a costly halt much to the elation of the Chinese commander and his crews, but he was no fool and fully aware that efforts would be made to catch him. The *Sparrows* had proved their lethality: it was time to get them out. Much to the *Mujahideen*'s disgust he withdrew in time to make good his escape before the Russian airborne troops were landed at Zebak. The *Mujahideen* could melt away into the countryside: the Chinese could not and had no intention of trying to do so. During the three hundred mile retreat, through the Pamirs back into Sinkiang, the Russians did not manage to overhaul them but winter did. Though obviously exaggerated, the Chinese Commander's report, which was published in Peking several years later, was an epic of dogged determination and endurance entitled '*Retreat from Faizabad: 2021*'.

The Kandahar and Kabul operations followed but they took place in well trodden guerrilla country and achieved nothing decisive. Dost Mohammed handled his troops and aircraft well and could justifiably claim a number of significant successes that enhanced his reputation and improved the morale of the Afghan Army. But he made one major error of judgement which was to have consequences far beyond the borders of Afghanistan. It could have become the 21st century's Sarajevo in that it almost triggered the nuclear Third World War.

The Soviet High Command had found from their long experience of helping to pacify Afghanistan that the operational efficiency of Soviet formations dropped significantly if they were left for more than three winters on garrison duty.[2] The 54th Motor Rifle Division, which had occupied the Herat area on and off since the original Soviet invasion of Afghanistan in 1978, was due to be relieved again in the summer of 2021, but, due to the redeployment of many Soviet divisions in 2019, its original relief was no longer available. It would either have to stay in Herat for a fourth winter or Dost Mohammed must relieve it with a reliable Afghan division until another Soviet division became available in 2022. Dost Mohammed chose to provide an Afghan division in which he had full confidence. Though he did not say so within Soviet earshot he was delighted to get rid of a Soviet division even for a short time. He would not be able to carry out the relief before December, but this was considered acceptable by the Commander of 54th Motor Rifle Division, who started preparations for his division to return to Samarkand for re-equipment, retraining and the little rest that Soviet divisions are ever given.

When the *Mujahideen* offensive started around Faizabad in October, the Turkistan Military District Commander suggested to Dost Mohammed that 54th Motor Rifle Division should stay in Herat for the winter so that all available Afghan units could concentrate on dealing with the guerrillas. Dost Mohammed declined the offer. He had made his plans and had no wish to create confusion with order/counter-order, which always sapped military discipline.

Dost Mohammed did not take sufficient account of the 'leakiness' of his headquarters in Kabul. The *Mujahideen* became aware that the 54th Motor Rifle Division was to be relieved by the 77th Afghan Division in the second week of January 2022. They had plenty of time to exploit this intelligence in preparing for their Herat offensive. Preparations were not limited to the *Mujahideen* themselves; both the Ayatollah and General Khan played significant parts in setting up what turned out to be an almost bloodless coup in Herat.

General Taza Gul, the commander of the 77th Division, was a Pathan from the Khyber area, whose forebears had often fought the British in their North West Frontier skirmishes in the 1920's and 1930's. He still had relations in the Pakistan Army through whom clandestine approaches could be made to him. General Khan directed his Intelligence staff to find out whether Taza Gul could be 'turned' and, if so, at what price. And the Ayatollah used his *Shi'ite* agents to subvert the higher ranking officers of the division. This was not difficult because many, who had become Communists of convenience during the early days of the Soviet occupation, were now in middle age and beginning to hear the call of the religion of their childhood as old men are apt to do. Bazaar gossips worked wonders on the rank and file of the division. The Ayatollah's friendship with Nogi, the hero of Asia, and the rumours of Chinese weapons reaching the *Mujahideen* were all seen as the work of Allah. It was time to jump off the Communist band-wagon and to make *Jihad* as true followers of Islam, who alone would reap Allah's rewards in the life hereafter.

The *Mujahideen* did not rely entirely on their clandestine efforts to subvert Taza Gul's division. They stepped up their attacks in the Kabul and Kandahar sectors to draw as many Afghan troops away from Herat as possible while they infiltrated the Herat area during December, taking care not to alert the Soviet 54th Division. New Year came and went. The weather deteriorated and the relief of 54th Division began on 7th January. Any suspicions, which the Soviet troops might have had, that the sector had become unusually quiet, was put down to the weather. In any case why should they care; they were getting out, weren't they?

The *Mujahideen* allowed forty eight hours to elapse after the last 54th Division convoy drove away before starting to encircle the Afghan 77th Division's positions around the city. Taza Gul reported increasing *Mujahideen* pressure to Kabul, but Dost Mohammed seems to have had full confidence in 77th Division's abilities and did not judge it necessary to reinforce him at the expense of the more heavily pressed central sector. The first he heard of the débâcle at Herat was a Baghdad radio accounce-ment that said: 'The city of Herat is once more in the hands of the faithful: Allah be praised.'

There was no reference to heavy casualties on either side. It would be nice to be able to write that religious conviction led to the fall of Herat on 20th January. Money rather than *Korans* changed hands. Taza Gul and a large part of his division surrendered to the *Mujahideen* when called upon to do so, and were helped to escape to Mashad in eastern Iran. They were flown from there to Baghdad where they received a truly Islamic welcome.

Dost Mohammed was a brave man. He reported the loss of Herat at once to Turkistan Military District, accepting full responsibility for mis-judging Taza Gul,. He asked for the immediate return of 54th Division. The Soviet Commander in Tashkent misjudged the temper of the 54th Division just as badly.

On arriving back in its barracks in Samarkand and the adjacent towns 54th Division had already started to send off its time expired conscripts whose release had been delayed by the problems of finding the division an earlier relief. The first home-leave parties of regular soldiers were also about to depart. There was a general end of term spirit prevailing through-out the division when the order arrived to stop all conscript release and leave parties, and for the immediate return of the division to Afghanistan to retake Herat. In a spontaneous outburst officers and senior N.C.O.'s were murdered by their men, and the divisional commander and his staff were taken hostage by the mutineers. The units in which non-Russians predominated were worst affected, but Muscovite units also took part in the initial outburst, though they were more easily dealt with by the three Guard Motor Rifle Divisions sent to quell the mutiny.

It may seem surprising that a mutiny could occur in a Soviet division, but no army has ever been totally proof against such defections and the Red Army is no exception. It is, after all, made up of human beings, who will always react violently, if pushed beyond an indefinable breaking point, no matter how ruthless its discipline may be.

The world might never have heard of the Mutiny at Samarkand, as it is now known, if it had not been for sizeable bodies of 54th Division soldiers of Turkmen origin who managed to escape across the Afghan frontier and joined the *Mujahideen*, providing a propaganda coup for the Islamic Fundamentalists. Moscow had the good sense not to deny the incident, but belittled it as a minor affair, embroidered and exaggerated by the Western media.

It would have been a minor incident, soon forgotten in the stirring events of the 2020's, had it not been symptomatic of the deeply rooted anti-Europeanism and a wish to return to their own traditional culture that was surging through the minds of the people of Soviet Central Asia. What Nogi-ism was to eastern Asia, Islamic Fundamentalism was to western Asia. The antagonism was centred upon Asiatic dislike of all things Russian, and upon a growing confidence that liberation from Muskovite thraldom was the will of Allah and hence inevitable. The Russians were beginning to face the same weight of ethnic nationalism under which the paternalistic British Empire had crumpled. The mutiny at Samarkand revealed to the world the growing tension between the Soviet citizens of Russian and Asiatic descent, and the less ready acceptance of Muskovite dominance east of the Urals.

Though future historians will probably highlight the Mutiny at Samarkand as the trigger of the world crisis of 2022, it was the way that Herat fell that incensed the Kremlin. There was an immediate return to the harsh cold war rhetoric of the 1950's and '60's as Moscow accused the Baghdad Pact in general and the United Stages in particular of counter-revolutionary activity within the recognised frontiers of the Soviet Union. On 1st February 2022, Moscow began blaring out its message to the west.

> '*The Soviet Union will not stand idly by while the agents and provocateurs of American imperialism push the drug of religious superstition to Soviet citizens in their unprincipled attempts to undermine Marxist-Leninism by counter-revolution. Unless the Baghdad Pact powers bring their hostile subversion to an end, the Soviet Union will take appropriate measures of self-defence!*'

What those measures were to be soon became evident from satellite photographic cover and communications intelligence. I had by this time been appointed a full colonel in the Chiefs of Staff Secretariat in the

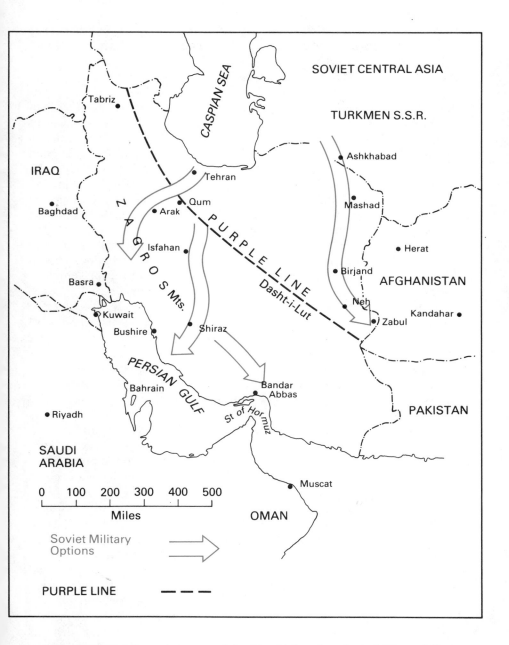

MAP 10: Soviet operations to seal the Iran Afghan frontier in 2022; and the
Purple Line of 2023

Ministry of Defence, so I saw most of the action of this crucial period through the eyes of the British military policy makers. The Joint Intelligence Commmittee's assessment of Soviet activity in February and March 2022 showed a steady build-up of their forces in Iran where they had been in occupation of Tehran since their invasion in 2017, and in Central Asia. There were three main concentrations of armoured units with supporting tactical airforces. These were at Qum just south of Tehran, at Ashkabad on the north eastern frontier of Iran, and at Herat, which had been retaken by a Guards Tank Division. The JIC view was that the Soviet High Command was deploying in a way that would give it two principal options. It could order a limited offensive southwards from Ashkhabad and Herat to seal the western frontier of Afghanistan; or it could adopt the more ambitious course of advancing from Qum as well and heading via Isfahan and Shiraz for Bandar Abbas on the Straits of Hormuz thus closing the Persian Gulf to Western and Japanese oil traffic. Although they did not discount it all together, they thought a thrust south west from Qum to the Iran and Iraq oil fields was unlikely because the passes in the Zagros Mountains were strongly held by Baghdad Pact forces, including a strong Israeli contingent at Arak on the main road and rail links from Tehran to Basra.

At the Chiefs of Staff meeting on 15th March the Deputy Chief of Defence Staff (Intelligence) pointed out the prescience of the CIA's 2019 paper which had predicted a Soviet threat to Western European oil supplies if the Ayatollah succeeded in setting Soviet Central Asia ablaze. It had not yet burst into flames, but the splutter at Samarkand had been enough to produce that reaction already. The British Defence Adviser at the British Embassy in Washington reported that there was considerable nervousness in the Pentagon and State Department about the Soviet build up and a feeling of annoyance that SACEUR had still not managed to produce even a plan for the creation of a NATO strategic reserve to look after Western European interests overseas. Europe's oil supplies were clearly in danger and yet only the United States and United Kingdom could respond to the threat.

American frustration with Western European procrastination was thoroughly justified. The NATO Council had agreed unanimously in 2020 that the equivalent of the United States Rapid Deployment Force should be formed to protect Western European interests. They also agreed that the force must be manned by regular servicemen to give it the efficiency and speed of reaction needed by such a force. A further two years had drifted by and none of the Western European member states had been prepared to face the cost of increasing the numbers of very expensive regulars in their defence forces. A system of joint funding was suggested, but the idea was abandoned when the American delegation made it quite clear that Congress was most unlikely to accept a share of the bill: America was already doing more than her fair share of the defence of the NATO area by keeping 300,000 regulars in Southern Germany.

At American insistence, the issue was placed once more on the NATO Council's agenda for its March 2022 meeting. It was not discussed because reports were coming in of unusually large Soviet logistic movements into Poland from Western Russia and the westward movement of Soviet aircraft normally based in Byelorussia into Poland. The Warsaw Pact communication networks were showing increased activity and agents in East Germany were reporting the retention of time-expired conscripts in Soviet units. With all these indicators of Soviet military activity pointing in the same direction, SACEUR declared 'Simple Alert' amongst NATO forces, as the preliminary to 'Reinforced Alert', which meant general mobilisation in Western Europe and the despatch of American based reinforcements across the Atlantic. Western European minds in the NATO Council concentrated almost exclusively on Soviet military preparations in Eastern Europe. The affairs of the Middle East and the possibility of setting up a NATO force for operations outside Europe were almost forgotten as the acrid smell of *sauve qui peut* began to permeate the Council chamber. Was there not time to strike a collective bargain or do individual deals with the Soviet Union before it was too late?

This Soviet diversion – for that is what it was – to pin down NATO's forces before striking in the Middle East was hideously successful. April, May and June were months in which the Kremlin alternated raising and lowering political and military tension until they had the North Atlantic Alliance in unforgiveable disarray. Then on 4th July 2022, as the United States was in the midst of the annual Independence Day celebrations, Soviet forces thrust forward from Ashkhabad; and Moscow radio announced that the Soviet Government had lost patience with Western prevarication and was invoking its legitimate right to self-defence by sealing off the Western frontier of Afghanistan from further contact with the West.

President Hoffmeyer had to act regardless of the views of his Western European allies, if his policy of negotiating from strength and United States support of the Baghdad Pact were to retain any validity. He did warn his NATO partners, but he went futher in the case of London. He authorised the United States Joint Chiefs of Staff to brief their British colleagues fully on U.S. intentions and plans. I happened to be Secretariat duty officer for the night 4th/5th July. We had had a busy and exciting day as intelligence of the Soviet action came in and assessments were made of its implications for us and for NATO as a whole. It was at about 8 p.m. when a call came through from the British Defence Adviser in Washington, saying that the American Chiefs would welcome a combined meeting with the British Chiefs as soon as possible. The Pentagon wanted to use some United States units stationed in Britain, and it would also be grateful for air staging facilities and logistic support for aircraft and troops

being flown to the Middle East. Could I arrange a transatlantic video conference for 10 p.m. London time?[3]

I rang the Chief of Defence Staff, Field Marshal Sir Colin Campbell, at his
flat in Kingston House, on the south side of Hyde Park.[4] He was not at all
surprised by the request.

'Good', he said, 'that will just give me enough time to consult the PM.
Please confirm to Washington and set the wheels in motion. Ask everyone to
assemble in the conference room by 9.30 so that I can have a quick word
before the Americans appear on the screen.'

I don't think I had realised until this time how strong that indefinable
Anglo-American special relationship really was. The Chiefs all knew each
other well. As their respective careers had developed they had met each other
on frequent occasions as the years rolled by, during joint exercises, during
exchange postings, during briefing tours and often working together on
international staffs in NATO. It was an easy relationship, which had its
origins not only in common early history and language, but in the traditions
created by working so closely together during the Second World War.

The Chiefs of Staff Conference Room, in which the British Chiefs and their
immediate advisers assembled at 9.30, had changed little since Admiral Lord
Louis Mountbatten designed in the early 1960's. It was a long narrowish room
dominated by a triangular shaped table. The wide end of the table was at the
far end underneath a large projector screen, on which maps and other graphic
material could be displayed. Its sides tapered towards the Chairman's seat at
the other end with enough room for about eight seats on either side. Behind
the Chairman's seat was a small platform with another eight or so seats for
advisers called in from time to time to speak on some particular item on the
agenda. The only real change since Mountbatten's day was the replacement
of the projector screen with one of the largest television screens I have ever
seen. Images on it could be life size.

At the preliminary meeting, Sir Colin told his colleagues that the Prime
Minister wanted to offer the President all the help he could with political and
military support. The PM would have liked to have been able to provide a
token force for operations in the Persian Gulf area, but he, Sir Colin, had
pointed out that all Britain's strategically mobile forces had been withdrawn
to the United Kingdom and were poised ready to reinforce NATO's northern
flank in Scandinavia. As he said this, he turned to the Vice Chief of Defence
Staff, who was responsible for deployment and operations, for confirmation.

The VCDS was quick to take up his cue:

'However politically attractive it may be to a Conservative Government to
support a Republican Administration, the despatch of even a token force to
the Persian Gulf should be resisted on military grounds. It would be most
unwise to weaken the Northern Flank. A Soviet move into Northern Norway
would present a far graver threat to the security of the British Isles than the
loss of Persian Gulf Oil.'

Sir Colin Campbell nodded and added:

'The most we can offer the United States Chiefs is staging facilities and logistic support, and that is all that the PM has agreed to so far.'

At 10 p.m. exactly, the television screen at the end of the room lit up and the conference room seemed to double in length as the U.S. Chiefs of Staffs appeared, sitting round a very similar table with their Chairman, Admiral Douglas McLean, at the head of it, with the usual stand of American colours behind him.

After a short introductory banter by the two chairmen about upsetting American Independence Day celebrations, Admiral McLean sketched out the United States' plans and intentions.

'The President,' he said, 'has ordered the immediate activation of the Baghdad Pact contingency plan "Black Gold" of which the British are aware. A corps of two airborne divisions will be flown into Isfahan to form a central reserve for the Baghdad Pact forces holding southern Iran. At the same time the United States Indian Ocean Task Force is to land its Marines at Bandar Abbas to help defend the Straits of Hormuz. A patrol line of nuclear submarines has been established off the Yemeni coast to intercept any Soviet warships from Aden that may try to interfere.'

'Is the President satisfied that the recent Soviet sabre-rattling in Europe is a diversion to pin down NATO forces during their operations in Iran?' asked Sir Colin.

'Hell, no,' was the reply, 'That is why we are not asking our European partners for help. SACEUR could still order 'Reinforced Alert'. Europe may well be the real target.'

The conference then changed gear as each United States Chief explained what help his department would like from his British counter-part, and the 'nuts and bolts' of Anglo-U.S. military co-operation were tightened up. It was well after midnight when the screen went blank and we all settled down to issuing the necessary instructions down the British chain of command.

As the news of the American landings at Isfahan flashed round the globe, the world held its breath. Although the American troops were covered by a screen of local Baghdad Pact forces, the danger of a direct confrontation between American and Soviet ground forces was very high. If contact did occur, it would be the first time the United States and Red Armies had faced each other in anger since the aftermath of the Second World War. The consequences were unpredictable. Escalation to all out nuclear conflict might be only hours away. Tension grew worse as the United States Marines started landing at Bandar Abbas and the Soviet naval squadron from Aden was reported sailing north to challenge the United States Naval Task Force, covering the entrance to the Persian Gulf. A clash at sea looked inevitable.

Calls for restraint and offers of mediation flooded into Washington and

Moscow from all the leading political figures. Without the United Nations Security Council, the world was bereft of any mechanism for enforcing a pause for second thoughts. The Pope, Karl Tell, Jawal Gandhi and other well known peacemakers offered their good offices. None was listened to until Chu and Nogi stepped in. Chu's message was hard and uncompromising: 'Stand fast, or China will enter the conflict.'

He did not say on whose side his forces would intervene, because Nogi, playing the treble to Chu's base, invited both superpowers to meet in Tokyo under his chairmanship.

'To resolve their differences and to protect the peace of the world.'

By this time the Soviet armoured forces from Ashkhabad had passed through Mashad and Birjand and had leading elements at Zabul, virtually sealing the western Afghan frontier, which was their objective. They had not attempted to thrust south from Qum, so contact with the Americans had been avoided. Having achieved their primary aim virtually without loss, thrown western Europe into disarray, and forced the United States to commit its hardest hitting military force to a wild goose chase, the Kremlin blandly accepted Nogi's invitation without any reference to Chu's threat. Washington had no other option but to accept as well. Not to have done so would have been to invite nuclear war.

Nowhere was the irony of Nogi acting as mediator between the superpowers perceived more clearly and treated more cynically than in the offices of the Copps. It was Copps policies that had brought about the conflict in the first place: now it was their task to advise Nogi about how to resolve it to the advantage of the Hong Kong Powers!

We have to depend upon Oyama's evidence to piece together the back stage lobbying and tortuous negotiations which went on behind the facade of the Tokyo conference of August 2022, because no official documents have been published as yet by the participants. The Copps' hidden aim during the conference was, as Oyama put it:

'To strengthen Asia's position at the expense of the superpowers.'

In preparing Nogi's briefs for the Conference, the Chinese and Japanese teams did not find agreement easy since they reflected, quite naturally, the growing divergence of view between Chu and Nogi. Chu had always been the Chinese imperialist, while Nogi saw himself as a Samurai seeking better world government. Chu was becoming more and more militant, while Nogi was donning the robes of a peacemaker, dedicated to the creation of a new world in Japan's own image, far removed from the Great American dream or the Marxist-Leninist Utopia.

In the first Chinese draft of the brief it was suggested that it would be to the Kong Kong powers advantage to keep the superpowers locked in an eyeball to eyeball confrontation in Iran, so that they would be less able to interfere in the development of Nogi's co-prosperity ideas, or in Chu's first direct political and military moves to regain the Ch'ing frontiers of China. They cited the precedent of the Korean Armistice Commission. This had lasted almost half a century and, in its early years, had enabled China to pin down American forces and hamstring American Far Eastern policy at minimal cost to China. They recommended a truce line drawn down the central Iranian desert, the Dasht-i-Lut, from Qum in the northwest to the triple junction of the Iran, Afghan and Pakistan frontiers in the south east. The truce commission and supervisory force could be provided by such well known neutral busy-bodies as India and Yugoslavia, and the costs could be shared equally between the superpowers. Such an arrangement would be just as effective as any of the former United Nations' peace keeping forces and more amenable to Sino-Japanese pressure!

The Japanese draft took a diametrically opposite view. The establishment of a truce line could only be a necessary but preliminary step. The world was expecting far more than that from the authors of the Charter of the China Seas. The successful negotiation of a superpower disengagement and withdrawal not only from the Soviet's 'back yard' in Iran, but also from the American's 'back yard' in Central America as well, was the prize for which Nogi should strive. Its attainment would be a direct help to the Ayatollah, who would be able to re-occupy Tehran, and to Archbishop Bolivar, who would be freed from U.S. constraints in Latin America. M'Bundu would profit too if the agreement could be extended to a superpower arms embargo in Africa. Much greater indirect benefits would flow from Nogi's enhanced reputation. He would be able to use his success as the foundation upon which he could start rebuilding a new world government based on the precepts set out in the Charter of the China Seas to replace the United Nations, which he and Chu had pulled own.

The final Copps brief for Nogi as chairman of the Tokyo Conference was enevitably a compromise between the two views. It was accepted that negotiations for a mutually balanced withdrawal by the superpowers would be slow and tedious, requiring great patience. The establishment of a truce line was, therefore, an essential preliminary step and should be the first item on the conference agenda. A long bargaining period would then begin with Nogi limiting discussion at first to withdrawals from Iran only. The Americans, the Copps thought, might be more than satisfied with a Russian withdrawal from Iran as the *quid pro quo* for a similar U.S. withdrawal, though they would probably indulge in window dressing on the human rights theme by demanding freedom of Islamic worship within the Soviet Union. The Russians on the other hand, would not be satisfied. They would argue that an American withdrawal from Iran, which was only marginally important to the defence of the United States, was hardly equivalent to a Soviet withdrawal from an area which was *vital* to the security of the Soviet Union. The conference would thus widen itself into a geo-political market place in which far reaching but unpredictable bargains might be struck.

The Conference opened on 12th August 2022. The truce line proposed by Nogi, which became known as the Purple Line – a mixture of Soviet red and American blue – was accepted after a period of haggling over its exact delineation and over the terms of reference of the Indo-Yugoslav Truce Commission, both countries having accepted that thankless task thrust upon them by Nogi. The subsequent debate on the longer term disengagement went much as the Copps had predicted, but was settled more quickly than they expected. Both superpowers had looked into the nuclear abyss and had recoiled. Some new *modus vivendi* was obviously needed and a deal, very like the package agreed with Karl Tell in 2019, was struck. There would be a phased and mutually balanced withdrawal programme from Iran and Central America, and a separate self-denying arms supply limitation agreement was concluded which, in theory at least, would do much to reduce tension in the flash points of the world.

By the turn of the Year, Nogi felt, like Karl Tell before him, that he was on the verge of his greatest triumph. The Purple Line was established; the Truce Commission was at work; and the final details were being settled in the Mutual Balanced Force Withdrawal programme. Some observers, however, were suggesting that all Nogi had done by imposing the Purple Line was to move the Soviet frontier southwards: the Russians would soon find a series of excuses for not withdrawing their troops and the whole of Northern Iran would, over the subsequent years of prevarication, become virtually part of the Soviet Union, as Afghanistan had done.

These cynics were nearly proved right, but not in the way that they foretold. Karl Tell's peace package had failed through the bungling in Washington which led to the Soviet space station crisis. Nogi's package collapsed due to a vicious power struggle that developed in the Kremlin where the Politbureau was divided upon the strategic nuclear risks being run to gain tactical advantages in Central Asia. The amenability of the Soviet delegation at the Tokyo Conference reflected the temporary triumph of its younger liberal members over the hard-liners of the Old Guard. But the liberals went too far. Their very success in reaching agreement for a superpower disengagement was their undoing. By the time the draft agreement was debated in the Kremlin, the fear of nuclear war had receded and the hard-liners counter-attacked. They argued that the 1917 Revolution had been betrayed; that the Soviet Union had ceased to pursue the Marxist-Leninist philosophy of world revolution; that anti-capitalist fronts should have been maintained in Iran and Central America; and that disengagement was fundamentally wrong and against the best interests of the Soviet people. This was all good Communist rhetoric. What annoyed the hard-liners most was the kid-glove handling of the growing Asian xenophobia in the Central Asian SSR's. In trying to persuade their colleagues to ratify the Tokyo agreement, the liberals gave way to the hard-liner argument that withdrawal from Iran would open up Central Asia to penetration by Islamic Fundamentalism. The conciliatory policy agreed in 2019 must be reversed and the Security Forces ordered to purge all Moslem militants within the Soviet Union. Events were to show that any chance that there might have been of Nogi succeeding where Karl Tell had failed, was swept away by that concession. With it also went, at least for the time being, the possibility of a United States-Soviet agreement to unite against the Sino-Japanese challenge, which many observers were confidently predicting.

Nogi's package was never ratified. Before detailed planning for the first phase of the disengagement could start, reports began to circulate in February 2023 of mass arrests of Islamic sympathisers in the historic centres of Moslem culture in Soviet Central Asia like Bukhara, Samarkand, Tashkent, Kokand and Alma Ata (*See Map 9*). These KGB operations led to spontaneous rebellions against all things Muskovite, which were put down by the Red Army with a brutality reminiscent of Stalin's purges in the Ukraine in the 1930's. In the upsurge of anger that engulfed the non-Communist world, Nogi's carefully balanced package fell apart. The two men most affected, other than Nogi himself, were President Hoffmeyer and Chairman Chu. Hoffmeyer and his Republican supporters realised that his chances of re-election in 2024 had been blighted by events. The American electorate rarely awards failure, however well intentioned. His policy of negotiation from strength had resulted in the United States living more dangerously than most voters liked or felt justified in terms of American self-interest.

In contrast, Chu Cheng saw the strategic balance swinging in his favour as his Copps team had predicted. The superpowers, pinned in confrontation on the Purple Line in Iran as well as on the Iron curtain in Europe, would be less able to curb Chinese ambitions elsewhere. Nogi for the time being had shot his political bolt. The initiative in the Sino-Japanese alliance had passed to Chu, who was ready to exploit his opportunities for re-establishing the Ch'ing frontiers and re-imposing tributary status on China's neighbours under the guise of Nogi's Co-prosperity spheres.

Hoffmeyer's expectations were further reduced and Chu's opportunities improved when in July 2023 the Soviet Union announced publically that an indefinite delay in the release of conscripts from active to reserve Red Army formations had been ordered. In the past such extensions had been unannounced, but this time there was obviously a premeditated attempt to warn the West and the Hong Kong powers not to try to exploit Soviet difficulties in Central Asia, nor the consequential internal tensions which were developing within the Warsaw Pact, as its members sensed that Moscow's embarrassment might have opportunities for them too.

In Washington, Brussels and London the retention of Soviet conscripts –

one of the key Intelligence indicators of Russian preparation for war rekindled the dread of nuclear war. Hoffmeyer decided that the Rapid Deployment Force in Iran was becoming like Berlin, a Soviet hostage, but unlike Berlin it could be easily reinforced within the grounds rules of the Baghdad Pact and reinforced it must be.

And so, in the middle of a pre-election year, the United States was sending more servicemen than ever overseas, principally to strengthen the Baghdad Pact, but also to fill in gaps in its military contribution to NATO. Chu could only chuckle: the superpowers were still facing in the wrong direction.

Notes

1. It will be remembered that Afghanistan had been an autonomous Soviet Socialist Republic since 1998.
2. British battalions, by contrast, were not expected to stay in Berlin for more than one winter without deterioration of morale.
3. Video conferences were by secure fibre optical cable across the Atlantic.
4. Sir Colin Campbell's successes in East Africa had led to rapid promotion. He had become Chief of General Staff in 2018 and then Chief of Defence Staff in 2021.

10

Undermining the Super Powers: Plan White Lotus (2024–2025)

*'At General Oyama's reception this evening to mark
the first anniversary of the decision to set up the
East Asian Treaty Organisation, EATO, on the lines
of NATO, Marshal Tzu Te, Supreme Allied Commander,
East Asia, gave me a message which could be
significant in the years to come.'*

Diary entry for 1st January 2026

When analysing the events of the mid-2020's I was in two minds about the most appropriate title for this chapter. At first I thought *The Decline of the Superpowers* would be apt. The power of the United States and the Soviet Union had certainly declined relative to Asia, and perhaps Afro-Asia, in terms of both wealth and dynamism. It was not just the obvious economic growth and political confidence of Nogi's and Chu's Eastern Asia that impressed me. The Ayatollah's Islamic Fundamentalism was winning converts from Communism in Central Asia, and M'Bundu's Black African Homelanders were at last reaping the benefits of abandoning their confrontation with Kenya and Tanzania. Even in Latin America, there had been laudable progress in closing the gap between the deprived majority and the privileged minority. Although the Bolivarists had not managed to increase their vote in Mexico and were stalled in Central America by the United States intervention in Panama, they had won the battle for hearts and minds in Ecuador, Peru and Bolivia where Bolivarist Governments had been installed.[1]

I was, I think, influenced in this view by personal experience. My time in the Chiefs of Staff Secretariat came to an end early in 2024 when I was appointed British Military Attaché to our embassy in Tokyo as a brigadier. The vibrance of Japanese society and its burgeoning confidence contrasted so starkly with the cynicism I had experienced in New York and the *laissez faire* attitudes of Whitehall which I had just left. I used to meet Nogi quite frequently at diplomatic functions and I got got know General Oyama well in his official capacity as Deputy Chief of the Japanese Self-Defence Staff. I certainly had no inkling of his secret capacity as joint Chairman of the Copps military cell; nor for that matter did any of my colleagues in the Tokyo diplomatic corps.

It was my conversations with Oyama at this time and reading his book later that made me change this chapter's title to *Undermining the Super-powers*. Although there was undoubtedly some natural ageing and disenchantment in American and Russian society, which accounted for the lustreless performance of the two superpowers as they faced each other across the Iron Curtain and the Purple Line, and as they tried to out-manoeuvre each other in Africa and Latin America, it was the positive policies of Nogi and Chu that began to upset the world balance of power in a decisive way in 2025.

American disillusion was demonstrated in the 2024 Presidential Election campaign. Hoffmeyer's Republicans chose the slogan 'Strength Pays' as the logical successor to their over-used claim of 'Negotiating from Strength'. The firm, resolute action by the Republican Administration during the Iranian crisis of 2022 had saved Western oil supplies in the Persian Gulf and had checked Soviet ambitions in Europe. President Hoffmeyer's robust defence of freedom would not have been possible without the United States military strength, which the Republican Party had played such a major part in sustaining over the years. America would always be safe in Republican hands.

Hoffmeyer was misjudging the American mood. The Democratic slogan writers counter-attacked by adding just two words to the Republican slogan: 'Strength Pays – *for what*?' What had been achieved by American sabre rattling, asked Patrick O'Dwyer, the Democratic presidential candidate, who was inordinately proud of his Southern Irish ancestry.[2] British bayonets had never achieved lasting peace in Ireland: what mattered was the hearts and minds of the people. American bayonets would never bring peace to the world either. American servicemen had been in Panama since 2017, but the people of Central America were no nearer enjoying the peace that comes from political fulfilment. 2025 would mark the eightieth anniversary of the entry of American forces into Germany in 1945. 300,000 were still there, enabling Western European Governments to keep their defence budgets low and their economic competitiveness high. And now the world had been brought to the brink of nuclear catastrophe through the misguided policies of the Republican Administration in the Middle East. Those who rely on the sword usually die by the sword. The pen has always proved the mightier in men's affairs, and now the 21st century world television networks had reduced the power of the sword still further. The

United States must, of course, maintain the sharpest of swords, but it must remain sheathed as a weapon of last resort. A Democratic Administration would return America's sword to its scabbard, and let ideas and ideals, for which the United States was renowned, flourish again. Disengagement and peace through prosperity rather than military strength would be the policy of President O'Dwyer.

The issue that won the 2024 election for O'Dwyer was conscription. The regular forces of the United States were suffering the same over-stretch that the British forces had experienced in the 1960's and '70's when they were acting as world policemen during the British withdrawal from empire. The need for some form of selective draft to keep the U.S. forces in Europe, Iran and Panama up to strength became a live issue by mid 2024. President Hoffmeyer's solution was to increase regular recruiting by improving pay and conditions for the American serviceman. O'Dwyer countered by demanding a reduction in United States overseas commitments and insistence that America's allies in NATO should carry more of the West's military burden. The American electorate preferred O'Dwyer's song and awarded him a landslide victory.

Nogi and Chu were not slow to recognise the opportunities presented to them by the change in American mood and by the horrific Stalinesque repression being practised by the Soviet Union against the followers of Islam in Central Asia. Nogi, however, had used up too much of his political capital in his successful creation of the South East Asia Co-prosperity Sphere and his worthy attempt to act as conciliator between the superpowers over Iran. He had been wearing the velvet glove of the published clauses of the Treaty of Hong Kong. It was now time for Chu to uncover the iron fist hidden beneath its still secret protocols. The target date for Sino-Japanese war readiness, 2025, was only a few weeks away when O'Dwyer was elected to lead the United States onto the road of disengagement and Chu had made ready to display the Chinese steel beneath the velvet of Nogi-ism.

On 1st January 2025 senior ministers and officials of the Chinese and Japanese governments met for the annual Copps conference in Peking at which it was customary for the Joint Chairman to report progress to Chu and Nogi. There was nothing secret about such meetings or the communiqués that were issued at their conclusion. They were usually a bland resumé of the continuing political and economic successes of the Co-prosperity venture. As far as the public were concerned, the 2025 conference was no different and the communiqué issued at its conclusion was as uninformative as ever. Alert observers might have noticed that it lasted a day longer than usual, but this was explained away by the expansion of Co-prosperity business.

During the extra day Tzu Te and Oyama appeared for the first time to brief ministers on their carefully matured plans for the discreet change

MAP 11: Plan White Lotus: 2025

from velvet glove to mailed fist now that military preparations were nearing completion. The plan they presented was as ambitious in its aims as *Barbarossa*, Hitler's plan for the invasion of Russia, but there any similarity ended. As religious subversion within the Soviet Union was to play a major role in the Copps military plan, it was code named *White Lotus* after the great Buddhist rebellion against the Ch'ing dynasty in the 18th century.

Of the two leaders of the Copps military cell, Tzu Te was the tactician and Oyama the strategist, and their appearance reflected their aptitudes. Tzu Te was a large man with the heavy black eyebrows and determined mouth of a field commander: Oyama was small, bespectacled and intellectual. Both men had a sense of humour and were highly articulate, but Tzu's style tended towards the raucousness of the barrack room, whereas Oyama's had the quiet subtleness of the academic world.

Tzu Te, the senior of the two, spoke first, sketching the principles behind the equipment, organisation and training of the Co-prosperity Defence Forces. He and Oyama had made a close study of the Second World War successes and failures of the German and Japanese forces. They admired the tactical brilliance of the *Wehrmacht's Blitzkrieg*, and the dedication and endurance of the Japanese forces that conquered South East Asia in 1942. The Germans had paralysed their victims with the speed, venom and depth of their combined tank and dive bomber attacks. The new Sino-Japanese forces would do the same thing but in a different way. Their target acquisition equipment, *The Eye of Heaven*, which used the latest supra-technology, would unerringly pin-point the enemy's weapon systems; the *Crows* would suppress them; and the helicopter-borne units armed with *Sparrows* would deliver the *coup de grâce*. The dedication of the Chinese and Japanese servicemen was being focused on the concept of the rebirth of Asia and on the important part that they were to play in bringing it about. The cry of 'banzai' had been replaced by the simple word 'Asia', shouted at the tops of their voices.

At the end of his presentaiton of military technology, Tzu Te intrigued his audience by suggesting that beam systems, developed for use in space, might be applicable to the land/air battles on earth. He would not elaborate, but ended with the cryptic remark: 'We have high hopes that the *Dragon's Tongue* project will come to fruition in time for the later phases of *White Lotus*.'

At this stage of the briefing Oyama took over to paint the strategic environment in which the two men envisaged their 'New Model' forces operating. The Hong Kong Treaty powers, he pointed out, had already achieved nuclear security through their massive investment in offensive and defensive strategic systems. They were virtually immune to nuclear blackmail, but they could never be secure from conventional attack until three strategic aims had been fulfilled. As he spoke the three headings appeared in turn on the screen behind him:

'1. RECOVERY OF THE MANCHU HOMELANDS'

'Those north and east of the Amur River, were ceded under duress to Tsarist Russia in 1858 when the Russian frontier was moved south of the Amur River and the Russian city and naval base of Vladivostok was founded. The whole of the old Manchurian maritime provinces, now called Primorsk and Khaborovsk, must be recovered.'

2. OCCUPATION OF SAKHALIN, THE KURILS AND THE KAMCHATKA PENINSULA

'Japan can never be secure until these Russian-held base areas are demilitarised and administered by Japan.'

3. LIBERATION OF INDO-CHINA

'China cannot be secure either until Russian bases at Kam Ranh Bay and Da Nang are closed and Vietnam, Cambodia and Laos accept the guidance of Peking rather than Moscow.'

'The strategic aims of *White Lotus*,' Oyama recapitulated, 'are to pluck these three blooms without disturbing the water of the nuclear lily pond in which they flower, and, indeed, the whole world lives.'

'The first is the bloom of greatest quality,' he continued, turning directly to the Ayatollah's representative, 'and it is the most difficult to reach. By supporting Islamic Fundamentalism we plan to build three stepping stones to reach it: through Moslem insurrections in Afghanistan, Soviet Central Asia and Outer Mongolia.'

'Of the other two, the third is the easiest to reach and can be plucked at any time by stretching out an arm from Southern China. The second is just as easy to reach from Japan, but should be plucked last.'

Oyama then went on to analyse how the stepping stones should be placed.

'Lenin used to say that the revolutionary road to London ran through Calcutta,' he began. 'Tzu Te and I suggest to you that the route to Vladivostok across the nuclear lily pond starts in Baghdad.'

The Ayatollah's *jihad* in Afghanistan, he said, was blazing and was being stoked rather than dowsed by Soviet repression. The same could be said of Central Asia, though the insurrection there was less advanced and needed additional political support. The Chinese government had agreed that Sinkiang 'at the request of its people' could become an Islamic state within the Chinese Peoples' Republic, and this would be announced publically in the communiqué at the end of the conference. No special political measures were needed in Outer Mongolia where the long standing irredentist movement was gaining more and more support as the Soviet repression in Central Asia gathered momentum. Action there would have to be timed carefully. There were twenty Soviet divisions in Outer Mongolia. Until some of these had been drawn westwards by Soviet difficulties in Afghanistan and Central Asia, or the Soviet will to resist was seen to be weakening, the Outer Mongolian Government was unlikely to defect from Moscow to join Peking. When it did, it would need Chinese military support on a large scale to win its independence. That support was being positioned.

Oyama then turned to the plucking of the main Manchurian lotus bloom. The scope for political finesse was limited and there was little or no Islamic influence that could be exploited. The population of the maritime provinces was largely Russian. Success could only come through military action. Plans were being laid and troops trained for a two phase offensive: a threat northwards across the Amur River on a wide front to sever the two tracks of the Trans-Siberian Railway, which formed the main Soviet Line of Communication to their Eastern Maritime Provinces; and then a direct attack on Vladivostok itself. When Vladivostok fell it would be time for the Japanese amphibious strike forces to take Sakhalin, the Kurils and the Kamchatka Peninsula.

'But,' Oyama concluded, 'great strategic concepts rarely go according to plan. The unexpected always happens. The timings, sequence and intermediate objectives of Plan *White Lotus* are flexible: only the ultimate objective – Vladivostok – is fixed.'

Tzu Te, the tactician took over the briefing once more to describe in broad outline the preparations made so far for military action. One of the keys to success was the creation of a road, rail and air network from Harbin in Manchuria to Kashgar in Sinkiang along which Chinese reserves could be moved east and west more quickly than the Soviets could use their trans-Siberian communications. It had been an immensely costly venture, but it had been completed successfully in 2024.

There had not been much change in the frontier garrisons or in the static security framework within China, both of which had been low on the military re-equipment programme. Most money and effort had been concentrated upon the creation of five air-mobile strike forces and a Central Strategic Reserve. They were:

1st (Central Asian) Strike Force in Sinkiang.
2nd (Mongolian) Strike Force in Inner Mongolia.
3rd (Manchurian) Strike Force around Harbin.
4th (Cantonese) Strike Force in Kwangsi.
5th (Yunnan) Strike Force around Kunming.
Central Strategic Reserve around Suchow.

The Japanese Self Defence Forces were similarly organised with two amphibious Strike Forces and a Strategic Reserve:

Amphibious Strike Force, North would be responsible for operations in Sakhalin, the Kuriles and the Kamchatka Peninsula.
Amphibious Strike Force, South was to reinforce the defence of the South East Asia Co-prosperity Sphere.
Central Strategic Reserve was most likely to operate northwards.

When Tzu Te had completed the military presentation of *White Lotus*, Chairman Chu rose to apply the high level political gloss from the Chinese point of view. He reminded the conference that the longer term political aim of the Hong Kong Treaty powers was the fulfilment of the Charter of the China Seas by the creation of a new world government more appropriate to the needs of the 21st century. The danger was that the existing superpowers would unite to re-impose the antiquated United Nations Charter and its veto system that was so much to their advantage. They must be kept divided and defeated in detail, as the military say, by both political and military means.

Keeping them divided and, indeed, at each other's throats should not be difficult. Restlessness among the members of the Warsaw Pact and the continuing rumblings about German unification, should keep their horns locked together across the Iron Curtain; and there would be no relaxation on the Purple Line as long as the Russians stayed in occupation of Tehran. A decision had yet to be taken as to which superpower should be brought to heel first. However, Chu himself was in little doubt that it should be the Soviet Union, using *Plan White Lotus* as the means. He had high hopes that the United States, under O'Dwyer's Presidency, might be brought round to accepting the Charter of the China Seas as a reasonable basis for negotiation by political rather than military pressure.

He then revealed that he and Nogi had discussed their personal division of responsibility and had concluded that Peking would mastermind the undoing of the Soviet Union, using military action if necessary, while Tokyo concentrated upon neutralising American opposition, principally by political means.

Nogi had the last word. In his winding up speech, he thanked the military staff for their lucid presentaiton of *White Lotus* and confirmed his agreement to the division of responsibility between Peking and Tokyo. He then said that he had been concerned for some time about the position of the Copps military cell.

'Tzu Te's and Oyama's work cannot remain secret for much longer,' he said. 'If they are to direct the Co-prosperity military effort effectively, they must be seen to be doing so publically and on behalf of both governments and their allies.'

He then proposed the setting up of a military command for the Alliance similar to NATO, which would be called the East Asian Treaty Organisation initially. If success smiled on the Alliance, it might become the Asian

Treaty Organisation or even the Afro-Asian Treaty Organisation. The Copps military cell would provide the foundation members of the EATO military staff.

Turning directly to Chu, he said:

'I wish to propose here and now that General Tzu Te should become the Supreme Commander, East Asia, with General Oyama as his deputy. I hope Chairman Chu will agree to Tzu Te's promotion to the rank of Marshal on assuming the appointment.'

There was spontaneous applause in which Chu joined with genuine enthusiasm. Nogi's final words were:

'I call upon Chairman Chu to assume the role of political director of *White Lotus* while I continue with the development of the Co-prosperity concept in the Third World and to attract as many as possible of the superpowers' satellites into our orbit.'

Oyama had been wise to stress, during the *White Lotus* briefing, the need for strategic flexibility to meet the unexpected. It was to be the 4th or 5th Strike Forces in Southern China that saw military action first, rather than the 1st and 2nd in Central Asia. He had said that the Vietnamese bloom could be picked at any time by stretching out an arm from Southern China, but the general impression Tzu Te and he had given was that he expected Central Asia to be ablaze first.

Unexpected events usually cast their shadows before them, but they are only visible to historians in retrospect. At the time, men either fail to recognise the import of the events leading up to a crisis or choose to ignore them. In 2021 the Kremlin had reacted with malign hostility to the formation of the South East Asia Co-prosperity Sphere and had started to bring political pressure to bear upon Thailand and Burma through its Vietnamese satellite to pre-empt their joining Nogi's creation. Moscow had some success in both countries where the various political parties took opposing views on the merits of Nogi-ism.

In Rangoon there was no great interest in the issue, but the Soviet Ambassador was able to report that the anti-Nogi-ists had the upper hand and that Burma was unlikely to leave its neutralist orbit. The situation was very different in Bangkok. Japanese capital and know-how had been pouring into Thailand since the mid-1970's. However, with laudable restraint, the Japanese had avoided political involvement in Thai internal affairs. Their economic success was a shining example of all that was best in Nogi-ism: all levels of society in Thailand benefited from the Japanese economic stake in the country. Nevertheless, the Thai people have an acute awareness of trends in international politics, which had enabled Thailand to maintain its independence throughout the European colonial era. In 2025 they were split on whether to seek 'association' with the South East Asian Co-prosperity Sphere or not. (Being a Buddhist state they could hardly become full members unless its Islamic connotations were dropped.) The Thai Government, headed by Prince Chandra and backed by the Army, favoured Nogi-ism and opened negotiations for 'association'. The main opposition came from senior naval and air force officers, who accused Prince Chandra of diminishing Thai sovereignty, and from cliques in the business community, whose trading monopolies might be endangered.

Vietnamese agents were not slow to take advantage of the crack that was opening up in the Thai political establishment. Radio Hanoi started a virulent anti-Nogi-ist propaganda campaign beamed on Thailand, and the Soviet embassy in Bangkok made it clear to the Thai Government that flirting with the Co-prosperity concept might strain Thai-Soviet relations to breaking point.

In May 2025, Nogi was advised by the Japanese Ambassador in Bangkok that negotiations were deadlocked due to internal opposition which was unlikely to be broken without his personal intervention. Conscious that under the *White Lotus* plan he was responsible for using the velvet glove to cover Chu's mailed fist, he accepted an invitation from Prince Chandra to visit Bangkok on 25th June to initial the heads of the 'Association' agreement. The announcement of his visit unleashed a new wave of internal criticism in Bangkok and external abuse from Hanoi. The Thai opposition claimed that the Prince was selling Thailand's independence for a mess of potage in the form of a bowl full of Japanese electronic components; and the Vietnamese announced that they could not be expected to face with equanimity the prospect of being encircled by satellites of the Hong Kong Treaty powers. The Vietnamese, Hanoi Radio claimed, prized their independence every bit as much as the Thais and would look to their friends in the Soviet Union to help them preserve it. To add substance to their threat, they announced joint Soviet-Vietnamese-Cambodian amphibious exercises off the Cambodian coast in the Gulf of Siam.

Nogi was about to take off from Tokyo for Bangkok on 24th June when news reached him that there had been an anti-Nogi-ist coup in Thailand and that Prince Chandra had been replaced by air force General Phumi as Prime Minister. Nogi returned to his office in Tokyo, and a few hours later heard that Vietnamese troops had crossed the Thai border to support the new Government of Thailand 'in its just stand against Japanese neo-imperialism.'

Nogi was momentarily abashed by Vietnamese sabre rattling: Chu was not. Marshal Tzu Te was directed to start the implementation of the *White Lotus* contingency plan for picking the Vietnamese bloom straight away. 4th (Cantonese) Strike Force was brought to immediate readiness for an advance on Hanoi via Langson, and 5th (Yunnan) Strike Force was to move down the old Burma Road to threaten Lashio and possibly Mandalay. Tzu Te was warned that both offensives, if they were launched, would have the limited object of frightening the Vietnamese, Thai and Burmese

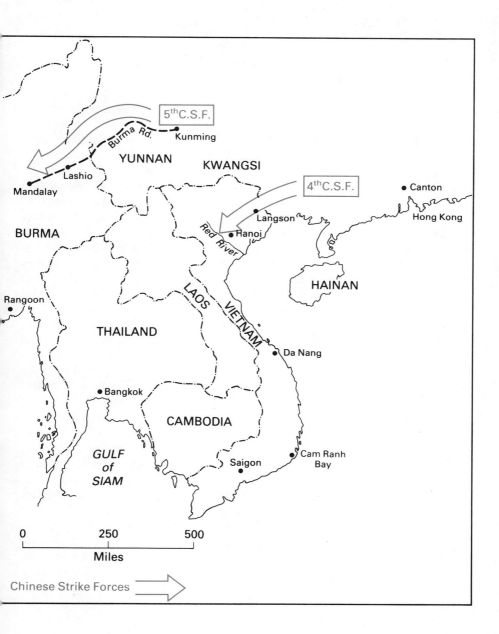

MAP 12: The Chinese Invasion of Vietnam, 2025

Governments and of demonstrating to the world at large the awesome capability of China's military forces. *Crow* as well as *Sparrow* class weapons were to be used at maximum intensity, but the 'Hawks' would be kept in reserve. They were only to be fired if the Soviets intervened from Da Nang or Cam Ranh Bay, and then only on Chu's personal authority.

The Vietnamese invasion of Thailand was a grave error of judgement. It united all Thais behind Prince Chandra and enabled him to topple General Phumi in a counter-coup. On the advice of the Japanese Ambassador, Prince Chandra called upon the Hong Kong Treaty powers to help Thailand resist Vietnamese aggression. Chu responded by demanding withdrawal of Vietnamese troops from Thailand and was met with a contemptuous silence from Hanoi. 4th Chinese Strike Force crossed the Vietnamese frontier on 1st July and was in Langson that evening.

The Chinese 2025 invasion of Vietnam echoed their 1962 invasion of India. It was just as punitive and equally successful in demonstrating China's power, ability and willingness to strike her Asian neighbours. It also partially unveiled the performance of the new and advanced Sino-Japanese weapon systems, and the frightening efficiency with which they were handled. The Vietnamese frontier defences crumpled under the weight and accuracy of the initial *Crow* salvos. This was understandable because they had been exactly pin-pointed before the invasion began, but the accuracy of the *Eye of Heaven* target acquisition systems in the mobile fighting that took place on the road to Hanoi was just as good. It enabled them to use their *Crow* salvos to suppress the Vietnamese surface-to-air missile batteries and anti-helicopter weapon systems before 4th Strike Force's heli-borne assault units were committed. Hitler's *Wehrmacht* had panicked its enemies with the noise and concentrated destructive effect of its *Blitzkreig*; the Japanese had relied on encircling their opponents; the Chinese now combined the two methods to destroy Vietnamese morale. The noise, accuracy and devastation of the *Crow* suppressive fire might have been tolerable by themselves, but not when coupled with air-borne encirclement. In the earlier engagements, the Vietnamese made the Chinese pay dearly for their successes, but fear is cumulative in its effect and Vietnamese demoralisation snowballed. Panic engulfed the defenders of Hanoi, which fell on 10th July. The Vietnamese Government panicked too and fled south to Ho Chi Minh City (Old Saigon).

The day after the fall of Hanoi, Chairman Chu announced that the Chinese forces would halt on the Red River 'to give the Vietnamese Government time for self-criticism.' He also informed the world that the 5th Strike Force had entered Lashio via the old Burma road, but would delay its advance on Mandalay to give the Burmese Government time to consider 'the advantages of friendly relations with the Hong Kong Treaty powers.'

The political establishments in Saigon and Rangoon were as divided as

Bangkok's had been over the merits of Nogi-ism. In both capitals there were pro-Moscow, pro-Peking and neutralist political factions. The fall of Hanoi, without any sign of Russian military intervention on the Vietnamese behalf, swelled the ranks of the pro-Peking cliques in both capitals. The Burmese Government, with no Soviet bases on its soil, had no difficulty in accepting 'friendly guidance from Peking in the cause of Asian unity'. In Saigon it took a pro-Peking *coup d'état* to reach the same conclusion and to go further by demanding that Moscow should withdraw its forces from Vietnamese soil. Few observers expected the Kremlin to do more than prevaricate, but surprisingly Moscow followed the precedent set by their withdrawal from Egypt in the 1970's when requested to do so by President Sadat. They did not make the British mistake of trying to maintain military bases in countries hostile to their presence. They agreed to evacuate Cam Ranh Bay and Da Nang by 2028, provided all Chinese troops had also been withdrawn from Vietnam by that date, no doubt expecting the political pendulum to swing back in their favour as deep seated Vietnamese fears of Chinese domination and inevitable Chinese arrogance once more soured Sino-Vietnamese relations.

Moscow was not the only capital to be disadvantaged by the Chinese punitive invasions of Vietnam and Burma. Delhi became understandably alarmed about the arrival of Chinese troops in Northern Burma, and sought United States and Commonwealth political and military support. President O'Dwyer did not believe there was any real threat to India, and, in any case, he had no wish to take on additional strategic commitments so soon after his election victory won on the disengagement issue. The British Government was equally sceptical, but Britain's historic ties with India could not be ignored, despite the many occasions on which India had sided against her since Independence in 1947. The Chiefs of Staff, however, advised that British military resources could only be provided at the expense of the formation and training of the NATO Strategic Reserve, which was at last showing satisfactory progress. They recommended that it would be more appropriate for Australia and New Zealand as Indian Ocean/Pacific powers to go to India's assistance.

In Australasia there had been mounting anxiety about the true nature of Nogi-ism. The successful creation of the South East Asian Co-prosperity Sphere had worried Canberra and Wellington as much as Moscow. Would it pose a threat to Australian and New Zealand interests in Asia and perhaps, in due course, to their security as well? Both Governments recognised that they had a stake in maintaining Asian stability. The Indian request for support, and the British reluctance to weaken their forces committed to NATO, led to an ANZAC force arriving on the old battlefields of Kohima and Imphal on the Indo-Burmese frontier as a symbolic gesture of Commonwealth solidarity with India.

Tzu Te and Oyama were far from dissatisifed with events as they had unfolded during the first half of 2025. If the Soviet agreement to leave Vietnam by 2028 was fulfilled, they would have plucked the third of the three *White Lotus* blooms earlier than they expected. In the second half of the year, the campaigning season in Afghanistan brought more *Mujahideen* successes, and the trickle of refugees and defectors crossing into Sinkiang from Soviet Central Asia, which had been spasmodic thitherto, was becoming a significant migration. Several Soviet divisions had left Outer Mongolia without replacement, suggesting that the Russians might be finding Asian nationalism as difficult to crush within the Soviet Union as the Americans had found it to be in Vietnam in the 1970's. The stepping stones to the main *White Lotus* bloom were being slid into position.

At the turn of the year, Oyama gave a reception for all Tokyo's military attachés to celebrate the first anniversary of the decision to set up EATO. Tzu Te was guest of honour as it was also the anniversary of his appointment as Supreme Allied Commander East Asia and his promotion to the five-star rank of Marshal. At many receptions of this type my hosts often made a point of introducing me to the guest of honour because, as a sucessful female military officer, I was a diplomatic curiosity! On this occasion I sensed there was more to it. I knew Oyama well enough to realise that he had something important on his mind when he came over to me and asked whether I would like to be introduced to the Supreme Commander. I noticed also that Tzu Te's aides were clearly keeping other people away from the Marshal as Oyama led me over to meet him.

Tzu Te looked every inch a Supreme Commander with an imposing presence and a natural charm that flowed from personal self-confidence. When we shook hands, I congratulated him on the success of the 4th Strike Force's operations in Vietnam. He laughed and said:

'Yes, it was gratifying, but, as I am sure you appreciate, it did not all go according to plan. We have a lot to learn in this electronic age. It was a very useful troop trial, but no more than that; but it did teach the Vietnamese a lesson. Fear works wonders in all walks of life.'

I suggested that other people had learnt a lot of lessons too. He laughed again and said that was why he wanted to meet me.

'I don't know why you British rushed to India's help. Jawal Gandhi exaggerates. We are posing no threat to India. India has never been a Chinese tributary, even during the greatest days of the Ch'ing dynasty.'

'Nor is there a threat to Australia and New Zealand. We all admire the British Commonwealth for its multi-racialism and its sense of common purpose that gives it unity without the shackles of imperial power. It is the exemplar of the Co-prosperity concept of Chairman Chu and Prime Minister Nogi. We, Asians, cannot abide the arrogance of the Russians and Americans.'

He turned to Oyama as if seeking his support. Oyama picked up his cue beautifully:

'We, in Japan, have always looked back with pleasure on the Anglo-Japanese Alliance of 1902, which was destroyed by American jealousy in the 1920's. Our ideals and political systems have so much in common, and technologically we are on the same wave length, as the *HOTOL* success has shown.'

It is the job of all diplomats, military as well as political, to pick up and relay signals to their Governments. I realised that Tzu Te and Oyama had just delivered a deliberately contrived message which they expected me to pass on to the British Ambassador. I thanked them for their confidence in our British way of life and gave way as an aide appropriately brought up the next guest for introduction.

Few diplomatic messages delivered verbally at a social function can be taken at their face value. They have to be de-coded, preferably by those who have the full facts at their fingertips, which I certainly did not. Instead of going back to my flat after the reception I drove to the Ambassador's house where I knew he was giving a farewell dinner party for the First Secretary, who was leaving Tokyo on promotion. I had been invited but had had to refuse because Oyama's reception took precedence. When I arrived at the residency the men were still drinking their port, but Sir Miles Brown invited me to join them rather than the ladies in the drawing room.

The great danger of being a diplomatic courier is to allow one's imagination to garble the message. Was I certain, Sir Miles asked, that Oyama had deliberately engineered the meeting and that Tzu Te's aides made a special effort to keep other guests away during our brief conversation? A fleeting doubt momentarily crossed my mind, but I managed to assure him that this was so. Was I equally sure, the new First Secretary asked, that he was not just delivering a warning about the startling success achieved by the new Sino-Japanese weapon systems? Their effect was reputed to be more psychological than lethal, and Tzu Te was perhaps trying to add to their psychological impact by exaggerating their performance.

I must have given convincing answers to this port-fuelled inquisition because after dinner Sir Miles took me into his study to draft a cable to the Foreign and Commonwealth Office, reporting the exact wording of the conversation so that the Joint Intelligence Committee could consider its implications. Sir Miles gave it as his view that the message was genuine and that it was possibly a probe to see whether Britain could be persuaded to play a 'constructive' role in the growing conflict between Asia and the two existing superpowers.

Thus the first seeds were sown, which were to germinate a decade later when the Treaty of London was signed in 2035 – but that is anticipating the story of the Apocalypse.

11

The White Backlash
(2026–2028)

*'The White backlash, which we have always
feared, has begun: the old Boer Republics
have declared UDI, and are backed by
the French in Shaba.'*
Diary entry for 2nd April 2028

Looking at the world from the British Embassy in Tokyo, while at the same time seeing the diplomatic cables from other British Embassies around the globe, made me appreciate the importance of the Foreign Office clichés about maintaining world stability. Both the Chinese punitive invasion of Vietnam and the Chinese support being given to the Ayatollah's *Jihad* in Central Asia via the newly established Islamic province of Sinkiang looked dangerously de-stabilising to me. The Japanese electorate certainly thought so too.

'If Chu goes too far,' a Japanese acquaintance of mine remarked, 'all our achievements will be swept away for a second time in eighty years by nuclear weapons. The Chinese do not understand the price we may all have to pay for their ambitions.'

A public expression of Japanese anxiety came during the annual and still deeply emotional Remembrance Day ceremony at Hiroshima. Despite the solemnity of the occasion, a massive anti-Nogi-ist demonstration was staged by radical extremists that led to ten days of street violence in several Japanese cities, including Tokyo. They were only calmed by a personal appearance by Nogi on television. He announced that he was setting out on a world pilgrimage to seek support for the immediate rebuilding of a new world security organisation based upon the principles set out in the Charter of the China Seas. Knowing that it was fear of Chu's actions that lay at the root of the recent unrest, he produced his now famous analogy of the Magnolia tree:

194

'Co-prosperity, is like a Magnolia Tree. It will only thrive if carefully tended, and it will not flower if it is over-hung by neighbouring trees. They must be pruned back when necessary. Chairman Chu was quite right to use his pruning hook on the Vietnamese tree to enable South East Asian Co-propserity to bloom.'

Nogi had been Prime Minister since 2013 and he knew that, although his doctors had managed to keep his own heart condition under control, his twelve years in power had hardened the arteries of his party and taken a toll of its electoral popularity. He needed an outstanding diplomatic triumph to ensure his own survival and to assuage Japanese and international fears that Nogi-ism was turning into little more than a cloak for Sino-Japanese aggression. Chu's mailed fist had become too blatant and had frightened world opinion. It was up to Nogi to correct the balance with his velvet glove.

While Tzu Te concentrated upon the control of *White Lotus*, Oyama became the *éminence grise* behind Nogi's peace offensive and the organiser of his world tour, which was reminiscent of the Kennedy tours of the 1960's, when the United States was grasping world leadership. Nogi's public image was to be of *A man of Peace and Co-prosperity*, intent on bringing stability to an increasingly unstable world. There were four areas of instability: the Purple Line, the Iron Curtain, Latin America and Southern Africa. Success in just one of the four would be seen at home and abroad as a major diplomatic triumph for Nogi-ism. Oyama suggested that Nogi would be wise to avoid entanglement in the Islamic *Jihad*, which was being directed by the Ayatollah with Chu's support. He should also avoid overt interference in European affairs. He would not be welcome and, in any case, Chu was depending upon tension between the superpowers in Europe to hold Soviet forces in the West while he pursued his *White Lotus* plans in the East. Oyama, therefore, recommended concentrating on the two lesser targets of helping the Archbishop to bring Co-prosperity to Latin America and M'Bundu to do the same thing in Africa.

While Nogi agreed with Oyama's strategic arguments, he felt that his life's work would not be complete unless he could start the rebuilding of the world's security organisation. He would not get much help from the superpowers, who were well content to go on dominating the world without Third World interference. He had high hopes, however, that he might find kindred spirits in western Europe, who must be as irked as he was with superpower hegemony. In particular, the British, with their long history of involvement in Afro-Asia and their attachment to liberal-morality, would be useful allies. After all, the principles, upon which their Empire and later their Commonwealth had been based, were not far removed from Nogi-ist Co-prosperity. He felt sure he could find the basis of renewed Anglo-Japanese political understanding through personal contacts in London.

Oyama was too much of a courtier to tell Nogi that he and Tzu Te had already come to the same conclusion and had conveyed a very similar message through me to London at Oyama's reception nine months earlier. He merely smiled and agreed that Nogi should visit London and Western European capitals first, then the Americas, and finally Southern Africa.

No British Government, or any other government for that matter, can ever resist the temptation to play international peace-keeper if the opportunity arises. Sir Miles Brown had no difficulty in persuading the Foreign and Commonwealth Office to invite Nogi to London at the beginning of his world tour. Although November was hardly the best month in which to visit England, Nogi's time was far from wasted. His quiet engaging personality brought him many British friends. Just the right notes were struck and he left London feeling that he had established a *rapport* with British Ministers and their officials. Common bonds were forged between the governments of the two most important off-shore islands of the Eurasian continent. The clock seemed to have been turned back over a century to the happier days of the Anglo-Japanese Treaty of 1902.

Nogi's visits to Bonn and Paris were less cordial. Japanese trading policies did not endear them to the West Germans; and, although they were still as reluctant as the Japanese to strut on the world stage, they were equally averse to anyone else interfering in their *Ostpolitik* and cautious steps towards German re-unification. They made it quite clear to Nogi that they were not interested in his Co-prosperity concept or his Charter of the China Seas.

The French were even cooler. They knew that Tokyo had replaced Moscow as the principal sponsor of M'Bundu's Homelander Union. The Homelander failure in East Africa had enabled the Black American expatriates, who had streamed across the Atlantic in the early years of the century, to regain the ascendency in Kinshasa and to oust the old fashioned Moscow orientated members from M'Bundu's government. Instead of continuing with attempts to overthrow the Francophile government of Shaba by guerrilla warfare and subversion, M'Bundu accepted expatriate advice that economic development was more important than territorial aggrandisement. Black American capital and technology began to flow across the Atlantic again; and after the Okinawa Conference Sino-Japanese aid came across the Indian Ocean as well. By 2026 a minor economic miracle had occurred in Black Homelander states and irredentist factions in Shaba started to press for re-union with Zaire and the Homelander Union much to the annoyance of the French. Nogi's reception in Paris reflected the French mood. There was no meeting of minds: only an agreement to differ.

Nogi returned home briefly for the Christmas and New Year holiday period, which always brings a lull in the world's diplomatic activity, before flying off eastwards across the Pacific to start his American tour. He was again in a depressed mood when he met Oyama in Tokyo. He sensed that the Western world was becoming introverted and more intent on its own interests than on the problems of world stability. There had been some debate in the original planning of his itinerary about whether he should visit Washington first or fly direct to Bogota. Oyama had argued for Washington on the grounds that President O'Dwyer might be offended if he placed Bogota before Washington. Nogi had disagreed. He did not want to look like a United States emissary when he met the Archbishop. Now he was delighted that he had reversed Oyama's proposal. His European experience made him determined to project himself as the champion of the Third World as well as being a man of peace and co-prosperity.

When Nogi reached Bogota in January 2027 he found the Archbishop in an equally despondent mood. His old friend Domingo Garcia had just died after a long lingering illness. The years of anti-American guerrilla operations had taken a toll of Domingo's ebullience and confidence in his Marxist upbringing. At the last cabinet meeting before he died, Domingo had warned his colleagues that they were not being treated fairly by Moscow and Havana. They must either come to terms with the Americans or seek aid from Tokyo and Peking. Nogi's visit could not have been better timed, because the Archbishop had himself come to much the same conclusion. Soviet interest in Latin America was waning as their troubles in Central Asia grew, and he had good reason to believe that the Cuban's were syphoning off the dwindling flow of Eastern Bloc supplies consigned to the Bolivarist guerrillas in Panama. It was time for the Bolivarist movement to change sponsors.

At their first meeting, the Archbishop did some frank talking. The Bolivarists had been grateful for the efforts of Karl Tell in 2018 and of Nogi himself in 2022 to enforce an American withdrawal from Latin America, but they had gone about it in the wrong way. They had tried to negotiate a superpower withdrawal package. What was wanted was a genuine American change of heart and acceptance of Bolivarism for what it really was – a nationalist movement aiming to rid South America of its Spanish and Portuguese heritage of privilege and exploitation. The Christo-Communist label that had been tied round the movement's neck had been justified in the early days. The Church's collaboration with the Communists was but a stepping stone to power. The movement was at heart Christo-Socialist. With United States help, the movement could transform Latin American society: continued hostility would drain United States' resources. Bolivarism was now too deeply rooted to be overturned by outside interference in Latin American affairs.

Nogi was equally forthright in his reply. If the Archbishop wanted his help, he must be prepared to sever his links with both Moscow and Washington, and his movement must become independent, aiming at creating a Latin American Co-prosperity sphere. Nogi would use his good offices in Washington to persuade President O'Dwyer that Bolivarism was no longer Communist inspired or supplied, and was genuinely Christo-Socialist and Nationalist. In return, he would expect the Archbishop to help him in his efforts to rebuild the world's security system upon the foundations of the Charter of the China Seas. Bolivarist Governments were, of course, welcome to buy arms and seek economic aid from the Hong Kong powers. He and Chu were prepared to offer very favourable terms, but they did not believe in interest free loans or outright gifts. Co-prosperity meant standing on your own feet through corporate effort. The details of any aid package that was needed to offset the loss of Eastern Bloc support could be worked out over the next few months through diplomatic channels.

Nogi left Bogota for Washington confident that he had gone a long way towards detaching Latin America from both superpowers and that it would only be a matter of time before the Bolivarist movement was drawn into the Co-prosperity orbit. Moreover, he had something positive to offer President O'Dwyer: the Archibishop's agreement to negotiate with the United States, under Japanese auspices, on all differences preventing the establishment of friendly relations between Washington and Bogota.

It all seemed so simple and logical to Nogi while he was in Bogota, but when he reached Washington he was warned by the Japanese Ambassador to expect a tough and difficult two to three days. A body of opinion had been building up, particularly in Congress, which resented his presence in the U.S. capital. The view was that he and Chu were becoming too big for their boots and needed cutting down to size. The Chinese invasion of Vietnam and Nogi's peace offensive were seen, quite justifiably, as two sides of the same coin: the coin of Sino-Japanese ambition. U.S. public opinion was also critical of Nogi's interference in the affairs of the Western Hemisphere. One influential commentator in the *New York Times* warned Nogi:

'*Beware of generating a White backlash. Co-prosperity is not wanted here.*'

The timing of Nogi's visit to Bogota had been fortuitously opportune. The same could not be said of his arrival in the United States. President O'Dwyer was facing the mid-term elections without having achieved any of the military disengagements he had promised in 2024, and the Republicans were making political capital out of his failure.

O'Dwyer's embarrassment was all the greater when he received a personal and Top Secret memorandum from the Secretary for Defence warning him that, unless there was a major reduction in United States military commitments overseas, the draft would have to be reintroduced. Since the Democrats had won the Presidential election of 2024, there had been a slump in regular recruiting for the Armed Forces. Such was the depth of political disillusion which had swept the United States over the last five years that even higher pay and better conditions were unlikely to bridge the growing gap. America's young men just did not want to join the Services. 'The only alternative,' the Secretary for Defence pointed out, 'was to cut back in Europe, Iran and Panama, or eliminate one of these commitments altogether.'

The usual Presidential reception took place on the White House lawn although there was snow on the ground. Both leaders made mercifully short speeches, extolling each other and their respective countries, and then retired for their first meeting away from the blaze of publicity. They had two particular things in common: each needed a personal triumph in foreign relations for internal political reasons, and each held a concealed card in his hand which might bring that triumph about, if played with sufficient finesse.

The first meeting was as cold as the weather outside. The President had been briefed to be frostily non-commital: the United States had no interest in resuscitating or rebuilding a veto-less United Nations, and Japanese interference in Western Hemisphere affairs was deeply resented. Even Nogi's well known charisma did not warm the atmosphere. It was made quite clear to him that United States did not view the Hong Kong powers as a stabilising influence, nor the Charter of the China Seas as particularly helpful in preserving world peace. The first session ended with an agreement to turn away from generalities and to deal with specifics at the next session.

At the second meeting Nogi decided to play the secret card in his hand. The United States might not like his visit to Bogota, but he had established a useful *rapport* with the Archbishop, who had assured him that he was severing his links with the Soviet Union and the Eastern Bloc, and would welcome collaboration with the United States. His movement had swung away from its Communist origins and was now becoming Christo-Socialist. The Archbishop was not pressing for the withdrawal of American troops, but for greater understanding by the United States of his motives, which could eventually lead to their voluntary withdrawal.

The United States Secretary of State and Defence Secretary, who were attending the meeting, poured cold water on Nogi's suggestion. They had heard it all before. What proof had he of the severance of links with Moscow? American intelligence sources suggested just the opposite. And there was no hard evidence of any real acceptance of social democracy amongst the leading Bolivarists. Nogi could see no sign of American hostility to Bolivar and all his works diminishing, but, with his own personal position at stake, he fought back, arguing that the United States had little to lose by exploring *rapprochment* with the Bolivarists. The second session ended without much to show for the hours spent in debate or the piles of briefing material consumed by both sides.

Nogi went off to meet the Japanese community in Washington that evening at an Embassy reception feeling that he was faced with failure. He was quite unaware that the President was in the Oval Office confronting his principal advisers and wielding the card that Nogi knew nothing about. During the second session O'Dwyer had realised that Nogi was quite unconsciously offering him a way out of his acute mid-term dilemma of trying to cut back apparently irreducible commitments or drinking the political hemlock of re-introducing the draft despite all his election promises. By the time he retired to bed that night he had forced the Defence Secretary to admit that a withdrawal from Panama would, at least temporarily, balance his manpower books, and he had won the Secretary of State's agreement to accept Nogi's good offices next day.

The third and final session was a charade. The American team put on a display of reluctance to accept the validity of Nogi's assumptions, but showed a willingness to probe Bolivarist intentions with Nogi's help. The Japanese for their part played down any hopes that disengagement might be achieved, but expressed gratification at the American willingness to meet the Archbishop's negotiators. During the drafting of the final communiqué the American officials strove to exclude the words 'Prime Minister Nogi's good offices' to avoid any suggestion that an Asian political leader had intervened successfully in the affairs of the Western Hemisphere. Nogi made it quite clear that his reputation in Asia was just as important as O'Dwyer's in the Americas. They both needed this diplomatic triumph which should be shared equally between them.

The U.S./Bolivarist negotiations, which began in April 2027, proved long and tortuous, but did, in the end, lead to a United States acceptance of the legitimacy of the Bolivarist movement and to the voluntary withdrawal of U.S. troops from Panama in 2028. Christo-Socialism became the predominant influence in Latin America. By the time the Archbishop died in 2030, a South American Co-prosperity Sphere had been established under another name. The Treaty of Bogota, which was signed by all the South American states shortly before his death, brought the Latin American Common Market into being. One of the four horsemen had reached his 'new heaven and new earth!'

But this happy outcome still lay in the mists and uncertainties of the future. The immediate effect of the Washington visit on Nogi was traumatic. He felt that he had been talked down to by the Americans, and had been treated with the disdain meted out to the European 'Red Devils' by Chinese Emperors in the 18th century. There had always been a love-hate relationship between the Japanese and Americans ever since Commodore Perry had negotiated the U.S.-Japanese Treaty of 1854, which ended Japan's self-imposed isolation from world affairs. As Nogi left Washington a lot of hate and very little love pulsed through his emotions. He was determined not to seek any American support in future for the creation of his brave new world.

Nogi set off for the southern African leg of his world tour in June 2027. Unlike his arrival in Bogota, where he had found a very depressed Archbishop, he was greeted by an obviously elated M'Bundu when he reached Kinshasa. His host had just received an invitation from President Joseph Yombi of Azania to fly to Cape Town to initial the heads of agreement for the formation of a Southern African Co-prosperity Sphere on Nogi-ist lines.

M'Bundu and most Black Africans had high hopes that the Co-prosperity agreement would lead eventually to the fulfilment of Noah Johnston's dream of a United States of Southern Africa, free from the inhibiting influence of tribalism. To the White and Coloured communities, however, the timing could not have been worse. In 2030 the entrenched clauses in the Azanian Constitution were due to lapse at the thirty-five year point. The separate White electoral rolls would be replaced by universal franchise, in which there were to be no racial distinctions. To be submerged, at the same time, in an even larger and increasingly successful Black dominated common market was more than some of the White tribes, particularly the Afrikaners, could stand. During the preliminary negotiations between M'Bundu and Yombi, these fears had not been fully articulated. By the time of Nogi's visit, what had been no more than a cloud on the horizon, had become a billowing thunder storm lowering over the Azanian political landscape.

Nogi was naturally delighted that his philosophy was spilling over into Africa, and with the economic miracle wrought in Southern Africa by the Sino-Japanese aid programme, but he was alarmed by the White reaction in Azania, in Francophile Shaba and in Europe. The wounds inflicted during the long struggle to end *apartheid* in the 1980's and 1990's were only partially healed and were still festering in the old Boer Provinces of the Orange Free State and the Transvaal. Japanese intelligence sources amongst the business communities warned him that clandestine links were being forged between the Afrikaners and the French in Shaba, and that sympathies in Paris, Bonn and the Hague lay with the White minority.

When Nogi reached Cape Town a week after his visit to Kinshasa, he was invited by President Yombi to address the Azanian parliament as the father of the modern Co-prosperity concept. In his speech he concentrated on the merits of corporate individualism and its prospects in overcoming Africa's tribal problems. In the first half of his speech, he adopted the tactic of telling his audience what they wanted to hear and they applauded him. Then his mood became sombre as he adjured them to read the Charter of the China Seas very carefully, and not selectively. It called for majority rule, but it also insisted upon adequate safeguards for the interests of minorities. He had no intention of interfering in the internal affairs of Azania, but as an old friend and fellow Afro-Asian he felt himself in duty bound to say:

'In my view, it is too early to dispense with the entrenched clauses in your 1995 Constitution. It would be a great act of statesmanship, Mr President, to extend their validity for at least a further decade while you

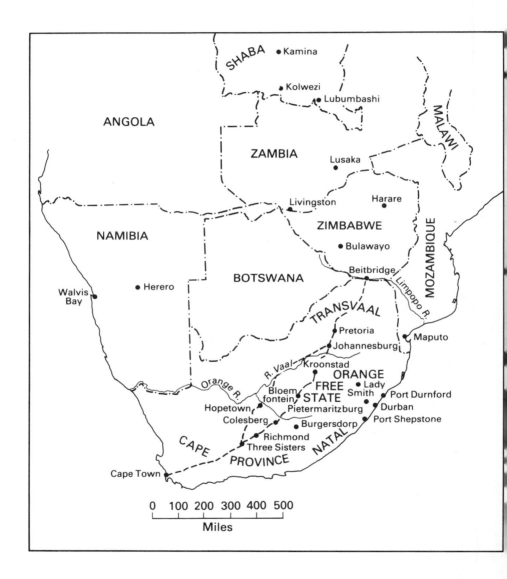

MAP 13: Afrikaner UDI: 2028

consolidate your Co-prosperity. Success will lead to success, and the entrenched clauses will become increasingly irrelevant as the years pass and prosperity spreads more evenly.'

Nogi's speech will probably be seen to have been as historic as Macmillan's 'Wind of Change' speech, delivered in the same chamber almost seventy years earlier. Macmillan's fell on determinedly deaf White ears: Nogi's fell on equally unresponsive Black ones with even more disastrous consequences.

Moderate opinion in Africa and the world at large accepted the good sense of Nogi's speech, but the militant minorities at either end of the racial spectrum were exasperated by it. The Black nationalists saw it as an insult and the White extremists as a sell out. The Whites demanded not just a ten year postponement, but the permanent entrenchment of their tribal rights. If Joseph Yombi had acted at once with a proposal along the lines Nogi had suggested, moderation might have prevailed. It was, however, too big a step to take without careful political preparation. He hesitated and was lost.

Throughout the rest of 2027 political attitudes hardened. Action and reaction were, as ever, equal and opposite, and misunderstandings, cross-purposes and downright deceit abounded as the political cauldron bubbled. Azania split as the United States had done before the American Civil War. The new Mason-Dixon line ran along the Orange River and the western borders of Natal. The rights of the White Afrikaners replaced abolition of slavery as the *casus belli* and lip-service was paid by both sides to the preservation of the Azanian Union.

Since 1995 the Azanian provinces of the Cape and Natal with their British traditions had become comfortably multi-racial and proud of their sucessful racial integration. They viewed Nogi's proposed extension of the White franchise as reasonable, but unnecessary and not entirely welcome. In the old Boer provinces the extension was not seen as just reasonable: it was considered vital. The ending of *apartheid* thirty years earlier had not led to a multi-racial society in the lands of the *Voortrekkers*. Racial discrimination was outlawed, but in its place had come a natural pecking order in which the Afrikaners exerted their supremacy by force of personality, strength of purpose and a paternalism which few Black Africans could match. The Black population showed by their votes in recent Transvaal and Orange Free State elections that they preferred the peace of natural *apartheid* to the miseries of the struggle against offical *apartheid* which had originally brought Azania into being.

The keys to Azanian stability lay in the composition and loyalty of the security forces. If they had been re-organised on truly multi-racial lines in 1995, it would have been very difficult for the Afrikaners to take the law into their own hands. The Army and Police were, however, organised on traditionally British territorial lines. The Army's regiments were recruited territorially and had geographic titles, and the Police were both recruited locally and owed their allegiance to the provincial rather than national governments. Moreover, the boundaries and responsibilities of the four major Army Commands coincided with those of the four provinces. The Constitution only laid down that units were to reflect the racial balance of the area from which they were recruited and this was rigorously imposed. Above regimental level, however, ability rather than ethnic origin was the criteria for senior officer promotion, though the latter was taken into account in deciding the appointments to which they were posted.

As tension rose in the autumn of 2027, increasing numbers of Afrikaner officers serving in posts south of the Orange River or in Natal either resigned or applied for postings to the north. Military and police loyalties began to polarise as they had done before the American Civil War, and the authorities in Cape Town did the same as the Federal Government in Washington had done in 1860: they closed their eyes to the implications and hoped that by so doing not to exacerbate the crisis through advertising its existence.

World opinion polarised too. Most Europeans and Anglo-Saxon North Americans sided with Pretoria, while American ethnic minorities and the Afro-Asians united solidly behind Cape Town. There was clear evidence of the growing White backlash that Nogi and Chu had always feared. The danger was that Oyama's nuclear lily pond might be disturbed, not by trying to pluck one of the three *White Lotus* blooms of Asia, but by stretching out too far for the less important Co-prosperity flowers in Africa. Nogi realised that M'Bundu's and Yombi's determination not to be deflected from their chosen course, was driving the Afrikaners back into their traditional *laager* stubbornness. He again counselled delay, this time to the signing of the actual Co-prosperity Sphere Treaty. But such was the wave of Black political emotion stirred up by the White world's support of the Afrikaners that neither of the Black leaders could pull back. Yombi flew to Kinshasa on 20th January 2028 and in a gesture of defiance signed the Co-prosperity Treaty amidst great pomp and ceremony and to the applause of Afro-Asia.

Next day Paul Vervaal, the undisputed leader of the Afrikaners in the Transvaal and Orange Free State Provinces, proclaimed Afrikaner UDI from the steps of the vast Voortrekker Hoogte (Voortrekker Heights Memorial, the most hallowed Afrikaner shrine) outside Pretoria. In his speech Vervaal spoke of his confidence that the whole of the White Western world would support the restoration of the old Boer Republics under his leadership.

While Vervaal was speaking, the Afrikaner members of the Security Forces in both provinces were putting into effect their carefully planned operation for seizing power. Plan '*High Veldt*' was the brainchild of General Hans Heemskirk, who was GOC of the Transvaal Military Command and principal adviser to Vervaal. He envisaged three phases in the military operations that would be needed to give the two republics a secure future. *High Veldt I* was the disarming of non-Afrikaner soldiers and policemen. *High Veldt II* was the invasion of Natal to secure an outlet to the sea at Durban in case the international community tried to impose sanctions. And *High Veldt III* was the crossing of the Orange River and a decisive advance on Cape Town where terms would be dictated to the Azanian Government. Heemskirk saw himself emulating Frederick the Great, operating on interior lines and beating all who opposed him by swift concentrations of force. Surprise was to be his greatest ally.

High Veldt I was startlingly successful. All armouries, heavy weapons, aircraft and ammunition depots were seized by the Afrikaner members of each military and police unit. Those military and police patrols, which happened to be out of barracks at the time, were disarmed as they returned. Non-Afrikaners were given the option of discharge or continued service in an unarmed capacity, which meant menial service in the army, and community and traffic work in the police. Within forty eight hours *High Veldt I* was complete. It had been a faultless and bloodless coup.

And so it might have remained if the usual random coincidence of events had not decreed otherwise. At Nogi's instigation, Yombi offered to negotiate with Vervaal rather than treating him for what he was: a rebel guilty of high treason. In a speech in the Cape Town Parliament on the day after Boer UDI had been declared, Yombi stressed that the doors were not closed to an extension of the White franchise. A two thirds majority might still be obtained for the amendment to the Constitution. Indeed, no motion had been put, as yet, to Parliament to decide the issue. He then quoted Abraham Lincoln's speech at the same stage in the run up to the American Civil War:

> *'In your hands my dissatisifed fellow-countrymen, and not in mine, is this momentous issue of civil war. The Government will not assault you. You can have no conflict without yourselves being the aggressors. You have no oath registered in Heaven to destroy the Government, while I shall have the most solemn one to preserve and defend it.'*

The Afrikaner response to Yombi's appeal was the pre-planned launching of *High Veldt II* on 1st February 2028. There were a number of senior Afrikaner officers in the Durban garrison, who had deliberately not resigned and were feigning complete loyalty to Azania in general and Natal in particular. Thanks to their treachery, Heemskirk scored his second Afrikaner victory. He captured Durban unopposed with a ruthlessly executed advance by land and air. Most of the people of Natal were apathetic and only wished to avoid being drawn into the conflict. The Asian community, however, felt they had too much to lose by pandering to the Afrikaners. Their leaders sent urgent appeals to Nogi and Jawal Gandhi calling for international intervention.

High Veldt III should have been launched by 15th February, if Heemskirk was to keep to his schedule and maintain the momentum of his offensive. Unexpected events in Shaba dislocated his programme. Anti-White hostility, stirred up by the Afrikaner UDI, gripped Zaire and the rest of the Homelander Union. The French communities scattered throughout Shaba were the nearest and most obvious White targets for revenge. The Black Homelander guerrillas, who had been waging the desultory anti-French campaign in Shaba for years, joined hands with the Shaba Gendarmerie to attack the French. Paris reacted quickly, putting into action French plans for just such an emergency. French paratroopers seized the old Belgian airbase at Kolwezi and air transported forces were flown in to start the rescue of French nationals. At the same time, the French Government appealed to Pretoria for help. The Afrikaner columns that should have crossed the Orange River were diverted northwards and crossed the Limpopo instead. Brushing aside Zimbabwe and Zambian opposition they made for Lubumbashi (old Elizabethville) via Bulawayo, Livingstone and Lusaka. Surprise was again on their side. They arrived in time to turn the tide of the rebellion in favour of the French with a brutal show of force in which a large part of Lubumbashi was destroyed and little quarter was given. They could not, however, withdraw until more French troops had been flown in. *High Veldt III* was, in consequence, postponed indefinitely.

The delay to *High Veldt III* proved fatal to Heemskirk's dreams of a quick and decisive military victory. It allowed time for international reaction. The French, though not contributing to the military forces of NATO, appealed to Brussels for help. The recently created NATO Strategic Reserve was an obvious weapon in Western European hands if there was sufficient unity of political purpose to make its deployment to Southern Africa in a peace keeping role practicable. Such unity was just not there. The French, Dutch and Belgian, were pro-Afrikaner. The West Germans sided with them too, but they were more concerned with exploiting any opportunity that might present itself for German re-unification. The Scandinavian and Mediterranean countries were neutral and disinclined to agree to the deployment of their troops outside Europe. The United States and Britain took the view that NATO intervention could only be at the request of the recognised government of Azania and be aimed at re-establishing constitutional government in the rebel provinces. Any inclination there may have been within the United States Administration and the British Government to go to the help of Whites in Southern Africa was firmly quashed by mass demonstrations against Pretoria in London and Washington, and by the results of the electronic opinion polls which showed an overwhelming support in both countries for the Azanian Government.

I had just returned from Tokyo to take up the appointment of one of the three Directors of Defence Intelligence in the Ministry of Defence with the rank of Major General, so I saw NATO's disarray almost at first hand. I was even more closely involved in sifting reports of secret meetings between representatives of East and West Germany, which had been going on for several months. German reunification has ceased to be a distant possibility: it was hanging like the sword of Damocles over Europe. Could it be accomplished without triggering the nuclear holocaust? As each Russian division left Eastern Europe for Central Asia, our expectations of Warsaw Pact defections grew.

One thing we did not expect was the turn of events in southern Africa. After a life time of military service, I thought little could shock me, but I was wrong. The Rand massacres, as they are now called, began on 13th April 2028 and the killing went on for three days. Whether they were engineered or spontaneous is still uncertain, so many of the key witnesses did not survive. There had been unrest in the gold fields ever since Vervaal had declared UDI, but it seemed to have been contained. It has been suggested that Homelander agents provoked the trouble at the Ransdorp mine, but it is just as likely that it was triggered by some local incident or by the news of Afrikaner brutality in Lubumbashi. What is certain is that the management offices were attacked by a large crowd of angry miners and over fifty of the White staff, including five female secretaries, were hacked to death before help could reach them. It is equally certain that over three thousand Black men, women and children died in the reprisal raids launched by the Afrikaner Security Forces against the nearby African townships. The 20th century massacres at Sharpville and Soweto were minor affairs in comparison.

That one brutal spasm of African action and Afrikaner reaction alienated sympathies in Europe, North America and Japan. There was no United Nations to reflect and focus world opinion, so calls for intervention were diffuse. The Azanian Government appealed to Washington and London; the Afrikaners to Paris, the Hague and Bonn; the English speaking South Africans of the Cape and Natal to London; and the Asian communities to Tokyo and Delhi. On 24th April 2028 London *Times* thundered:

> '*Europe cannot just watch as Pretoria and Johannesberg burn; nor can the Afrikaners be allowed to mow down the unarmed Black majority. The Azanian Government must be given the support it needs to bring the Vervaal rebellion to an end. If no-one else will do so, London and the Hague with their historic links with South Africa should do so. What is the use of the NATO strategic Reserve if it cannot be used to help maintain world stability?*'

The British Government, as the original sponsor of the Azanian settlement and constitution, did take the lead, but soon found the military cupboard remarkably bare. The NATO strategic reserve did exist, but the Dutch component was *persona non grata* to Azania and SACEUR was not prepared to release the German component because of the growing tension over German re-unification. The United States Rapid Deployment Force was in an emaciated state, with many of its formations tied down on the Purple Line in Iran. India, which had such large communities in Cape Province and Natal, should have been able to provide a contingent, but their government was mesmerised, like a chicken facing a cobra, by the Chinese Strike Force in Upper Burma.

It was at this point that the seeds sown during Nogi's visit to London in 2026 and his disastrous visit to Washington in 2027, began to germinate. The Japanese Ambassador asked to call on the Foreign Secretary. He proposed a joint Anglo-Japanese initiative. Britain's past connections and Japan's current links gave the two offshore islands a common interest in ending the genocide in Azania. At the British Prime Minister's invitation, the U.S. Secretary of State and the Japanese Foreign Minister flew to London on 2nd May to convert the Japanese political initiative into practicable measures for intervention.

The plan, which emerged from the London meeting, was simple, if not elegant. The British would provide a task force to support the Azanian Government in Cape Province and the Japanese Southern Amphibious Strike Force (earmarked for South East Asia in Plan '*White Lotus*') would help the Azanians in Natal. The United States Fleet would cover both operations to prevent interference by the Russians, and the American strategic air transport force would help to fly in British and Japanese units and logistic supplies. The operation was deemed so important by the United States, British and Japanese Governments and the politico-military problems were so great that they decided to appoint the very experienced Field Marshal Sir Colin Campbell, who was just retiring from the chairmanship of the NATO Military Committee, as Commander-in-Chief of the Azanian Assistance Force (AAF)[1] His jointly agreed directive, dated 7th May 2028, instructed him:

> '*to direct and co-ordinate the military actions of the AAF to bring the Afrikaner rebellion to an end with minimum loss of life.*'

The Japanese Government, appreciating the political sensitivity of this first Japanese military operation since the Second World War, appointed General Oyama to be Campbell's deputy. Both men flew out to Cape Town with their personal staffs within days of their appointment to make plans for the reception of their forces and to co-ordinate action with the Azanian military authorities.

Colin Campbell's first task was to ensure that Cape Province was made a secure military base for operations across the Orange River. By this time we, in Defence Intelligence, had enough hard information about Heemskirk's plans to know that he would launch *High Veldt III* into Cape Province as soon as he could recover his forces from Shaba. It would be a race between the British Task Force arriving by air and sea and the Afrikaners extricating themselves by land and air through Zambia and Zimbabwe. Campbell agreed with the Azanians that he should concentrate the British troops astride the main Cape Town Road at Colesberg with a lay back position at Richmond. The Azanians would cover the flanking approaches at Burgersdorp to the east and Hopetown to the west. Zambia and Zimbabwe were asked to do what they could to impede the Afrikaner withdrawal from Shaba.

Campbell's second task was to engineer an unopposed landing for the Japanese at Durban, which was still firmly held by the Afrikaners. Provided he won the race with Heemskirk for the Orange River, he would invade the Orange Free State to pin Heemskirk down before the Japanese Southern Strike Force threatened Durban. If the Afrikaners did not abandon the port, the Japanese would land at Port Durnford and Port Stiepstone, sixty miles north and south of Durban respectively, and advance on Pietermaritzburg to cut off the city's garrison.

Heemskirk was no fool. Enough of the joint Anglo-Japanese plan had been leaked – some of it deliberately – in the world press to make him realise that he could not hold Durban indefinitely. He authorised his commander in Natal to pull back to Ladysmith to cover Pretoria, *as a last resort*, if Durban was assaulted by superior Japanese forces. His plan was to give the British a bloody nose first on the Orange River and then switch his main effort to stopping the Japanese advance from Natal.

'The best laid plans of mice and men . . .' The front line states' efforts to stop the Afrikaner withdrawal from Shaba proved futile. 1st British Parachute Brigade was just arriving at Colesberg and the 5th Air Portable Brigade at Richmond when Heemskirk struck on 10th June. Neither brigade had been in action since the days of Eagle Force, a decade earlier. The Parachute Brigade did receive a bloody nose and fell back to Richmond, where the combined force checked the Afrikaner rush. Steps were being taken to fall back again to Three Sisters when the Afrikaners unexpectedly withdrew, leaving the British to lick their wounds and to reappraise the fighting qualities of their old Boer opponents.

Campbell's plan seemed to have gone awry and the world press were not slow to pillory him, but Heemskirk's turn was to come next. When the Japanese Strike Force ships appeared off Durban on 12th June the Afrikaner commander misunderstood or deliberately disobeyed the 'last resort' phrase in his instructions and withdrew to Ladysmith, allowing the Japanese to come ashore unopposed to receive a rousing welcome from all sections of the Durban population and most especially from the Indians, who were delighted to see their fellow Asians playing a full part in world affairs.

Campbell may have been caught tractically off balance in Cape Province, but his overall strategy was sound. Heemskirk could not disengage quickly enough on the Orange River to move the *High Veldt III* troops back to defend the Transvaal before the Japanese started their advance from Durban. The Afrikaners were as unprepared as the Vietnamese had been for the Asian style *blitzkreig* launched by the Southern Japanese Strike Force. It was a replica of the Chinese advance on Hanoi and just as successful. Oyama flew over to Durban from Cape Town and accompanied the Strike Force Commander when he entered Johannesburg on the 19th June and Pretoria a day later.

Vervaal and Heemskirk escaped southwards. They set up a new seat of Afrikaner government at Kroonstadt and asked Cape Town for terms. The Afrikaner rebellion seemed over, but the struggle, which had started with so many similarities to the American Civil War, was to end in much the same way as the Boer War had done in the first years of the 20th century. On British and Japanese advice, Yombi adopted a conciliatory attitude and placed reconciliation high on his agenda. He offered to extend the White franchise for ten years, as Nogi had originally proposed in his Cape Town speech, on condition that the Afrikaners laid down their arms and the two rebel provinces rejoined the Azanian Union.

Vervaal was a political realist and recommended acceptance of these terms as reasonable. The failure of the Azanian Government to extend the White franchise for a further ten years had, after all, been the original cause of Afrikaner UDI. He agreed with Yombi that the only sensible way forward was through reconciliation. An attempt to fight on now that the Japanese held Pretoria and Johannesburg and the British were approaching Bloemfontein made no sense at all when such conciliatory terms were on offer.

Heemskirk and the hard-line military commanders would have none of it. They knew that the Azanian Government, even with the support of the AAF, would not have enough troops to crush a well directed guerrilla and urban terrorist campaign which would have the support of most of the White population. They argued that a mix of the old style Boer commando tactics on the Veldt and IRA type terrorism in the cities and towns would, in the end, preserve the Afrikaner way of life more surely than trusting in the magnanimity of Yombi and M'Bundu.

The two sides agreed to differ. Vervaal returned to Pretoria to sign an armistice with Oyama. Heemskirk set off for a secret destination in the high veldt where he established his guerrilla and terrorist command. Campbell and Oyama found themselves facing much the same situation as Kitchener had done after the fall of Pretoria in 1900. Kitchener had had to resort to a scorched earth policy with all the cruelty of his concentration camps to bring the Boers to the negotiating table. The Commandos of Botha, Kritzenger, Hertzog, De Witt and De la Rey had resisted the British Army for two years. Heemskirk did better. The AAF could not be withdrawn for seven long years and then only as part of the international settlement, which ended the Third World War. Unlike Archbishop Bolivar, M'Bundu had a long way to go before he reached his 'new heaven and new earth.'

Note

1. After completing his three year tenure as British Chief of Defence Staff, the Field Marshal became Chairman of the NATO Military Committee in 2025 and was due to retire at the age of 65 at the end of 2028.

12

The Battle of the Amur River (2029–2034)

*'The Chinese have crossed the Amur River.
It looks like 1904 all over again, but it
is not just a Russo-Japanese war, it
is a Russo-Asiatic conflict.'*

Diary entry for 13th May 2034

For three years (2026–2028), Nogi and Oyama had played the leading roles in the *White Lotus* drama. In 2029 Chairman Chu Cheng and Marshal Tzu Te stepped from the wings and assumed the supreme direction of Asia's bid for superpower status. Throughout the Apocalyptic final phase of the Third World War I was in Defence Intelligence in Whitehall.[1] I was, therefore, able to follow the course of events fairly closely. No Soviet or Sino-Japanese records have yet been released, so I have had to depend on my own extensive diaries, contemporary press reports and the invaluable memoirs of Nogi and Oyama for this account of the decisive battles which led to the emergence of the new world order without the human race committing nuclear suicide in the process.

Major political change is usually brought about in the Western World by General or Presidential elections. In the Communist Eastern Bloc it is Old Father Time who scythes down the old order to allow the new to sprout. Patrick O'Dwyer's election as American President in 2024 marked the beginning of America's period of disillusion, return to isolationism and relative decline as a superpower. In the Soviet Union, similarly fundamental change and a corresponding measure of decline was wrought by the death of the Soviet leader, Uri Shepilov, in February 2029.

Without a multi-party electoral system, the Soviet political establishment suffers the cyclical effects of old age. The leadership grows older and older until, as happened in the 1980's, death sweeps away the whole of the ageing generation and a 'young Turk', like Mikhail Gorbachev, takes over and brings his own age group to power. Gorbachev himself helped the process to repeat itself by living and retaining power until his eightieth birthday. He was then followed in quick succession by three septuagenarians the last of whom was Uri Shepilov. 2029 saw another 'Young Turk' upheaval in the Kremlin from which Alexander Karpov emerged at the age of fifty-six as Russia's new leader. His election was by no means unanimous and there remained a powerful body of old guard supporters in the Politbureau, led by Ivan Molotov, a descendant of Stalin's long serving foreign minister. As head of the KGB, Molotov was not a man whom Karpov could eliminate before he had consolidated his own power base.

There was no love lost between Karpov and Molotov. Karpov had been born in Omsk, east of the Urals, and had some sympathy for the non-Slav peoples of the Soviet Union. He and the younger generation, who had brought him to power, were appalled by the damage being done to the balance of Soviet society by the repression in Central Asia. Slav-Asiatic antagonism was growing in all walks of life and would tear the Union apart if the Kremlin could not come to terms with the Asiatic dislike of Slav dominance. Islamic Fundamentalism, in their view, was but a manifestation of the much larger problem of Asian resurgence inspired by Nogi-ism. Karpov and his supporters believed that the Stalin-like methods of repression had failed and it was time to try the alternative of reconciliation once more. Ivan Molotov, on the other hand, was a traditional Muskovite and the hardest amongst his hard-line colleagues. To him Islamic Fundamentalism was like couch grass that spread beneath the surface of Soviet Asiatic society. The only way to deal with the couch was to dig it out and burn it, however long it took.

The argument was won again by the liberals as it had been in 2022, but this time on strategic grounds. Nationalism in Europe, they claimed with some justification, was even more dangerous than its Asian equivalent. The weakening of the Soviet military presence in Eastern Europe to provide reinforcements for Central Asia was encouraging disloyalty within the Warsaw Pact. The Kremlin was not unaware of the clandestine talks that had been going on between the two German governments; nor of the increase in incipient unrest in Poland and Rumania. The Soviet Union was in danger of having to fight on two fronts unless a *modus vivendi* could be achieved in Central Asia before serious defections started in Eastern Europe.

Marshal Turkochevic, the Soviet Supreme Commander, who had Tartar blood in his veins, sided with Karpov. He warned the Politbureau that the fabric of the Red Army was being strained by Slav/Asiatic antagonism. The unity of the Soviet State depended upon the internal cohesion of the Red Army which could not be taken for granted as long as unrest prevailed in Central Asia.

The Molotov hard-liners did not accept the change of policy with good grace, but they decided to bide their time. If appeasement in Central Asia failed, Karpov and his liberal followers would pay for their mistakes in the usual Soviet way.

Reconciliation and co-operation, rather than hostility to the legitimate aspirations of the people of Central Asia, were the key notes of Karpov's inaugural speech to the Supreme Soviet. He pointed out that religion had only been discouraged and not proscribed in the Soviet Union. Those Soviet Socialist Republics that wished to give greater prominence to Islam were at liberty to do so, provided Soviet law continued to take precedence over the Moslem *Shari'a* whenever the two were in conflict. He was convinced that a satisfactory understanding could be reached that would restore racial harmony within the Soviet Union.

Our Kremlin-watchers in London noted that Karpov was offering the Central Asian Republics much the same terms as Chu had already given to the Moslems of Sinkiang. Karpov's speech was certainly well received inside and outside the Soviet Union. There was general relief in Central Asia that repression was to be phased out and some satisfaction in Afro-Asian circles that at least a partial victory had been won. During 2030 the Red Army units brought to Central Asia from Eastern Europe were returned to the Warsaw Pact order of battle. Those from Outer Mongolia and the Far East, however, were only pulled back into reserve in the Omsk area, along the Trans-Siberian Railway, ready to snuff out any resurgence of Moslem separatism in Central Asia if reconciliation failed. Responsibility for internal security was handed back to the MVD and KGB, whose troops were firmly established in the key cities of the region before the Red Army withdrew. There may have been a revolution in the Kremlin; nevertheless, events were to show that its effects were slow to permeate the lower echelons of Soviet bureaucracy and of the State Security Services, where the habits of a lifetime died hard and made official reconciliation more cosmetic than real. (*See map 11 for Omsk*)

The Islamic euphoria that welled up during 2030 began to subside in 2031 as the superficiality of Moscow's reconciliation became apparent to the people of Central Asia. Nothing had really changed. The godless Slavs still held the reins of power, and the MVD and KGB had not changed their spots. Increased autonomy was a charade. The Ayatollah of Baghdad was not slow to react to the growing anger in Central Asia. Karpov's reconciliation policy was to him a confession of Soviet weakness, which should be exploited. Karpov had given Islam an inch; he would see that Allah was helped to take a mile. With Chu's blessing, he paid a much heralded visit to Sinkiang in April 2031, during which he demanded not just increased autonomy for the Moslem SSR's of CentralAsia, but independence as true Islamic Republics in which the *Shari'a* and not Soviet law would be predominant. It was heady stuff, which, when added to the endemic cynicism of the people, ensured that discontent again began to heave beneath the veneer of Karpov's reconciliation policies. To make matters more awkward for the Kremlin reconciliation lobby, pro-Chinese elements in Outer Mongolia's capital, Ulan Bator, took courage and began to demand independence and the withdrawal of the few Soviet troops that remained within Outer Mongolia.

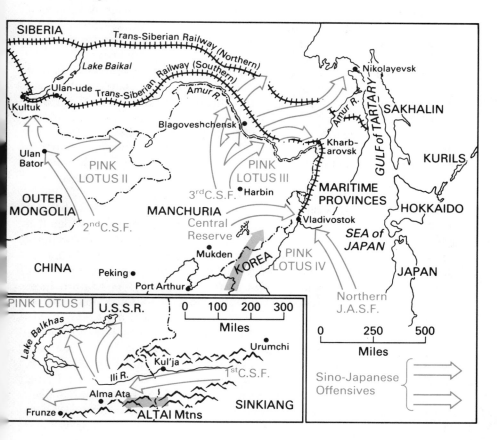

MAP 14: The Pink Lotus military plans: 2031

We, in Western Intelligence, had noted the moves of Soviet divisions back to the Eastern Europe with apprehension. The possibility of some form of diversionary military adventure in Europe could not be ruled out. On the other hand, we also picked up rumours of the outbreak of guerrilla warfare in the mountains of Central Asia to the east of the ancient Moslem cities of Alma Ata, Tashkent and Samarkand, which lay along the natural frontier with China. Reports suggested that the main centres of unrest were in the Alma Ata provinces of the Kazakh S.S.R., which was the area ceded to the Tsars by China in 1864. Had we known the contents of the secret protocols attached to Treaty of Hong Kong, we might have been able to make more sensible deductions. We saw only that further trouble in Central Asia would be an embarrassment to Alexander Karpov and might lead to his overthrow by Ivan Molotov's hard-liners. That Chu might be building up his case for the restoration of China's pre-1864 frontiers escaped us.

The significance of the unrest in Alma Ata and Outer Mongolia was not lost on Tzu Te or Oyama. Their agents and those of the Ayatollah had done their work well in softening up the first two targets of the *White Lotus* plan. They judged that the moment for decisive military action could not be far off, but they also appreciated that instability in the Kremlin meant that even greater care had to be taken not to ripple the nuclear lily pond. Every operation mounted must have a strictly limited and clearly announced objective that would not cause anyone in the Kremlin, however nervous, to reach for the nuclear button.

Within the overall strategic concept of *White Lotus*, Tzu Te's subordinate EATO commanders had elaborated four contingency plans which had been coded *Pink Lotus* I, II, III and IV, the *Pink* denoting their military connotation. *Pink Lotus I* was an intervention operation by the 1st Chinese Strike Force to secure the old western Ch'ing frontier, which lay on the shores of Lake Balkash and embraced the whole of Alma Ata province. *Pink Lotus II* was the occupation of Outer Mongolia by 2nd Chinese Strike Force at the request of the government in Ulan Bator. *Pink Lotus III* was the decisive battle, to be fought with no holds barred, to isolate the Manchurian Maritime provinces. 3rd Chinese Strike Force, the largest, best equipped and hardest trained, would cross the Amur River at Blagoveshchensk, cut both tracks of the Trans-Siberian Railway and exploit to the Pacific coast cutting off the whole of the former Manchu homelands that had been ceded to Russia under the 'unequal' Treaty of Aigun in 1858 which led to the founding of the Russian cities of Blagoveshchensk, Kharbarovsk and Vladivostok on the Amur River in the 1860's. The *Pink Lotus IV* was to be the *coup de grâce*, probably delivered by the Chinese Central Strategic Reserve and the Japanese Northern Strike Force, in which Vladivostok, Sakhalin Island and the Kuril Islands would be wrested from their Soviet garrisons. The participation of the Japanese amphibious forces would, however, depend upon the concurrent defeat of the Soviet Pacific Fleet.

In his memoirs Oyama confesses that he expected *Pink Lotus II* (the occupation of Outer Mongolia) to be launched first. The recurrence of guerrilla warfare in Central Asia would pin the Soviet reserves in the Omsk area, leaving Ulan Bator with a minimal Soviet garrison. A pro-Chinese *coup d'état* could be engineered there almost at any time of Tzu's choosing:

the establishment of an Islamic Co-prosperity sphere embracing Afghanistan and the Moslem SSR's was still only a distant Ayatollan dream rather than a practicable possibility.

Tzu Te, Oyama and our Kremlin watchers were taken completely by surprise by the upheaval, which occurred in October 2031, not in Central Asia or Outer Mongolia, but in the Kremlin itself. The 2031 celebrations of the October Revolution were about to begin in Moscow when Soviet television and radio switched quite unexpectedly to solemn funeral music and the announcers began to prepare their viewers and listeners for bad news. At 11 o'clock that morning it came: Alexander Karpov was dead. He was said to have had a massive heart attack from which he had not recovered, despite the heroic efforts of the Soviet medical profession.

'Comrade Ivan Molotov' the announcers intoned, 'has assumed the temporary leadership until a successor has been elected by the Supreme Soviet of the Soviet Union.'

No-one doubted that the KGB would ensure that Karpov's mantle would stay firmly pinned to Molotov's shoulders and it did. But what was in doubt and remains locked amongst the Kremlin's secrets is how he really died. He had been in sparklingly good health the day before at a reception given by the West German Embassy to mark the first visit to Moscow of the newly elected Chancellor of the German Federal Republic, Herr Otto Grünwald. Rumours spread rapidly through the Moscow diplomatic corps that cyanide had helped Karpov on his way, but several eminent authorities maintained that extreme anxiety brought on by the evident failure of his reconciliation policies had proved fatal to him. We may never know the true story and many a novel will be written about it in the future.

The return of the Slav hard-liners to power in the Kremlin brought with it an immediate reversal of Karpov's reconciliation policies. Marshal Turkochevik was astute enough a politician to survive the change, but many of his colleagues did not. He signed the military directive, ordering the divisions held in reserve around Omsk, to move south once more to support the MVD and KGB troops in crushing Islamic deviationism in the Central Asian SSR's and to bring the guerrilla war to an end. Appreciating that this could not be done successfully without cutting off the dissidents from their sources of supply, he ordered the Far Eastern Military District to provide troops to seal off the twelve hundred miles of the frontier of Sinkiang from Afghanistan to Outer Mongolia. It was a prodigious task, which was to pin down large numbers of Soviet troops throughout 2032 and 2033, and could not have been more welcome to Chu and Tzu Te.

Exactly a year after Karpov's death the Alma Ata Incident, as it is now known, occurred. Whether by mistake or miscalculation of Chinese sensitivities, the 65th Motor Rifle Division from Vladivostok, which was possibly unfamiliar with its sector of the frontier, crossed into Sinkiang in the Ili River valley, due east of Alma Ata, ostensibly in hot pursuit of dissidents.

It was mid-October so the Soviet Commander probably thought that with winter approaching there would be little Chinese reaction. They reached Kul'ja, some fifty miles inside China, before they were sharply checked by the Chinese frontier division in the area and forced to withdraw. (*See Map 14 Inset*)

This stupidity on the part of the local Soviet Commander gave Chu and Tzu Te the opportunity for which they had been waiting. Announcing that such deliberate incursions into Chinese territory could not go unpunished, Chu ordered *Pink Lotus I* to be implemented. Tzu directed 1st Chinese Strike Force to seize Alma Ata and to exploit to Lake Balkhash if Soviet resistance collapsed, as he believed it would.

1st CSF caught the Soviet forces completely off balance. They were deployed on counter-guerrilla operations with units widely dispersed, holding a static framework within which cordon and search operations were being mounted. There were no tank divisions immediately available and little artillery had been deployed. The only units facing east were the frontier guards and the scattered detachments of the Far Eastern divisions, which were attempting to seal the frontier. 1st CSF reached and took Alma Ata against only sporadic and ill co-ordinated opposition.

The Commander of the 1st CSF, General Sun Li-Jen, was the first to admit that surprise contributed most to his success. He expected a Soviet counter-offensive would develop in a matter of days and so he sought authority from SACEA to use his *Hawk* weapon systems to destroy any major Soviet concentrations as soon as they were detected by his *Eye of Heaven* target acquisition staff. Tzu Te had hoped that it would not prove necessary to reveal the *Hawk*'s real capabilities until *Pink Lotus III*, and, in any case, Chu's personal authority was still needed for *Hawk* release. Chu demurred. He believed he could forestall a Soviet counter-offensive by opening up a diplomatic offensive of his own in Moscow to still any ripples on the nuclear lily pond. General Sun was ordered to advance to Lake Balkhash and go onto the defensive on the old 1864 Ch'ing frontier. He was authorised to use his *Hawks* only as a last resort.

Sun never did need to use his *Hawks*. The Chinese Ambassador in Moscow handled Chu's *démarche* with consummate skill. First, he cast all the blame for the Alma Ata incident upon the faceless 65th Motor Rifle Division Commander. He then offered Chu's good offices to bring about a satisfactory settlement with the Ayatollah, which would bring the costly struggle in Central Asia to an end. He pointed out that no-one was reaping any profit from the current situation, least of all the people of the region. From this proposition he developed the idea of a package deal whereby the Soviet Union would accept the re-establishment of the 1864 Ch'ing frontier on Lake Balkhash in return for Chinese curtailment of military supplies to the Islamic dissidents in Central Asia. In short, the Ayatollah's usefulness in creating a diversion for *White Lotus* was over for the time being. His interests were to be temporarily sacrificed to prevent any unnecessary risks being taken of an escalation to nuclear war.

Few people were more surprised than we were in Whitehall when we heard that not only was a Chinese delegation going to Moscow to settle frontier differences in Central Asia, but a delegation from Baghdad was to join in the Moscow talks. The only explanations for the absence of any Soviet counter-offensive in Alma Ata that our Kremlin experts could suggest were that Molotov was reluctant to risk direct confrontation with another nuclear power, and that Marshal Turkochevik was equally hesitant about attacking an Asian enemy with Slav/Asiatic antagonism still an unknown factor in the Red Army's battle efficiency.

We soon had some confirmation of both theories. In the New Year of 2033 the irredentist faction in Ulan Bator started a successful coup that ousted the pro-Soviet government of Outer Mongolia. Declaring that the Chinese government would support the legitimate aspirations of the Mongolian people, Chu authorised Tzu Te to order *Pink Lotus II*. In the midst of the bitterest winter weather the helicopter borne elements of the 2nd Chinese Strike Force landed at Ulan Bator just as the last Soviet troops and embassy staff took off for Ulan Ude, the headquarters of the Soviet Trans-Baikal Command on the southern track of the Trans-Siberian Railway south east of Lake Baikal. Moscow made no attempt to reverse the coup. The Kremlin had neither the intention nor the resources to do so. They had other more far reaching plans under consideration. Outer Mongolia was added to Alma Ata as the price the Soviet Union would have to pay for possible but not certain peace in Central Asia.

The negotiations for the settlement of the Vietnam War in the 1970's had been long and tortuous: the Moscow talks on Central Asia were even worse. Both sides recognised that the gulf between them was too wide to be bridged without a further trial of strength, and both were manoeuvering for the advantage like a couple of heavyweight wrestlers.

Chu was the first to make a lunge. At a state dinner in Peking, held to mark the fifteenth anniversary of the signing of the Charter of the China Seas on 12th August 2019, and attended by Nogi and all the senior officials of the East Asian Treaty Organisation, he stated publically for the first time the Hong Kong Powers determination:

> *'to re-establish Asia's power and dignity by restoring China's territorial integrity and bringing political fulfilment to the followers of Islam.'*

It did not take long for the international community to decode Chu's cryptic remarks. He was aiming to recover the Ch'ing frontiers for China and most of Central Asia for the Moslem faith.

No-one expected the Kremlin's response to be anything but hostile. We were dumbfounded when Molotov appeared on Moscow television shortly after Chu's speech to announce that the Soviet Government had agreed to the re-unification of Germany and was withdrawing from its sector of Berlin so that the city could, once more, become the capital of a re-united Germany whose eastern frontier would remain on the Oder-Neise line.

History is often said to repeat itself. Molotov's announcement had the ring of his grandfather's pact with Ribbentrop in 1939, which triggered the Second World War. In 1939 Hitler had made his unholy alliance with Stalin in order to rape Poland before turning on Britain and France. He had then turned about and attacked his Russian ally. It took little imagination to see that the younger Molotov was repeating Hitler's ploy. He was clearing the Soviet Union's European flank in order to settle matters with Asia.

Chu's speech and Molotov's announcement caused the utmost confusion and doubt in all Western capitals. Peking and Tokyo were, by contrast, gripped by the urgency of the situation. Nogi and Oyama flew at once to Peking for a hastily called EATO summit meeting with Chu and Tzu Te. The decision to forestall the redeployment of Soviet forces from West to East was unanimous. None of the leaders present was in any doubt about the enormity of the risk of nuclear war developing if *Pink Lotus III and IV* were launched, but it was now or never. Tzu Te and Oyama gave a combined military view that the Politbureau in its divided state would not risk the nuclear devastation of Moscow, Leningrad and Kiev to save Blagoveshchensk, Kharbarovsk and Vladivostok, provided the limited nature of the Sino-Japanese offensive was made unmistakably clear to the Kremlin. Chu and Nogi concurred and authorised *Pink Lotus III.*

The original tactical plan for *Pink Lotus III* had envisaged 3rd Chinese Strike Force under General Hor Lung's command crossing the Amur River on a wide front either side of Blagovskchensk, severing both tracks of the Trans-Siberian Railway and cutting off the whole of the Maritime Provinces by a thrust along the Amur to its mouth at Nikelayevsk. Molotov's agreement on German re-unification meant that Tzu Te must guard Hor Lung's western flank from Soviet reinforcements that would be rushed eastwards from Europe as soon as *Pink Lotus III* was launched. He had the means ready to hand. The 2nd Chinese Strike Force under General Chang Chu in Ulan Bator had seen little action so far, and the Soviet Trans-Baikal Military District was known to have sent most of its troops westwards to the Central Asian front. Chang was to cut the Trans-Siberian Railways at either end of Lake Baikal, and then form a defensive front facing west to stop the arrival of Soviet reinforcements.

Tzu Te's order to his Strike Force commanders had a simple clarity about it:

'1st CSF *(Sun Li-jen) at Alma Ata, to stand on the defensive ready to use its Hawks at the first sign of a Soviet counter-offensive in Central Asia.*

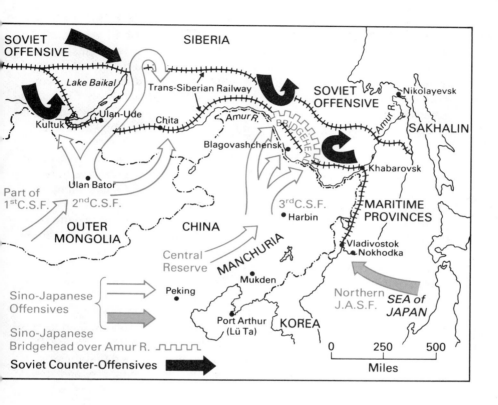

MAP 15: Pink Lotus III, The Battle of the Amur River:
23rd August to 18th September 2034

2nd CSF *(Chang Chu)* at Ulan Bator, to strike northwards to cut the *Trans-Siberian Railways* north and south of Lake Baikal, and to form a defensive flank facing west.

3rd CSF *(Hor Lung)* at Harbin, to launch the main assault across the Amur river and to cut off the Maritime Provinces by an advance along the Amur to its mouth on the Pacific Coast.'

Once the Amur was sealed, *Pink Lotus IV* would be launched against Vladivostok from the west by General Tu Lu Ming with the Chinese Central Strategic Reserve, which was to move north to Harbin as soon as 3rd CSF launched its attack across the Amur. The Northern Japanese Amphibious Strike Force under General Shozo Sakurai would land at Nakhodka and would attack Vladivostok from the east, provided the Soviet Pacific Fleet had been defeated by that time.

In his final briefing of his commanders Tzu Te followed Field Marshal Montgomery's phasing that he used for the Battle of El Alamein: the Break-in, the Dog-fight and the Break-out. He expected the Break-in across the Amur would go quite quickly as they would have the benefit of surprise, but the Dog Fight phase would be long and difficult. Its outcome would depend upon the degree of success the Soviet High Command achieved in redeploying its forces from Europe to the Far East. Speed was essential and Chang's defence of the western flank at Baikal would be crucial.

In one respect the launching of *Pink Lotus III* at the end of August 2034 was about a year too soon. There had been delays in the *Dragon's Tongue* beam weapon development programme, which Tzu Te had mentioned during the Copps briefing of ministers in 2025. Troop trials had only just been completed, and production had barely started. The Singkiang trials regiment had forty-five prototypes, organised in three battalions of fifteen equipments each, but there was, as yet, no agreed tactical doctrine for their use, nor were Strike Force officers aware of their capabilities. All that was known outside the weapon development staffs and the trials regiment was that the *Dragon's Tongue* was a direct-fire beam weapon, which could kill unprotected troops, destroy optical sighting systems and derange electronic equipment out to a range of about three kilometres against land targets and rather more against low flying aircraft and helicopters.[1] In pre-*Pink Lotus* war games, senior Chinese officers had been warned that the Soviets might already have such weapons in equally small numbers, and it was generally agreed that the counter should be greater use of reverse slope positions and neutralising strikes by *Crows*.

Tzu Te had a difficult decision to take: should the *Dragon's Tongue* trials regiment be committed in any phase of *Pink Lotus III* or not? The EATO Chief Scientific Adviser, Liao Kai-Sen, was against its deployment, which he considered would be premature. The regiment was only partially trained; the equipment was prototype and hardly reliable; and logistic support was inadequate for more than one major action. On the other hand *Pink Lotus III* might be the decisive battle of the Third World War and fortunes might be tipped either way by the side that used beam weapons first. Their effect on morale might be decisive.

In view of the subsequent claims by Chang Chu, the commander of 2nd CSF, that he rather than Tzu Te won the battle of the Amur River by his action at Kultuk, it is worth recording Liao Kai-Sen's account of Tzu Te's pre-battle decisions.

'*The Generalissimo summoned me before his final briefing conference to discuss the possible use of the* Dragon's Tongue *regiment.*

'I know,' he said, 'you are opposed to risking it, but if I do decide to use it, in which phase would you, as a scientist, recommend its first use: in the Break-in, Dog-fight or Break-out?'
'I thought for a few moments and then said:
'You have the Hawks *to give you surprise for the Break-in. The* Crows *and* Sparrows *are ideal for the Dog-fight. I would use the* Dragon's Tongue *for the Break-out, when you will need to spring a further surprise.'*
'Tzu Te also thought before answering.
'While I agree in principle, the phase that I am most worried about is the Dog-fight, and, in particular, Chang's chances of holding the Western flank at either end of Lake Baikal against counter-attacks thrown at him by Soviet troops as they arrive from Europe.'
'I could but agree: certainly the battle could be won or lost by Chang's success or failure in holding the Baikal flank.
'I will meet you half way;' Tzu concluded, 'I will hold the regiment in reserve under by own hand, but I will direct its commander to prepare for two eventualities: support of the Break-out, which will mean offensive action; or defensive support to Chang's 2nd CSF at Baikal. I realise that it will not be able to do both for logistic reaons.'
'It was Tzu Te who decided to use the regiment against my advice; and it was he who made the critical decision on 1st September to commit it on the Baikal front, again in spite of my opposition. Tzu Te deserves the credit for the correctness of his military judgement: Chang, however, has a right to claim the credit for the way in which he handled the Dragon's Tongues *on 5th September at Kultuk.'*

The significance of Liao Kai-Sen's evidence will emerge during my account of the Battle of the Amur River.

At the final EATO Council meeting there was a short discussion as to whether Chu should once again announce the strictly limited objective of *Pink Lotus III* before the offensive began, thus prejudicing surprise; or immediately after it had begun, which would heighten the risk of a nuclear exchange. On balance, reducing the nuclear risk was considered to be the more important. The venue for the announcement would be the Sino-Soviet Conference, which was still going on in Moscow.

On 20th August the head of the Chinese delegation in Moscow stated that his government's patience was exhausted. He had been instructed to withdraw his negotiators unless substantial progress could be made towards an equitable agreement that would restore China's territorial integrity. The Chinese Government could not be held responsible for the breakdown of negotiations if no new Soviet proposals for the annulment of the Treaty of Aigun were received within forty eight hours. There was no Soviet response, and on 22nd August the Chinese delegation and the Chinese Ambassador in Moscow left by air for Peking. Three hours after their departure, when their aircraft was well clear of Soviet airspace, Chairman Chu appeared on Channel I of the International Television Service to speak, the announcer said, 'To the Chinese people and the world on a matter of great importance and urgency.'

After giving a low key and balanced summary of the Sino-Soviet negotiations in Moscow and the Chinese version of the reasons for their breakdown, Chu came to the crux of his address:

> 'China hereby abrogates the unequal Treaty of Aigun. At midnight tonight all territories ceded under that Treaty to the Tsar in 1858 will revert to Chinese sovereignty. Any military operations that may occur will be limited by the Co-prosperity Defence Forces to the restoration of Chinese territorial integrity, and any loss of life will be the responsibility of the Soviet Union. There is one hour left for the Soviet Government to accept the peaceful restoration of the Chinese peoples' undoubted rights over the lands usurped by the Tsar 176 years ago.'

At midnight, Chinese police units appeared at all the recognised crossing points on the Amur River. They were fired upon, as they fully expected. What they did not expect was the vivid flashes of intense white light which lit up the night as they withdrew. This was hardly surprising as only a very few men had ever seen *Hawk* missile warheads fired operationally.

It was, in fact, about quarter past midnight on that fatal morning of 23rd August 2034 that Tzu Te authorised the start of *Pink Lotus III*. He had Chu's authority to order the initial *Hawk* strikes as soon as he had confirmation that the cross border police probes had been fired upon. At 0018, to be precise, *Hawk* missiles fitted with anti-airfield warheads struck all the main Soviet military airfields east of Lake Baikal, and anti-tank and anti-personnel salvos hit most of the known Soviet military centres that lay along the southern track of the Trans-Siberian Railway within the battle areas from Baikal to Khabarovsk. Despite the Chinese ultimatum and the precipitate withdrawal of the Chinese delegation from Moscow, tactical surprise was complete and the damage inflicted by the *Hawk* attack gave the 2nd and 3rd CSF's the initial advantage. The Chinese air forces also gained the upper hand and were able to concentrate upon stopping reinforcements being flown in from the West. By the end of the first forty eight hours, the Break-in phase was complete. The southern track of the Trans-Siberian Railway had been cut by 2nd CSF at Ulan-Ude and by 3rd CSF east of Blagoveshchensk. Both forces were building up for their advance to cut the northern track of the railway.

Although Tzu Te had warned his Strike Force commanders to plan for a prolonged attritional Dog Fight phase, he had hoped that the surprise effect of the *Hawk* attack, coupled with the racial antagonism that was known to be simmering within the Red Army, might lead to an early collapse of Soviet resistance. It did nothing of the sort. A number of the *Hawk* strikes fell wide of their targets and in some cases malfunctioned as was to be expected from a weapon being used for the first time on the battlefield. Moreover, the attack brought Slav and non-Slav in the Soviet units together in a common determination to drive out the Chinese invaders. Soviet resistance regained coherence both on land and in the air and Chinese losses began to mount. Both Strike Forces did reach the northern track of the Trans-Siberian Railway. Hor Lung's 3rd CSF managed to consolidate its grip on both tracks, but Chang Chu's hold on the line at the northern end of Lake Baikal looked precarious. As a precaution, his engineers prepared a fifty mile stretch of the track, including three major bridges, for demolition.

In Moscow, the Soviet High Command pressed for authority to use tactical nuclear weapons, but the knowledge that the anti-missile defences of the major Soviet cities were at best only ninety per cent effective, and that the Russian heartlands west of the Urals were not under threat, made Molotov hesitate. After the initial set backs, reports from the Soviet commanders in Siberia showed a welcome recovery. Molotov decided the battle could be won by conventional means and directed all his efforts to moving reinforcements by land and air from West to East, secure in the knowledge that Chinese and Japanese centres of population were just as vulnerable as their Soviet equivalents.

At El Alamein the contestants on either side had been numbered in tens of thousands and their casualties during the Dog Fight phase in thousands. During the Battle of the Amur River hundreds of thousands of Soviet and Chinese troops were locked in the Dog Fight with casualties mounting by tens of thousands. But it was not just a contest between two equally matched armies and air forces. It was also a contest between rival technologies. The Soviets still put their trust in the tank, battleship and manned aircraft: the Sino-Japanese depended upon the supra-technology of their target acquisition systems, guided missiles and the homing sub-munitions in their warheads.

By the end of the first week of *Pink Lotus III*, Tzu Te was facing a crisis of confidence at the EATO tactical headquarters in the deep underground complex built specially for it near Mukden, the scene of Oyama's great grandfather's triumph over the Russians in 1905. Both Hor and Chang reported growing exhaustion amongst their troops. All their tactical reserves had been committed and although, as good Commanders, they were regrouping to gather fresh reserves, they could detect no sign of an incipient Soviet collapse. On the contrary, Chang expected to be counterattacked by Soviet tank formations, which were assembling at the southern end of Lake Baikal, and Hor was reporting a similar build up in the Amur

Valley west of Khabarovsk. Regretably, the Chinese air forces had failed to stop the fly-in of Soviet reinforcements from the West.

On 1st September, Oyama flew from Tokyo to Mukden at Tzu's request to review and, if need be, revise their plans for *Pink Lotus IV*. The two men decided that there was no alternative but to cancel the Chinese participation in the Vladivostok assault so that their Central Strategic Reserve could be used to win the Battle of the Amur River. Oyama agreed to carry out *Pink Lotus IV* entirely with Japanese forces, but to do so the Soviet Pacific Fleet had first to be lured to its destruction in the Sea of Japan. This was to be done by electronic deception, which would simulate the track of a major assault convoy heading for Sakhalin across the Sea of Japan three days before the Japanese Northern Task Force was actually due to set sail. It was hoped that the Soviet heavy ships would put to sea from their Far Eastern bases to cut off the Japanese force. The long range naval version of the *Hawk* family, the *Sea Eagle*, and its target acquisition systems based on Hokkaido, would be used for the first time against naval surface forces. The outcome would probably change the complexion of naval warfare for the rest of the 21st century.

The EATO Operations Staff estimated that regrouping and preparation for the Break-out phase would take ten days. In the meantime, Hor and Chang were to go onto the defensive. Sun's 1st CSF would thin out in Alma Ata and send reinforcements to Chang to strengthen his Baikal block, and Hor would be reinforced with formations from the Central Strategic Reserve, which Tzu Te directed should be used for a concentrated attack to break-out down the Amur Valley towards Kharbarovsk with the ultimate aim of sealing off Vladivostok from the north. Tzu Te was then faced with the critical decision on whether to commit the *Dragon's Tongue* Regiment to Hor for his break-out, to Chang for the defence of the Baikal block, or to neither, keeping it in reserve against the unexpected. Chang played no part in the choice, despite his claims to have done so. Tzu took the decision, against Chiang Chung's advice, to send the regiment to Chang's 2nd CSF. The code word for Hor's break-out offensive was *HARVEST TIME*, and for the Japanese landings at Vladivostok it was *HARVEST HOME*.

Soviet electronic and other sources of intelligence provided the Supreme Command in Moscow with enough pointers to enable Marshal Turkochevik to deduce correctly that the Chinese had gone onto the defensive to regroup for a further offensive to break through the encircling Soviet forces. They also gave him the planted evidence of the Japanese deception plan to invade and repossess Sakhalin Island. He took two fatal decisions: to launch an immediate counter-offensive against the Chinese on land without waiting for more formations from the West to arrive; and to intercept the Japanese at sea by ordering the Far East Fleet to enter the confined waters of the Sea of Japan.

While the Dog-fight phase of the Battle of the Amur River was being fought out, political and diplomatic battles raged around the world. Spontaneous popular demonstrations on a massive scale took place in most major cities demanding '*negotiations not war*' and the creation of World Government. In cities with large etchnic minorities – black, coloured or white – many a '*peace*' demonstration turned to riot, looting and general mayhem as racial emotions flared in support of one side or the other. And behind the closed doors of Cabinet Offices and Foreign Ministries, politicians and officials sought to reap what advantages they could from the frightening situation. The risks of the nuclear holocaust grew with every day that passed, and yet neither side was willing to negotiate because each believed that it had military victory within its grasp.

One voice was heard above the clamour and was, in fact, amplified by the world's media. Nogi re-donned his cloak as the Asian peacemaker. Apart from the fully justified Chinese demands for the restoration of their territorial integrity, the East Asian Treaty Organisation had no territorial ambitions and was not seeking to impose unconditional surrender as Roosevelt and Churchill had done in the Second World War. The EATO war aim was the acceptance and implementation of the principles laid down in the Charter of the China Seas for a more equitable world order. Chu and he were ready to go anywhere, at any time, to start rebuilding the structure of world security.

The response to Nogi's plea was the roar of massed tank engines in the Amur Valley and at either end of Lake Baikal as the Soviet counter-offensive started on 5th September. The Sino-Japanese *Sparrow*, *Crow* and *Hawk* weapon systems had only given the Chinese Strike Forces marginal tactical superiority over the Red Army and Air Force during the Break-in. In the defensive Dog-fight phase their lethality was to prove decisive. The Soviet counter-offensive was mounted with the concentrated tank and infantry formations so beloved by the Russians, and were supported by well orchestrated air and artillery programmes. The carnage was appalling on both fronts. Billowing black smoke of burning tanks, vehicles and aircraft, which turned day into night, bore witness to the efficiency of the intelligent homing sub-munitions of the missile warheads when used in defence.

Despite Soviet losses, Chang's 2nd CFS was soon in trouble north of Lake Baikal and he was forced to pull his northern front back, having demolished enough of the railway to make it unusable for many months. At the southern end of the Lake, his defences were crumbling fast under the Soviet saturation attacks, mounted by formations from Europe and Central Asia in Marshal Turkochevik's main effort. Had it not been for the arrival of reinforcements from Sun, the EATO Western flank might have collapsed under the weight of the Soviet offensive before the *Dragon's Tongue* regiment could reach the battlefield. Chang decided to use the beam weapons as Rommel employed his formidable 88 millimetre Flak guns in the 1941/2 Desert War: as a lethal screen, through which his tanks would fall back, and on which the pursuing Russian tanks would impale themselves. Chang deployed the *Dragon's Tongue* on a thirty kilometre front in the Valley of the Irkut River that runs westwards from Kultuk at the south western tip of Lake Baikal. In the ensuing battle, which is now descriptively known as the Kultuk Cauldron, the *Dragon's Tongues* were too few to have more than a psychological effect. Most of the damage inflicted on the massed Soviet tank and armoured infantry formations was the work of the *Hawks, Crows* and *Sparrows*, but the balance was certainly tipped in Chang's favour by the surprise impact of the beam weapons, which shattered Soviet command and control at tank level and helped to decimate the supporting infantry. Chang's southern block held – just. There was no Soviet break-through round the bottom end of Lake Baikal, on which Marshal Turkochevik was depending to destroy the Chinese bridge-head over the Amur River.

While the battles of the Kultuk Cauldron were being fought out, Hor Lung's 3rd CSF rode out the less intense Soviet counter-offensive, mounted from Kharbarovsk by formations brought up from Valdivostok, which had been only marginally reinforced by troops flown in from the west. One military commentator, describing the appalling losses suffered by Soviet troops in the Dog-fight phase drew a parallel between the British offensive on the Somme in 1916 and the Soviet counter-offensive around Lake Baikal and in the Amur Valley. The Russian tank losses matched those of the British Infantry. On 5th September 2034 the tank joined the horsed cavalry as one of the 'has beens' in the history of land warfare.

At sea, naval history was written two days later. The Soviet Naval High Command decided not to risk their heavy ships in the confined waters of the Sea of Japan, but they sailed cruiser, frigate and submarine forces to intercept the Japanese passage to Sakhalin. The Battle of the Gulf of Tartary, which followed, was reminiscent in its out-come of the fateful Battle of Tsusima in 1905 when the Russian battle fleet was destroyed by Admiral Togo off Port Arthur, bringing the Russo-Japanese War to an end. This time there were no surface ship engagements. Three Soviet cruisers and four frigates were sunk by the *Sea Eagles*, fired from Hokkaido. The rest of the Soviet surface ships withdrew northwards to the comparative safety of the Sea of Okhotsk, leaving submarines to dispute the passage of the Japanese Amphibious Strike Force, which had not as yet put to sea. Surface warships had joined the tanks as artefacts of naval history. Manned strike aircraft were on their way to joining them in the air equivalent.

It was not until 10th September that Chang and Hor were convinced that they had defeated the Soviet counter-offensives. That evening Tzu Te issued the codeword '*HARVEST TIME, 11 Sept.*' At first Hor's attempt to break-out seemed as futile and costly as the Red Army's attempts to break into the Chinese bridgehead on the Amur. Then, quite unexpectedly, the Soviet collapse began. There was a trickle of surrenders on 13th; a stream on the 14th; and a flood on the 15th. Hor decided it was time to risk committing helicopter borne pursuit units, and Tzu Te ordered '*HARVEST HOME, 16th Sep.*'

A recent analysis of the battles shows that Slav/Asiatic cohesion within the Soviet armed forces, which had held up well during the initial Chinese offensive and had enabled the Soviet High Command to respond in kind, had not withstood the losses that they had suffered during the counter-offensive between 5th and 10th September. When the Chinese attacked again on 11th September in their break-out, comradeship had buckled and the will to resist had crumbled as Slav blamed Asiatic and *vice versa*. It was surprising that the schism had not opened up much earlier.

Khabarovsk fell to Hor's helicopter forces on 17th September and the Japanese Northern Amphibious Strike Force was still at sea when the Soviet Commander, Far East, in Vladivostok was authorised by the Kremlin to ask for terms. The cease fire came at midnight 17th/18th September.

Two days later, the Soviet Armistice Delegation arrived at the EATO Tactical Headquarters near Mukden. Nogi and Oyama, whose great grandfathers had defeated Kuropatkin's Russian forces at Port Arthur and Mukden in 1905, had the satisfaction of watching Marshal Tzu Te, as Supreme Allied Commander, East Asian Treaty Organisation, receive the Soviet Commanders. He did so not as defeated generals surrendering their swords, but as potential partners in the creation of the New World Order envisaged in the Charter of the China Seas. Oyama, in his memoirs records feeling the presence of the spirit of his great ancestor willing him exploit Asia's victory, not just for China's and Japan's benefit, but for the world's as well.

Note

1. Each beam weapon system was carried by four tanks: one for the weapon itself and its cooling system and three carrying generators for power supply.

The New Heaven and New Earth

*'Then I saw a new heaven and a new
earth, for the first heaven and the first
earth were passed away . . .'*

Revelation of St John, Chapter 21
(Revised Version)

13

The Treaties of London (2035)

*'The Charge of the Four Horsemen had struck
the flank of the Soviet army, and the two superpowers
had fallen back, joining hands as they did so
to oppose the new threat.*

*Then I saw the leader of the Four Horsemen
raise his sword to halt the charge. And a lone
knight rode out from the superpower array to
request a parlez. His shield bore the leopards of
England and his saddle cloth was the Union flag.'*

Diary entry for 18th September 2034

The Third World War was over, or almost over. The European period of World history was also at an end. The third superpower had emerged and Asia was in a position to dictate terms to Europe and the world for the first time. The Four Horsemen had triumphed without blowing the world apart by triggering a nuclear holocaust. But would their vision of '*a new heaven and a new earth*' have any substance? Or would it remain, like the end of a rainbow, tantalisingly beyond their reach? Only time would tell.

It was no accident or random coincidence of events that led to the equivalents of the Dunbarton Oaks and Potsdam Conferences for the 21st century being held in London in 2035. Nogi had always admired the British way of life and political system. After all, Britain was the birthplace of *Magna Carta* and the homeland of Parliamentary democracy, and her long imperial experience made her the ideal bridge between the Western European World and the teeming millions of Asia. She had long since lost her desire to re-impose a *Pax Britannica* and she had no territorial ambitions. She still possessed the political will and military power to defend her own islands and its trade, and she also had the political instinct to make her way in the world by manipulating the balance of power as she had always done throughout her long history. She was part of the West, and yet her imperial past gave her ability to interpret and sympathise with the political ambitions of the East. The League of Nations had failed in the characterless neutrality of Switzerland, and the United Nations had collapsed in the noisy clutter and bustle of New York. If Nogi's dream of a new world order was to come true, it must be established in the right environment. London was *his* choice. His unhappy experience negotiating with President O'Dwyer in 2027 made Washington abhorrent to him.

The British Government and, indeed, the British people, were flattered by the role Nogi was thrusting upon them. Dean Aitcheson's quip about Britain having lost an Empire and failing to find a role, still rankled, because it was too near the truth. Nogi proposed that not only should Britain be the venue and act as host to the peace conferences, but she should also provide the secretariat that, in due course, would become the framework upon which the successor to the United Nations would be built.

The British Government attached such importance to Nogi's invitation that, when accepting, they suggested Lord Thamesdown, the Lord Chancellor, for the post of Secretary General. He was Britain's most eminent constitutional lawyer, who himself saw the appointment as so important that he was prepared to leave the Wool Sack to assume it.

Thamesdown was not a man who believed in starting with a blank sheet of paper: he preferred to rebuild fallen structures, using the sound and proven stones of the past, while discarding those that had collapsed under stress or had been eroded by time. At his suggestion, preparations for the three superpower summit, or 'Troika' as it became known, were made by an Armistice Commission drawn from the three major security organisations: NATO, the Warsaw Pact and EATO. Its task was to be twofold: to recommend how the new international boundaries should be drawn, and to draft the principles upon which the United Nations' successor should be constructed. Their work had to be consistent with the provisions of the Charter of the China Seas.

My appointment as Deputy Chief of Defence Staff (Intelligence) was nearing its end and I was contemplating retirement from the Army when I was summoned to the Foreign and Commonwealth Office to meet Lord Thamesdown. Would I, he asked, be prepared to join his secretariat to head the military section? He pointed out how valuable my experience on Karl Tell's staff in New York and as Military Attaché in Tokyo would be to him. Needless to say, I had no hesitation in accepting. It would be sad to leave the Army at the end of forty years service, but it was a challenge that I could not refuse. Many of the leading figures in NATO and EATO were known to me and, as head of British Military Intelligence, I had met most of their equivalents in the Warsaw Pact on paper in intelligence reports.

The Commission's offices were established in the Queen Elizabeth Conference Centre under the shadows of the Abbey and Big Ben. When I scanned the lists of the three delegations, which we were to serve, I was delighted to see that General Oyama was heading the EATO team. A number of the American and German officers in the NATO delegation were acquaintances, which would make working with them all the easier. The Warsaw Pact list meant little to me and I would have to depend upon Colonel Michael Vigor, an Eastern Bloc expert, who had been appointed to the Military Section both as interpreter and as a liaison officer with the Warsaw Pact delegation.

I will take credit for one suggestion which was to make more impact upon my life than I realised at the time that I made it. From my introductory talk with Lord Thamesdown I knew that he was keen not to lose any of the better features of the old United Nations Charter and its organisation. And so I recommended that he should invite Karl Tell to join the Commission as one of its political and legal advisers. He was delighted with the idea and issued the invitation, which Karl had as little hesitation as I did in accepting.

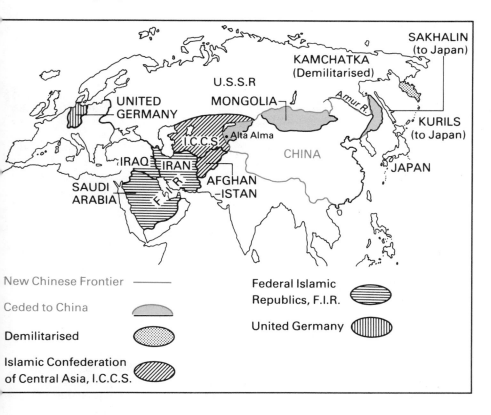

MAP 16: The new international boundaries of the First Treaty of London, 2035

Knowing that I knew Karl well, Lord Thamesdown asked me to meet him at Heathrow when he arrived from Switzerland. It was a sad meeting. As we waited in the VIP suite for his luggage to arrive, he told me that Ingrid had died two months earlier and that he would be living alone in London. Nevertheless, he was delighted to be joining the Commission so that he could drown his sorrow in constructive work.

At the first meeting of the Commission, Oyama made a conciliatory opening statement that avoided any suggestion of a victor-vanquished relationship between the delegations. The aim he said was to lay the foundations of a new, more prosperous and peaceful world. Nevertheless, he made it very clear that he was empowered to veto any proposals that did not conform to the provisions of the Charter of the China Seas. And he reminded us all that the Sino-Japanese forces were ready to resume military operations if EATO's fundamental demands were not met. The EATO powers, he explained, had five requirements which were not negotiable at official level and could only be challenged, if at all, at plenary session of the Troika. They were:

1. *The restoration of the Ch'ing frontiers of China by the return of all Manchurian territory south of the Amur River in the east, Outer Mongolia in the north and Alma Ata province in the west.*

2. *The restoration of Sakalin Island and the Kurils to Japan, and the demilitarisation of the Kamchatka Peninsula.*

3. *The creation of an independent Islamic Confederation of Central Asia, embracing the Kazakh, Uzbeck, Turkamen and Kirgiz SSR's. The new frontier of the Soviet Union would be along the northern border of Kazakhstan from the north end of the Caspian Sea to the Altai mountains.*

4. *The withdrawal of all foreign troops to within the boundaries of the sovereign states to which they belonged: in particular the withdrawal of U.S., British and Soviet forces from Europe; of U.S. and Soviet troops from Iran; and of U.S. troops from Central America.*

5. *The dismantling and destruction of all existing nuclear weapons and the prohibition of their future manufacture with adequate international control and inspection.*

Oyama had a further advantage. As usual the Copps had done their forward planning in their meticulous way, and he was able to table two draft treaties to form the basis of negotiations. The first was the peace treaty, which would define the new international boundaries and the programmes for the withdrawal of forces. The second would be the blueprint for the creation of the successor to the United Nations.

The clarity of Oyama's five principles left little room for argument within the Commission on points of substance in the First Treaty. There was the inevitable horse-trading over the detailed alignment of the new boundaries. The main bones of contention lay in the withdrawal programmes, particularly from Europe where the agreed re-unification of Germany and the withdrawal of United States, British and Soviet troops spelt the end of the Iron Curtain as it had existed for ninety years. It says much for the work of the Copps and the firmness of Oyama that an agreed draft was ready for presentation to the Troika at the end of May.

The Commissions work on the Second Treaty was much more controversial because Oyama was not in a position to enforce terms as representative of the victors. If the new United Nations was to work it would have to be established by consensus and not by *diktat*. Washington and Moscow favoured the simple amendment of the old United Nations Charter to accommodate the principles set out in the Charter of the China Seas. Peking and Tokyo took the opposite view, and insisted on taking a major step forward towards World Government. The decision was taken out of the Commission's hands by world opinion. No-one could have been in any doubt in the Spring of 2035 that people wanted a clean break with the past

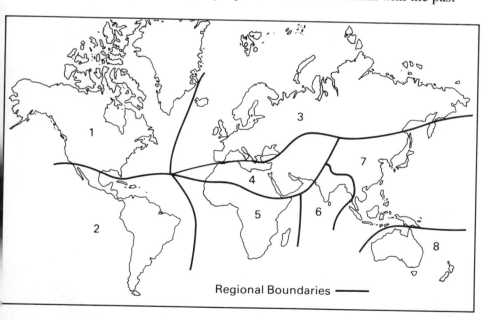

Map 17: The World Security Regions set out in the Second Treaty of London:
2035

and the establishment of a Supra-national Government. Many different names were put forward: World Co-prosperity Organisation, World Union, Global Confederation and so forth. In the end it was Karl Tell who suggested the simple and truthful title '*World Government*' and this was enshrined in the draft of the Second Treaty of London.

The main difference between the United Nations and the proposed World Government lay in the creation of a Security Executive in place of the Security Council, and the replacement of the General Assembly by a World Parliament in which member's votes would be weighted to reflect sizes of populations represented. The Security Executive was to be elected from MWP's (Members of the World Parliament) and to have portfolios as heads of international ministries. The fifteen members would be:

The Arbitrator General
The Peacekeeper General
The Inspector General of Armaments
The Treasurer General
The Economist General
The Inspector General of Health
The Inspector General of Education

and eight Regional Peace Keepers, elected from MWP's representing the eight regions into which the world was to be divided:

1. North America
2. Latin America
3. Europe, including Soviet Russia
4. North Africa, the Middle East and Central Asia
5. Africa South of the Sahara
6. The Indian Sub Continent
7. Eastern Asia
8. The Antipodes and Pacific

The Chairmanship of the Security Executive would rotate between the seven functional '*Generals*' and decisions of substance would need a two thirds majority before executive action could be taken.

The first plenary session of the Troika started on 1st June 2035. It was an impressive assembly of World leaders who sat down around the round table in Lancaster House where so many fateful international meetings had taken place in the past. Behind Chu and Nogi were M'Bundu, the Ayatollah and Archbishop Bolivar. Patrick O'Dwyer was supported by the Western European leaders, and Ivan Molotov had the Warsaw pact states and Cuba behind him. By common consent, the press had been excluded – much to their annoyance.

At Potsdam, the main bone of contention had been Poland: at Lancaster House it was Central Asia. The Russians accepted the Chinese occupation of all Manchuria south of the Amur River and of Alma Ata as a *fait accompli*, which could not be reversed except by military action; but they were still in occupation of Tehran and the northern half of Iran and had no intention of leaving unless they were accorded a satisfactory *quid pro quo*. Their price was the retention of the proposed Islamic Confederation of Central Asia as an autonomous state within the Soviet Union.

Ivan Molotov had two strong cards in his hand as he made his case for the retention of Russian sovereignty over Central Asia. The new state would not be economically viable unless it could depend upon the Soviet Union's railway network until new communications could be developed southwards to the Persian Gulf; and secondly it was by no means certain that the peoples of Central Asia wished to sever their links entirely with the Soviet Union. Holding up a copy of the Charter of the China Seas, he demanded a plebiscite to decide the wishes of the majority.

Chu trumped Molotov's communications card by offering the Soviet Union running rights over what would become the Chinese railway south of the Amur River to the ice free port of Vladivostok to help the economy of Eastern Siberia in exchange for similar rights for the Central Asian Islamic Confederation on the Russian railways. With the Ayatollah at his elbow he could not compromise on the plebiscite issue. He bluntly rejected Molotov's case on the grounds that the continued presence of Russian security forces in the Moslem SSR's would make a genuine expression of popular opinion impossible. He then issued a clear warning that China would re-open hostilities unless 'the just demands of the Islamic peoples of Central Asia' were met.

Lord Thamesdown intervened with the suggestion that the Armistice Commission should be directed to study the plebiscite proposal with a view to meeting Chairman Chu's justified worries about the fairness of such a poll. In the meanwhile, the conference should turn its attention to the draft of the Second Treaty.

It was noticeable throughout the debate on the First Treaty that the Americans had tended to side with the Russians, not so much because they agreed with the Soviet arguments but because they felt that Asian ambitions should be checked. At Potsdam the Soviets had been the bogey men against whom the other four of the big five – the United States, the United Kingdom, France and Nationalist China – ganged up. At Lancaster House it was the Sino-Japanese, who appeared to pose a threat to the rest of the world – as, indeed, they did.

The same ganging-up occurred in the debate on the Second Treaty, but with greater justification. The crunch issue was the proposed destruction of nuclear weapons and their future prohibition. Nogi and Chu had world opinion behind them in their determination to outlaw such weapons. Their case had been reinforced by the simple fact that nuclear weapons had not been used during the Third World War. Surely the time had come to put an end to this potential threat to the continued existence of human life on the globe?

O'Dwyer and Molotov took the opposite view. They could not ask their people to give up their only defence against Asian numerical superiority. They accepted the need for strictly imposed limitations but not total prohibition. It might be that some breakthrough in Star Wars technology could yet make nuclear weapons useless in the same way that gun powder had been driven out by high explosive, but until that time came nuclear weapons could neither be dis-invented or proscribed. Chu, in a surprisingly unguarded aside which was picked up by the microphones said to Nogi:

'We will see about that won't we?'

I, for one, did not fathom the meaning of the aside. Nor did Lord Thamesdown, who intervened once more to prevent an open rift between the two sides. He proposed a further study by the Commission to come up with an extended programme for the run down of nuclear arsenals that might provide an acceptable compromise.

As he was speaking, I saw a Japanese official enter the room and hand a note to Nogi. Nogi read it, smiled cynically and handed it to Chu. Chu looked at Nogi and nodded. There was total silence in the room as Nogi rose to speak:

'Gentlemen', he began in a grave voice, 'I think you will agree that this debate is now irrelevant. The World has entered a new technological era. One rocket launching site at Cape Canaveral and one at Tyuratam (Baikonur) has been vapourised as a demonstration of the breakthrough achieved by Sino-Japanese technologists with earth based beam weapons. Chairman Chu and I are aware that it will not be long before the U.S. and U.S.S.R. match our achievements. We are, therefore, prepared to place our technology at the disposal of the future Peacekeeper General to ensure a nuclear free and peaceful world.'

Nogi's words were drowned in the pandemonium that broke out as other officials came in to alert O'Dwyer and Molotov to what had happened at Cape Canaveral and at Tyuratam. The Second World War had been ended with the massive loss of life at Hiroshima and Nagasaki in 1945. The Third World War had been drawn to its conclusion just as decisively with minimal loss of life by the well timed Sino-Japanese demonstration of East Asia's claim to super-power status.

I met Oyama as he was walking back that evening from Lancaster House to our offices in the Westminster Conference Centre. I congratulated him on one of the World's best kept secrets. The Yangsi Gorge hydro-electric project had been used not only to provide the power for the earth based beam weapons, but to disguise the underground weapon emplacements and control systems. The reflectors had been positioned at the last minute in space by *HOTOL III*, a stretched and up-engined version of the Anglo-Japanese *HOTOL I and II*, which had been developed secretly by Sino-Japanese technologists.

'No,' Oyama said thoughtfully, 'not the best kept secret. Only one of them!'

I could not stop myself saying 'Oh?'

'When you come to write your story of this period, as I am sure you will, I will tell you about the rest.'

Oyama was as good as his word. When he heard that I was, indeed, embarking on this book, he sent me the paraphrase of the Secret Protocols of the Treaty of Hong Kong of which I have made full use. They certainly were the best kept secrets of our time.

There was no more argument or prevarication about the First and Second Treaties of London. They were both signed at Lancaster House on 4th July 2035. The British Government offered the site of St Thomas's Hospital and the old London County Hall on the south bank of the Thames opposite the Houses of Parliament for the construction of the World Parliament and the World Government offices. As I write this history in 2040, the buildings are about half complete: so is the establishment of the World Government itself, which is suffering all the usual teething troubles of any new organisation. I suspect that within its Constitution we have sown the dragon's teeth of the Fourth World War. For the moment the World seems a much more peaceful place. I doubt if such stability will last for long. The unexpected always happens in human affairs.

Nogi did not live long enough to enjoy the fruits of his success. As Robert Louis Stevenson once wrote, *'to travel is a better thing than to arrive, and the true success is to labour.'* For Nogi the Treaty of London was an anti-climax. The determination, that had powered his failing heart for so long, faltered. He collapsed and died on the *Golden Arrow* that was whisking him back to Tokyo for his triumphal return. Chu had re-established the territorial integrity of China: Nogi had done far more. He had created a new World order; he had given Afro-Asia its soul; and he had made the Japanese way of life the pre-eminent culture of the 21st century. London has become the neutral centre of world government, but Tokyo is the world's powerhouse of new ideas. Washington and Moscow are now the capitals of the second and third superpowers.

I, too, realised that I had come to the end of a journey. The Third World War had dominated the whole of my working life. But I was luckier than Nogi. I started off almost at once on another journey. This time I was not riding alone. I was married for a second time in the little Anglo-Saxon Church at Huish. I am now Kitty Tell!

We live at China Cottage across the fields from my grandparent's home at West Stowell. Without Karl's papers, diaries, memories and encouragement I could never have completed this book. Oyama visits us whenever he is in England. He has read my drafts and has made many constructive comments, which I have accepted and incorporated in the text.

As I walk over the downs above West Stowell with Karl and our two wire-haired dachshunds, just as my grandparents used to do, I can hear my grandfather's words:

'There comes a time when companionship begins to have its attractions.'

I had ridden alone for far too long, but it has been my good fortune to find true companionship with my dear Karl.

A chronology of the Third World War

YEAR	CHRISTO-COMMUNISM	BLACK NATIONALISM	ISLAMIC FUNDAMENTALISM	NOGI-ISM
1985) 1994) 1994		– Anti-Apartheid struggle – Brussels Treaty Re-negotiated		
1995	– Bolivar appointed Bishop of Cali in Colombia	– South Africa becomes Azania	– Iran/Iraq War ends with Shi'ite coup in Baghdad	
1996		– Gibraltar Accord		– Nogi wins first parliamentary seats
1997		– Angola becomes first Black Homelander state		
1998			– Council of Kerbala	
1999				– Anglo-Japanese HOTOL launched – U.S. evacuate bases in Japan.

2000	– Bolivar appointed Archbishop of Colombia – Black Homelander Union formed by Angola, Zaire, Congo and Gabon.
2001	– Commonwealth Task Force deployed to East Africa – Nogi becomes leader of Japanese opposition parties
2002	– Pope Xavier I elected – Shi'ite revolution in Saudi Arabia
2003	**WORLD ECONOMIC RECESSION BEGINS**
2004	– Christo-Communist Concordat
2005	– Assassination of Noah Johnston – Lynching of Ayatollah of Tehran
2006	– Bolivarist success in Colombian elections
2007	– Federation of Islamic Republics formed (Iran, Iraq and Saudi Arabia)
2008	– Homelander Namibia Coup fails

2009
- Somali invasion of Kenya: Battle of the Tana River

2010
- U.S. intervention in Bogota and Caracas

2011
- U.S. troops withdrawn

2012
- Bolivarists take seats in Mexican General Election

2013
- Homelander guerrilla campaign in East Africa begins
- Nogi becomes Prime Minister

2014
- Islamic *Jihad* in Afghanistan re-opens

2015
- Sino-Japanese Treaty of Hong Kong

2016
2017
- U.S. intervention in Panama
- Battle of Entebbe
- Soviet occupation of Tehran

2018		**UNITING FOR PEACE RESOLUTION IN U.N.**	– Charter of the China Seas
2019	– Ecuador Bolivarist	– Homelanders withdraw from East Africa	
2020			– Sino-Japanese 'Nuclear and Space Sufficiency'
2021		– *Muhjahideen* offensive re-opens	– South East Asia Co-Prosperity Sphere formed.
2022	– Peru Bolivarist	Mutiny at Samarkand – U.S. and U.S.S.R. intervene in Iran	
2023		**TOKYO PEACE CONFERENCE**	
2024	– Bolivia Bolivarist		
2025		– Soviet repression in Central Asia begins	– Chinese invasion of Vietnam
2026			– Nogi's peace mission begins
2027	– Treaty of Bogota signed by U.S.A. and Colombia		

2028
- Afrikaner UDI and Anglo-Japanese intervention

2029
- Karpov reconciliation policy starts in Central Asia

2030
- Archbishop Bolivar dies

2031
- Death of Karpov and renewal of Soviet repression in Central Asia

2032
- Soviet incursion into Sinkiang
- Chinese take Alma Ata

2033
- Outer Mongolian Coup

2034
- Battle of the Amur River

2035
THE TREATIES OF LONDON